Top Ten Reasons for Investi...

➤ **The Internet is here to stay**—The Internet is .... months and is spreading overseas like a wildfire. The amou.... of commerce passing through the Internet ranks in the billions of dollars and soon will pass the trillion-dollar mark. You can't afford not to consider the investment possibilities.

➤ **There are many opportunities to come**—One of the worst mistakes investors make is to fear that if they don't act now, they will not have another chance. Be patient. The Internet and all the associated industries will produce good opportunities for years to come. The more mature the Internet becomes, the more stable the stock market will become.

➤ **It is only as risky as you make it**—You control the amount of risk you want to take. Some Internet investments are no more risky than any other growing industry. If pure Internet investments are too risky for you, consider one of the many traditional companies that are big players in the Internet. You never have to take more risk than you can stand.

➤ **Do your homework**—The Internet is new and requires more research than older, established industries. Fortunately, a ton of information is available for your consideration. Stick with established, reputable information sources, and you will have all the information you need. This can be the most interesting and entertaining part of the investment process.

➤ **Keep greed and fear in check**—There's an old stock market saying: "Bulls profit, bears profit, but pigs get slaughtered." Greed is what drives prices through the roof and makes investors blind to reason. Fear can cloud your judgment just as badly. Having fun is the only acceptable emotion when investing in Internet stocks.

➤ **Watch where you step if you follow the herd**—The "herd" is more wrong than right. You should make your own investment decisions and pay little attention to television's talking heads and online gurus. Do your homework, and use your common sense—you won't need experts.

➤ **Hot tips are a way to get burned**—The Internet is a wonderful fountain of information, but it is unfiltered and unedited. Chat rooms and message boards are great places to share and receive information. However, you can never be sure who is posting the information or what their motives are. Many "hot tips" on the Internet are misguided at best and absolute fraud at worst.

➤ **Quality is always the least expensive choice**—Quality stocks are always your best bargain. Never buy an Internet stock based on its low price alone. Ten shares of a quality stock are worth more than 100 shares of junk for the same price. Remember, $10,000 invested in America Online when it went public is now worth millions. That $10,000 invested in (fill in something stupid).com is worth, well, what do you think?

➤ **Buy a piece of the future**—One of the most exciting aspects of investing in Internet stocks is that you are buying a piece of the future. Investing is ultimately about future returns, not past performance. You won't find many other market segments that are more tied to our future than Internet stocks.

➤ **Internet stocks are not for everyone**—Internet stocks may not be right for you. It takes a particular type of investor to look past the alternating hype and doomsday predictions to see the potential. If you like safe, predictable returns, consider another investment choice. Investors willing to step out just a little on the risk scale may find the rewards outstanding.

**alpha
books**

Internet Investing by the Numbers

- ➤ By 2004, global e-commerce sales: $7 trillion
- ➤ By 2004, U.S. e-commerce sales: $3.5 trillion
- ➤ By 2001, U.S. business-to-business sales: $1.2 trillion
- ➤ As of 1999, U.S. yearly Internet advertising revenue: $4.6 billion
- ➤ As of 1999, global Internet users: 304 million
- ➤ As of 1999, percent of U.S. adults on the Internet: 56

Where to Find Internet Stock Analysis

- ➤ **Morningstar.com (morningstar.com)**—News, analysis, and fundamental information
- ➤ **MSN Money Central (moneycentral.msn.com)**—News, analysis, and fundamental information
- ➤ **123 Jump.com (123jump.com)**—Internet stock news and Internet stock sector reports
- ➤ **Internet Stock Report (internetstockreport.com)**—Internet stock news, columns, and Internet stock lists
- ➤ **Internet.com (internet.com)**—Internet industry portal with links to dozens of information sources
- ➤ **ZDNet (zdnet.com)**—Internet news, columns, and sector sections
- ➤ **The Standard (thestardard.com)**—Comprehensive Internet news and opinions

Where to Find Comprehensive Financial News

- ➤ The New York Times Online (nytimes.com)—The granddaddy of all news reporting and always on top of financial news.
- ➤ CNNfn Interactive (cnnfn.com)—The financial arm of CNN. A comprehensive site that covers the markets completely.
- ➤ Bloomberg.com (bloomberg.com)—Bloomberg is one of the pioneers of online financial news services and is always worth a look.
- ➤ Morningstar.com (morningstar.com)—Morningstar.com is an acknowledged authority on mutual funds and, as more Internet mutual funds are formed, will be worth your time to read.

THE COMPLETE IDIOT'S GUIDE® TO

Investing in Internet Stocks

by Ken Little

alpha books

Macmillan USA, Inc.
201 West 103rd Street
Indianapolis, IN 46290

A Pearson Education Company

To my wife, Cyndy, the most important person in the world to me.

Copyright © 2000 by Ken Little

International Standard Book Number: 0-02-863941-3
Library of Congress Catalog Card Number: Available upon request.

02   01   00   8   7   6   5   4   3   2   1

Interpretation of the printing code: The rightmost number of the first series of numbers is the year of the book's printing; the rightmost number of the second series of numbers is the number of the book's printing. For example, a printing code of 00-1 shows that the first printing occurred in 2000.

Printed in the United States of America

Note: This publication contains the opinions and ideas of its author. It is intended to provide helpful and informative material on the subject matter covered. It is sold with the understanding that the author and publisher are not engaged in rendering professional services in the book. If the reader requires personal assistance or advice, a competent professional should be consulted.

The author and publisher specifically disclaim any responsibility for any liability, loss, or risk, personal or otherwise, which is incurred as a consequence, directly or indirectly, of the use and application of any of the contents of this book.

Publisher
Marie Butler-Knight

Product Manager
Phil Kitchel

Managing Editor
Cari Luna

Acquisitions Editors
Susan Zingraf
Mike Sanders

Development Editor
Nancy D. Warner

Production Editor
Billy Fields

Copy Editor
Krista Hansing

Illustrator
Jody P. Schaeffer

Cover Designers
Mike Freeland
Kevin Spear

Book Designers
Scott Cook and Amy Adams of DesignLab

Indexer
Angie Bess

Layout/Proofreading
Angela Calvert
Mary Hunt
Joe Millay

Contents at a Glance

Part 1: Why You Should Love Internet Stocks   **1**

  1   Why Internet Stocks Are Different   3
*Internet stocks are different. How and why they are
different is fundamental to successful investing.*

  2   Are Internet Stocks for You?   15
*Risks are associated with investing in Internet stocks, but
there are also opportunities for substantial gains.*

  3   The Internet   25
*Get an overview of the Internet, how it got so big, and
why it continues to expand, for an insight on the fertile
ground where Internet stocks grow.*

  4   Show Me the Money   35
*Venture capitalists and IPOs—we'll explain the contacts
that dreams are made of.*

Part 2: How to Love Internet Stocks   **45**

  5   Time for a Risk Check   47
*Risk tolerance is the psychological price you pay for
investing. Find out what buying Internet stocks will
cost you.*

  6   Doing Your Homework   59
*Internet stocks are well covered on the Internet and in the
media. Here's where you start your search.*

  7   Online Resources   69
*A great place to find information on Internet stocks is, of
course, the Internet.*

  8   The Basics of Evaluating Internet Stocks   81
*Internet stocks often defy conventional wisdom when
you're doing evaluations. Here's some unconventional
wisdom.*

  9   What Are They Selling?   91
*Internet companies have sales and not much else. Here's
how a sale-based evaluation model works.*

Part 3: Playing by the Rules   **103**

  10   Five Rules You Need to Know   105
*Learn the rules for evaluating Internet stocks that every
investor needs to know.*

11 But They Are Broke   117
    *Both young and not-so-young companies live on cash re-
    serves. Will earnings appear before the cash disappears?*

12 What's a Customer Worth?   127
    *Using a customer base to measure the value of an
    Internet stock is sometimes the only way that makes
    sense.*

13 What Price Growth?   139
    *Growth, or its potential, is often the only "almost tangi-
    ble" asset of many Internet companies.*

14 Technology Is Not the Answer   149
    The "gee whiz" factor will take a company only so far.

15 Management Is the Key to Success   157
    *Any 20-year-old can build a Web site, but it takes a keen
    business sense to turn ideas and technology into a real
    company.*

Part 4: IPOs, Mutual Funds, Day Trading, and Options   163

16 Jumping On the IPO Bandwagon   165
    *Getting in on an IPO before it is bid out of sight is not
    easy, but here are some ideas.*

17 Jumping Off the IPO Bandwagon   175
    *As a long-term investment, IPOs haven't done well, but
    there are exceptions.*

18 Mutual Admiration Society   185
    *Are Internet mutual funds the best way to sort the win-
    ners from the losers? Here's a mixed review of their per-
    formance.*

19 Day Trading for Fun and Profit   195
    *Day trading is one of the hottest deals going, despite the
    fact that most day traders lose money. You decide for
    yourself.*

20 What Are Your Options?   207
    *Internet stocks are finding their way into the options
    market. Here's how to use options to make money on
    Internet stocks.*

Part 5: Blue Chips and Micro Chips   221

21 New Tricks for Old Dogs   223
    *Can this dog hunt? Mainstream corporate America has
    decided the Internet may be more than a fad.*

22 Mixed Marriages   231
   What happens when the Internet and traditional com-
   panies merge can be a thing of beauty or a "learning
   experience."

23 What Price Glory?   241
   How do you place a value on a company's entry into the
   world of cyber commerce?

Part 6: Is That a Good Idea?   **251**

24 The Big Push   253
   Broadband delivery to the home and office is the bottle-
   neck, but it's also a golden opportunity.

25 Interactive Multimedia Toilet Cleaner Commercials   263
   Interactive multimedia ads tailored to each consumer are
   an advertiser's dream. The company that makes it work
   will clean up.

26 The Check Is in the Network   273
   Personal financial services such as bill paying, investing,
   and financial advice are the services that will make the
   Internet indispensable.

27 Work Is Where the Internet Is   283
   The Internet doesn't care whether you are in the office or
   at home, or whether those places are the same.

28 Online with Your Toaster   291
   Laugh if you will, but your whole house may soon be one
   big network that you can access from anywhere.

Appendixes

A Investment Review   301

B Glossary of Investing and Internet Terms   305

C Web Sites   321

  Index   327

Contents

Part 1: Why You Should Love Internet Stocks   **1**

1 Why Internet Stocks Are Different   **3**

What They Are 3
   Pure Internet Companies 4
   Hybrid Internet Companies 6
What They Are Not 7
What It Means to You 8
So What's the Big Deal? 10
What Makes Them Hot? 11
Will They Stay Hot? 13

2 Are Internet Stocks for You?   **15**

Let's Talk Real World 16
Internet Stock Myths 16
   For High Rollers Only 16
   I Will Lose My Shirt 17
   I Will Get Rich 17
   IPOs Are Pure Gold 18
Finding Them a Home 18
   Time Is on Your Side 18
   Investing or Speculating? 20
   Diversify or Die (Figuratively, Of Course) 20
How Much Risk Is There? 21
The "Gee Whiz" Risk Factor 23

3 The Internet   **25**

It's Magic 25
How Does It Do That? 26
All the Pieces 26
   The Interface 27
   The Connection 29
   The Backbone 30
   Software and Services 30
It Will Grow on You 32
   Necessity or Luxury? 33
   Offshore Opportunities 33
The Dot.Com Thing 34

4 Show Me the Money   **35**

Who Are These People? 36
What It Takes to Be a Venture Capitalist 37
Where They Find Deals 37
How They Work 38
Why Go IPO? 39
IPO to Go 39
How Much Does It Cost? 40
Who Fixes the IPO Price? 41
Where Does the Money Go? 42
What Changes for a Company? 43

Part 2: How to Love Internet Stocks   **45**

5 Time for a Risk Check   **47**

Safety Nets 47
Honest Talk About Risk 49
Enough Gain for the Pain 49
Amount Invested 50
Length of Time 50
Level of Risk 50
Types of Risk 51
Market Value Risk 51
Inflation Risk 52
Economic Risk 53
Your Personal Risk Tolerance 53
The Balancing Act 55
Different Types 55
Low-Risk Investments 55
Moderate Risk Investments 56
High-Risk Investments 57
Risk Is Your Friend 57

6 Doing Your Homework   **59**

Information Is Your Best Tool 59
Your Tool Box 60
The Good, the Bad, the Ugly 60
Newsletters 60
The Sting 61
The System 62
The Hook 62
The Line 62
The Sinker 63
The Rumor Mill 63

The Rip-Off 64
Sorting the Tools 64
  General News and Information 65
  Specific News and Information 66

7 Online Resources   69

Trolling for Stock 70
  A Quick Look 70
  Variables 71
  Preset Screens 72
  Custom Screens 73
Online Research 74
Overpriced Stocks 75
Founts of Facts 75
Morningstar.com 75
MSN MoneyCentral 77
The Tout 78
  Zacks.com 78
  InvestorPlace.com 79
The Old-Fashioned Way 79

8 The Basics of Evaluating Internet Stocks   81

Unconventional Conventional Wisdom 81
Reality Check 82
What You Are Buying 83
Dangerous Numbers 83
Using Numbers 83
The Biggies 84
Understanding What You Buy 85
What Do the Numbers Say? 86
  Do You Yahoo!? 87
  The Growth Hurdle 88
  Big Numbers 88
One More Reality Check 89
Brave New World 89

9 What Are They Selling?   91

Sales Come First 91
What Are They Selling? 92
The Joy of Cooperation 93
Share the Wealth 93
Connected or Not? 93
Sales As a Proxy for Earnings 94
Appearances Can Be Deceiving 95

Size Matters 95
Using a Stock Screen 97
How It's Done 97
   MSN MoneyCentral Screen 98
   Market Guide Screen 100
   Power Screen 100

Part 3: Playing by the Rules   **103**

10 Five Rules You Need to Know   **105**

Earnings Are Not Urgent 106
Earnings Estimates 106
I Can See Clearly Now 107
Cash Flow 107
Customers Are Different 108
Try It, You'll Like It 108
Stocks to Avoid 109
Advertising-Based Sites 109
Growth Is Not Optional 110
How Much Growth? 110
Unsustainable Growth 111
Stocks to Avoid 112
Technology Not So Important 112
Pay No Attention to the Man Behind the Curtain 113
Stocks to Avoid 113
Management Is Most Important 114
Logical Profit Plan 114

11 But They Are Broke   **117**

A Hole in the Bucket 117
Sea of Red Ink 118
Making Money 119
The Herd 120
How Long to Wait 120
How to Pick 'Em 121
Things in Common 121
Being First 122
Key Factors 123
Entertainment Tonight 124
Internet Everywhere 124
Content Rules 125
How Will They Make Money? 125
Who Are the Players? 126

12   What's a Customer Worth?   **127**

Counting Heads 128
Customer or Not? 129
Why This Is Important 129
Computing Value 129
Sales Per Visitor 131
Combination Plate 132
Playing the Percentages 133
Conclusions 134
Hard Sell 134
Mom and Pop 135
Three Examples 135
Customer Service Rules 136

13   What Price Growth?   **139**

The Great Growth Rush 140
Those Amazing Young Rockets 140
Growth High 141
What Can You Expect? 141
Handling Growth 143
Sucking Cash 143
Get On the Scale 144
Fractured Infrastructure 144
Earning Your Way 145
Some Warning Signs 146
Positive Signs 147
Forecasting Growth 147

14   Technology Is Not the Answer   **149**

Selling the Sizzle 150
It Does What It Says 150
The Personal Touch 150
Selling the Steak 151
Change of Clothes 151
Compounding Mistakes 152
Technology Slaves 153
Old Problems 153
Technology That Is Important 154
Fad or Fact? 154
A Popular Network 155

15   Management Is the Key to Success   **157**

Why Management Is So Important 158
Shameless Hustlers 158

Over 30 Need Not Apply 159
Finding Information 159
Stepping Down or Aside 161

Part 4: IPOs, Mutual Funds, Day Trading, and Options   163

16 Jumping On the IPO Bandwagon   165

Rocket's Red Glare 166
A Note of Caution 166
Why So High? 167
A Quick Review 168
Rocket Fuel 168
IPO Myths 169
  Offering Price *169*
  Fingerprints *169*
  Sound Retreat *170*
Getting In on the Deal 170
Alternative Sources 172
How Risky Is an Early Position? 173

17 Jumping Off the IPO Bandwagon   175

I Can See Clearly Now 176
Overconfidence 176
A Dilemma 177
The Future 177
Rethinking Our Definition 178
  Quality Stock *178*
  Long-Term Holding *180*
  What Do You Pay? *181*
Exit Strategy 181
  Going Long *182*
  Going Short *183*

18 Mutual Admiration Society   185

What Is an Internet Mutual Fund? 186
A Quick Review 186
  Diversification *186*
  Professional Manager *187*
  Internet Index Funds *188*
  Dow Jones Composite Internet *189*
  Goldman Sachs E-Commerce Index *189*
  Internet 100 ....*189*
  ISDEX *190*
Risk Upon Risk 190

Some of the Best 191
Who Should Own Internet Mutual Funds 192

19 Day Trading for Fun and Profit   **195**

The Day Trader's Dilemma 196
What They Really Do 196
Different Brokers 196
Commissions 197
The Space 197
Doing It at Home 198
Beware of Taxes 199
The System 199
Know the Fundamentals 200
Then the Technical Stuff 200
Support *201*
Resistance *202*
Different Looks 203
What It Takes 203
Playing Games 203
Emotions 204
The Rest of the Story 204
Price Trading *204*
Swing Trading *205*
Day Trading Internet Stocks 205
What Do You Recommend? 206

20 What Are Your Options?   **207**

Options on Internet Stocks 208
Options in a Nutshell 208
Pricing 209
Strike Price *209*
Time Factor *210*
Volatility *211*
Special Cases 211
Buyer or Seller 211
Buyers 212
Reasons to Buy 213
Sellers 214
Naked 215
Options Information 215
Overload 216
Using Options on Internet Stocks 217
Short-Term Speculating 217
Long-Term Speculation 218

xiii

Playing the Downside 218
Employee Stock Options 219
How Good Are They? 220
Diversify 220

Part 5: Blue Chips and Micro Chips 221

21 New Tricks for Old Dogs 223

Mixed Marriages 223
Nothing But Net 224
Clicks and Bricks 224
Nothing New 225
E-Tailing 225
From Bricks to Clicks 226
How You Do It 227
A Business Model 228
A Partnership 228
Late Bloomer 229
Looking Beyond the Hype 229

22 Mixed Marriages 231

Earth Shaking 231
Big Deal 232
What AOL Gets 233
What Time Warner Gets 233
The New Company 234
Potential Problems 235
Financial Concerns 235
Trouble in Paradise 237
The Bottom Line 237
What Will the Competition Do? 238
What Should Investors Do? 238

23 What Price Glory? 241

Internet Strategy 242
Understanding Commodities 242
Niche Markets 242
Portals 243
World Vision 243
Measuring the Impact 244
Well-Defined Goals 244
Realistic Costs 244
Realistic Time Frame 245
Follow the Money 245

What Can You Learn? 248
Second Best 248
Understanding Opportunity 249

Part 6: Is That a Good Idea?   251

24 The Big Push   253

Speed Defined 254
Speed Builds 254
Speed Sells 255
Advertising 256
The Options 256
Cable 257
DSL 257
Satellite 258
Wireless Cable 259
The Players 259
Place Your Bets 260
Some Issues 260
The Standard 260
A Future Vision 261

25 Interactive Multimedia Toilet Cleaner Commercials   263

In the Beginning 263
The Early Years 264
The Here and Now 264
An Advertising Primer 265
Test, Test, Test 266
So What? 267
Here to Stay 268
How It Is Changing 268
Growing Opportunity 268
The New Ads 269
A Gold Mine 269
Brave New World 270
Multimedia Mania 271
What Investors Need to Know 272

26 The Check Is in the Network   273

Internet Indispensable 273
Who Needs Banks? 274
Internet Banking History 275

What It Looks Like 276
Open an Account 276
Access 276
Good Deals? 276
Easy Bill Payment 276
Bill Presentment 277
Loans 277
Investments 277
Cash Is a Problem 277
Special Services—Not 278
The Future 278
Choices 279
Strategy 279
Security Issues 280
Personal Financial Services 280
Your Strategy 281

27 Work Is Where the Internet Is   283

Coming Full Circle 284
The End Is Near 284
Investors Take Note 285
Home Office Revolution 286
What Do We Need? 287
We Need ASPs 287
Business-to-Business (B2B) 288
The Missing Pieces 289
Networks Rule 289

28 Online with Your Toaster   291

Networks Rule 292
What's Next? 292
Computers 293
Internet Devices 294
Home Security 294
Environmental Systems 294
Appliances 295
Entertainment Systems 295
Hello, Jetsons 296
"Good Morning, Dave" 297
A Big Step 298
Investment Opportunities 299
No Utopia 299

Appendixes

A Investment Review   301

B Glossary of Investing and Internet Terms   305

C Web Sites   321

Index   327

Foreword

I'm writing this in late May on a small island (8.3 miles perimeter) in Northern Michigan called Mackinac. The place is like a time warp, back to a bygone era. The homes are mostly large and very Victorian. There are many gables, verandas, and wide porches. In fact, cars have been banned. This was done shortly after the first car appeared on the island in 1898. To travel, you either ride a carriage or bike.

It seems fitting to write here, because the Internet represents life in the fast lane. It seems that overnight a billion dollar company can be formed, creating a new industry or disrupting an existing industry.

In the past few years, making money from Internet stocks has been a no-brainer. Just throwing darts at dot coms was enough to retire early and buy the proverbial island. There was even the creation of a new career: day trading.

But as with any euphoric market, reality eventually sets in. This is what happened in the first part of 2000, as the NASDAQ underwent a savage plunge. Even the so-called Internet blue-chips have not been immune, such as Yahoo!, eBay, and even the mighty Cisco.

But the Internet is not a passing fad. It is real. It is completely transforming the world. For example, from my desktop computer I conduct much of my business using the Web. I have a cell phone, which allows me to browse the Web. Oh, there is my Palm VII. With it, I can browse the Web, as well as conduct my banking, messaging, and even online trading. In fact, even on the island of Mackinac, I was able to log onto the Net and do my work. The Web is all pervasive.

If anything, the recent plunge in Net stocks represents an opportunity. But be careful. There will be many casualties. After all, at the turn of the century, there were over 500 automakers. Of course, only a handful survived.

So to be a successful Internet investor means you need to do your homework. You need to understand the broad trends, the technologies, revenue models and the management teams. This is no easy task.

That is why this book, The Complete Idiot's Guide to Investing in Internet Stocks, is such a great help. The author, Ken Little, provides a comprehensive treatment of all the issues an Internet investor needs to know. He discusses the background of the Net, covering venture capital and IPOs. He also provides great analytic tools to make better investment decisions, such as ratio analysis. There is also discussion of online resources, so you can further enhance your knowledge.

Finally, he covers some of the market segments that are poised for growth. They include such hot topics as broadband (making the Net faster for such cool things as video); online financial planning (yep, there is no reason to go to the bank again); business-to-business (how industries are using the Net to create new sources of revenues, as well as create efficiencies); and home networks (wiring your home with Net technologies). Of course, this is an ever-expanding list. That's what makes Internet investing so fun and for many years to come, profitable.

Tom Taulli

Tom Taulli is an expert in the IPO field and has written about the stock market for a variety of publications including Barron's and Registered Representative. He writes on-line IPO columns for Microsoft Investor, TechInvestor, and StockSite, and is the founder of WebIPO, a pioneering Internet investment banking company. He is an often-quoted resource in IPO news stories and appears regularly on CNN and CNBC.

Introduction

My grandfather was fond of saying, "If it was easy, everybody would do it."

That was his way of suggesting that things worth doing often require more work than most people are willing to put in. My life experiences confirm his wisdom.

I know you are the type of person who is willing to put more effort into your investments than most. I know this because you have bought this book or are about to buy it. (Go ahead, buy it. For less money than two large pizzas, I will show you the secret of unlimited wealth. Yes, I also know that you are too smart to fall for a sales pitch like that.)

The news media have been full of news and advice about Internet stocks. You can tell which way the market is going by what the "experts" think are great ideas or the biggest scams since electric underwear.

You have figured out that investing in Internet stocks makes sense, given the tremendous impact that it has made and continues to make on our business and personal lives. However, the turmoil in Internet stock prices (one day up, the next day down) makes picking the winners from the losers difficult.

How would you like a secret tool that identifies the "can't-miss" Internet stocks and takes only five minutes to use? Let me know if you find one that works.

There are no sure-fire systems for consistently picking winners from any market sector, Internet or otherwise. However, you can make some educated choices in Internet stocks, and this book will get you started.

I will show you how to use traditional stock-evaluation tools and some hybrid tools that are more tuned in to Internet stocks. You don't need a CPA, CFP, BVD, or any other alphabet designation to make your own investment decisions.

You do need two tools to begin your adventure in investing in Internet stocks:

> **Information**—I'll show you where to get it.
> **Intelligence**—I'll show you how to use your own good smarts—and your common sense.

It will take a little time and effort, but you will be plugging in to the most exciting new economy since the transistor changed the way we thought about handling information.

Don't expect a smooth road. This is new territory for everyone, and the going can get bumpy at times. However, the rewards can be well worth the effort.

The days of throwing money at anything with a "dot.com" are over (thank goodness). Every day, the market for Internet stocks becomes more mature, and that means you will have more choices than ever.

Don't be in a hurry to get your money invested. You'll have plenty of opportunities for years to come in Internet stocks. Here is where your journey begins.

What You Will Learn in This Book

The Complete Idiot's Guide to Investing in Internet Stocks is divided into six parts.

Part 1, "Why You Should Love Internet Stocks," delves into the world of Internet stocks, sorting the myths from the facts. You'll look at how Internet stocks are different, and you'll "follow the money" from venture capital to the IPO. Along the way, you'll take some time to look in depth at the Internet itself.

Part 2, "How to Love Internet Stocks," is where we get into the nitty-gritty of analyzing Internet stocks using conventional tools. You will check your risk tolerance and learn how and where to get the best information on Internet stocks. Online resources can be a big help, and this is where you will find the best.

Part 3, "Playing by the Rules," looks at the key components of evaluating Internet stocks. You'll examine concepts such as "the smart way to lose money," and you'll look at how growth, customers, technology, and management can be used to evaluate Internet stocks.

Part 4, "IPOs, Mutual Funds, Day Trading, and Options," looks at some of the alternative ways of investing in Internet stocks. With the exception of mutual funds, these techniques are not for the faint-hearted. The sophisticated investor will find a world of opportunities using these techniques. On the other hand, mutual funds that invest in Internet stocks may be the answer for the investors with less interest in doing the legwork that stocks require.

Part 5, "Blue Chips and Micro Chips," examines the convergence or collision of Old Economy stocks and New Economy stocks. Some of the Old Guard have found this brave new world bewildering, while others have leveraged the Internet into a powerhouse tool for growth. If a pure Internet play is too risky for you, you'll find plenty of good opportunities in these mixed marriages.

Part 6, "Is That a Good Idea?" looks at the big areas of future growth on the Internet and tells how you can spot the market leaders of the future. These five areas don't even cover all the possibilities, but they do point you in the right direction as far as your thinking is concerned. The future is sooner than you think.

Following these parts, you will find three appendixes that cover a review of basic investing principals, a list of Web sites referenced in the book, and a glossary of all the terms introduced, plus some more for good luck.

Extras

In addition to all these goodies, *The Complete Idiot's Guide to Investing in Internet Stocks* has sprinkled throughout each chapter small snippets of information in boxed sidebars. These sidebars provide you with additional tips, definitions of key terms, warnings of potential dangers, and additional information that you may find helpful.

The signposts are up ahead—you are entering the sidebar zone:

Double Click

These sidebars contain useful tips on the current topic. They may be absolutely on track or just enough off to be interesting without being distracting.

Speak Up

Here's where you will find definitions of key terms introduced in the chapter. The definitions also appear in the glossary along with a number of other helpful terms.

Margin Call

The "Margin Call" items are warnings that you are on dangerous ground. They highlight pitfalls and erect warning signs where you need to be on guard.

Help File

These sidebars provide information of the "bet you didn't know" variety. They add to and amplify important points to give you an extra illumination.

Acknowledgments

This book is the result of the efforts of many people. Their contributions dramatically improved the book's concept and execution.

In particular, I would like to thank Susan Zingraf at Macmillan for working with me to get the book off the ground—her idea led to its writing. Renee Wilmeth, Senior Acquisitions Editor, provided a helpful focus to the concept. Thanks also to Mike Sanders at Macmillan, who took over the project when Susan moved on to a new position with Macmillan.

Special thanks also to Nancy Warner, the Development Editor. Her comments are always helpful and on target. This is the second book we have worked on together. I hope there are more.

A special thanks goes to my family, who endured two back-to-back book projects. (Cyndy, I'll get started on that to-do list real soon.)

Trademarks

All terms mentioned in this book that are known to be or are suspected of being trademarks or service marks have been appropriately capitalized. Alpha Books and Macmillan USA, Inc., cannot attest to the accuracy of this information. Use of a term in this book should not be regarded as affecting the validity of any trademark or service mark.

Part 1
Why You Should Love Internet Stocks

Investing in Internet stocks will be either the best idea you ever had or the worst idea you ever had. The outcome is pretty much up to you.

If you are one of those people who thinks that successful investing is a matter of luck and "hot tips," your experience with investing in Internet stocks will probably be short and painful.

However, if you believe that "lucky" investors are the ones who do their homework, take greed out of the equation, and set realistic goals, you may find investing in Internet stocks to be a rewarding experience—not only financially, but also emotionally and intellectually.

Chapter 1

Why Internet Stocks Are Different

In This Chapter

➤ Why Internet stocks are not General Motors

➤ Why Internet stocks are so important

➤ What makes an Internet stock hot

➤ Will Internet stocks stay hot?

Do you know the difference between gold and iron pyrite? Many of the California gold rush pioneers didn't either. The stories of gold lying on the ground for the taking lured many city slickers to the Wild West in search of their fortune. Most ended up broke.

To the uneducated would-be miner, iron pyrite looked like gold. Con men, preying on miners' greed, used the soft, shiny metal ore to convince prospectors that a claim was ripe for the picking.

The people who did find their fortune in the gold rush were able to tell the real gold from the fake gold.

In this chapter, we look at what makes Internet stocks different from the rest of the market—and how you can spot the gold among the fool's gold.

What They Are

Internet stocks represent companies that rely exclusively or substantially on the Internet as the backbone of their business model. They can be broken down into two very broad categories: pure Internet companies and hybrid Internet companies.

Both of these categories offer distinct and attractive investment opportunities, but they may behave in different ways to market conditions. (By the way, these categories are completely arbitrary on my part, but they serve the purpose of this book and would be understood by anyone knowledgeable about the Internet and the Internet economy.)

Pure Internet Companies

The popular image of a hot Internet company is a couple of goofy kids with an idea and not enough sense to know that it won't work. This scenario has repeated itself too many times to be an accident.

However, if that idea is going anywhere, it will need an experienced management team to get it there. For every 20-something multimillionaire Internet company tycoon, there are thousands of goofy kids who couldn't translate their ideas into workable businesses.

Margin Call

Internet stocks tend to be volatile—that is, they can rise and fall in value quickly and frequently. Be prepared for a bumpy ride.

Pure Internet companies represent the cutting edge of investing opportunities. By definition, these are young companies without long track records to analyze.

These companies represent the highest level of risk, but at the same time, they offer the greatest chance for spectacular reward. Your task is to identify which companies have what it takes to turn an idea into a viable business.

These companies may offer consumer, business, or technology services and products. Their distinguishing features include a business model that, for the most part, would not be possible without the Internet.

Amazon.com (ticker symbol: AMZN; amazon.com) is a well-known example of an Internet stock. This megabookstore has morphed into an online general store with a variety of goods and services for sale.

While there are plenty of catalogue booksellers, none can match the quantity of titles that Amazon.com is able to offer. However, that is just the beginning of the differences.

When you want to buy a book from Amazon.com, you also get a list of books that other people have bought along with your selection. While this is a nifty piece of technology, it is really a very old retailing concept called cross-selling.

Mail order catalogues would be hard pressed to match this level of cross-selling—and when was the last time you were in a store and got cross-sold by a clerk? It doesn't happen nearly as often as it should.

Does it work? I think the jury is still out on Amazon.com. The company has built an incredible business with more than 13 million customers at the last count, but they have yet to make a dime in profit.

This points out another characteristic of pure Internet stocks: Very few have any positive earnings, which makes buying them a leap of faith built on a common-sense approach to evaluating their prospects. Most Internet companies are not profitable for the same reason most off-line startups are not profitable. Building an Internet business can be a very expensive proposition.

Staying with our Amazon.com example, imagine what it costs to load several million books, music CDs, and all the other merchandise the company carries. Add in the cost of all the computer hardware, building a huge database that is integrated with accounting, shipping, and all the other systems needed to operate a huge business, and it is easy to see why they are in the red.

Yahoo! (ticker symbol: YHOO; yahoo.com) is another example of a pure Internet stock. As I'm sure you know, Yahoo! is a *portal*—that is, a gateway to other places on the Internet.

Although it's not an actual *search engine*, Yahoo! is the first place many people go to begin their hunt for information. Unlike Amazon.com, Yahoo! relies on advertising for its revenue.

The strength of Yahoo! is its clean design and speed of execution. If you are looking for information on a certain subject, Yahoo! leads you through multiple layers to finally zero in on Web sites that have the information you are looking for.

Yahoo! is often referred to as a search engine, but in fact, it is really an index of sites. The service combs the Web and finds interesting and informative sites to include in the index. When you use the search function, it looks within Yahoo! databases across the Internet.

Every step along the way is a new opportunity to display an ad. Page views, or the number of times a page is seen by visitors, are the online equivalent of circulation and determine how much the ad will cost the advertiser. The more page views, the more advertising revenue for Yahoo!.

DoubleClick (ticker symbol: DCLK; doubleclick.net) is another example of a pure Internet stock. The company provides Internet advertising systems of Web sites, and the systems deliver advertising to

Speak Up

A **portal** is a Web site that acts as a starting point for deeper levels of discovery. Portals often categorize information and direct the user to specific locations. Portals also offer additional services such as e-mail. Alta Vista (www.altavista.com) and Excite (www.excite.com) are examples of portals. A **search engine** is a specialized piece of software that searches the Internet for words, primarily in Web site descriptions, that match the request.

Speak Up

Business-to-business (B2B) is a fairly new phrase for a very old relationship. A B2B company sells products and services to other businesses. A wholesaler is a B2B company as well as an advertising agency.

the customer's Web site. DoubleClick is part of *business-to-business (B2B)* services, one of the hottest growing segments of the Internet.

Along with other service providers, DoubleClick is positioned to grow with the Internet. I'll talk more about these stocks in later chapters, when I examine infrastructure investment opportunities in Chapter 24, "The Big Push."

As you can see from this brief overview, the pure Internet stocks can be broken down into multiple subcategories, three of which are …

➤ Online retailers (see the section "Appearances Can Be Deceiving" in Chapter 9)

➤ Portals to other areas of the Internet (see the section "What Makes Them Hot" in Chapter 1)

➤ Business-to-business (see the section "How You Do It" in Chapter 21, "New Tricks for Old Dogs.")

We'll look at other subcategories later in the book.

Hybrid Internet Companies

Hybrid Internet companies started out in traditional business models but have integrated the Internet into their operations so completely that it would be difficult to return to the old business model.

Sun Microsystems (ticker symbol: SUNW; sun.com) is a computer and software manufacturer that has shifted its focus almost exclusively to the Internet.

The company makes computer servers and software for Internet clients. More than 40 percent of its sales in 1999 came from foreign clients.

Once known as the maker of high-end workstations, Sun Microsystems has transformed itself to focus almost completely on Internet-related business.

America Online (ticker symbol: AOL; aol.com) is the largest online computer company in the world, providing Internet access to some 20 million subscribers—roughly half of the market.

You might wonder why I put AOL in this category rather than listing as a pure Internet stock. Perhaps you don't remember, but AOL was around before the Internet (actually, even before the World Wide Web, as we know it) became popular.

Along with a couple of other providers, including CompuServe (which AOL now owns), AOL was providing online services before the Internet was widely available.

In fact, like Microsoft, AOL initially misread the future of the Internet and almost got left behind. Once the company righted the boat, it began an aggressive marketing campaign and moved into the number one spot quickly.

Then in early 2000, AOL bought Time Warner in a media deal unlike any other. The deal gives AOL access to Time Warner's huge inventory of content, including television, movies, cable systems, and more.

Can the button-down management of Time Warner mesh with the "casual any day you feel like it" style of AOL? Only time will tell.

What They Are Not

Internet company wannabes are a dime a dozen. Their Web sites are an afterthought, at best, and their approach to customers has all the finesse of two elephants in love.

However, a number of these disasters have managed to catch the eye of investors who left their common sense in the closet the day they bought these stocks.

Simply stated, putting "dot.com" on the end of your company name doesn't make you an Internet company, whether you built it from the ground up or simply decided that the world couldn't survive without your vision of an online toilet paper supplier.

In all fairness, many companies with an Internet presence don't position themselves as Internet companies. They are on the Internet because it enhances an existing business structure or because the Internet eventually may grow to be a substantial portion of their business.

Borders Group Inc. (ticker symbol: BGP; bordersgroupinc.com) is this type of company. The bookseller operates numerous bookstores under the name Borders and Waldenbooks, and has added an online presence with Borders.com.

Unlike Amazon.com, Borders.com grew out of an existing business structure. In 1999, Borders.com provided only 0.2 percent of the company's sales and none of its profits. The site is not bad and fairly functional, but this stock is not an Internet play and won't be for a long time, if ever.

Whether this is a workable model remains to be seen. For our purposes now, it is sufficient to note

Double Click

Hybrid Internet companies often report consolidated financial results. This can make it hard to understand the role of the Internet division in the overall well being of the company. Look for helpful online services such as Morningstar.com to uncover buried facts.

Margin Call

Changing a company built on classic manufacturing and distribution systems into an Internet company is harder than it looks. Be wary of the leopard changing its spots without a lot of spot remover and pain.

that it will be difficult for some companies to integrate the Internet into existing management teams and philosophies.

Compaq Computer (ticker symbol: COQ; compaq.com), on the other hand, desperately wants to be an Internet company—or, at least, more of an Internet company than it is. The large computer manufacturer has fallen way behind competitors such as Dell (ticker symbol: DELL; dell.com) in direct selling to consumers and businesses. Profit margins are lower, and costs are higher than those of online competitors.

Compaq's dilemma reflects the difference between starting out as a traditional company with traditional sales and distribution channels, and starting out as an Internet company. As late as 1999, it was almost impossible to buy a Compaq computer online (I know—I tried). The Web site was confusing and almost impossible to navigate. The bottom line was that you could enter only a vague description of the computer you wanted and then had to wait for a Compaq salesperson to call you back (some days later).

Compaq has made great strides and appears to be committed to a direct sales model, but it will be a while before it truly can be called an Internet company.

What It Means to You

None of the previous comments about companies have anything to do with whether they are good or bad investments. The comments simply suggest that if you are looking for an Internet stock, be sure that you are investing in an Internet company, not one that calls itself an Internet company or one that others think is an Internet company.

In virtually every chapter of this book, I will add to the ways you identify and evaluate Internet stocks. Most of these tools are objective (a company that generates almost no business from the Internet can hardly be called an Internet company), but some are subjective. These tools will exercise your common sense and give you confidence to make some calls on your own.

It may be stating the obvious, but Internet stocks are not General Motors (ticker symbol: GM; generalmotors.com). By that, I mean that they have a whole different perspective on how they interact with their customers.

GM is focused on the manufacturing, distribution, and marketing of its cars and trucks. GM has turned over the actual selling to independent dealers, so there is little contact with retail customers. GM's assets are in real estate and machinery. Distribution is by truck and rail. Even though the company has made some noise about offering GM products online, it is unlikely online selling will account for much in GM's total sales picture. (Frankly, until it's possible to deliver the smell of a new car's interior over the Internet, I'll do my car buying the old-fashioned way.)

GM's online selling efforts point out another problem that pure Internet companies don't have: pirating sales from existing outlets. For example, if Bob buys a GM truck over the Internet, the GM dealer in Bob's town has lost a sale. If the dealer loses too many sales, she may eventually go out of business or switch to some other manufacturer to represent.

This is not to suggest that GM will not benefit from the Internet. Its finance unit and other subsidiaries may achieve substantial benefits; in early 2000, the company announced a significant effort to move purchasing online along with other automakers. This business-to-business effort (more about this in Chapter 23, "What Price Glory?") may become a significant contributor to profitability, but GM still will not be an Internet company.

Brick and mortar companies that want to become hybrid Internet companies face similar challenges. Compaq Computer is struggling with this problem. Increasing direct sales will come at the expense of the retail stores that carry their products now.

However, some companies are managing to turn brick and mortar into *click and mortar* by combining the best of both worlds to their advantage. More about them in Chapter 14, "Technology Is Not the Answer."

Successful Internet companies focus their efforts on customer interaction and personalization. They offer solutions and shortcuts that make interacting with them as effortless as possible.

I use an online travel service to book all my airline tickets. Once I select the flight I want from the options presented, the service knows where to send the tickets—or, more likely, the electronic ticket confirmation (to my e-mail address). The service also knows that I like aisle seating and which credit card I use. If I need a rental car, the service knows what size car I normally get and any other travel details I have shared.

Margin Call

You can't read a business publication or a Web site or listen to television or radio news without hearing about the technology sector of the market. Technology stocks and Internet stocks are not necessarily the same thing. Amazon.com is an Internet stock, but it should never be mislabeled as a technology stock.

Speak Up

Click and mortar is a phrase coined to identify traditional companies that have integrated, or tried to integrate, the Internet into their existing structures. For example, Compaq Computer's Web site will direct customers to nearby retail stores for certain products.

My wife uses the same service and has her own preferences for travel. We could use a travel agent and get all these same considerations, but not readily on Sunday afternoon or whenever we want to make our reservations, and we wouldn't always be sure that we were getting the best fares.

Internet companies spend their money on the customer interface. The ones that do it well (Dell Computer, for instance) make buying from them as simple or as detailed as the customer wants it to be.

Dell uses basically a two-part strategy. For shoppers who want a bundle without having to answer too many questions, they offer preconfigured systems that include everything you need. These systems are the focus of their ads and carry a code that identifies them. If a customer sees an advertised system she likes, all she needs to do is enter the code off the ad into Dell's system.

The customers are offered a couple of upgrade opportunities, but not too many to overwhelm them. It's that simple. Enter the code and the shipping and credit card information, and you're finished.

For customers who want to configure their own systems, Dell offers complete control over the process. This is how I bought a computer in early 1999. I picked the processor I wanted, the hard drive, the memory, the video and sound cards, the monitor, any additional drives or add-ons, the modem, and the software.

The system I ordered was comparably priced with the preconfigured systems—best of all, I ordered it online on a Thursday evening, and the computer was delivered to my house (1,200 miles away) the next Tuesday.

That's why Internet companies are not General Motors.

Help File

Internet companies that compete with regular retail organizations have some distinct advantages and disadvantages. One advantage is low overhead because there is no storefront to maintain or salespeople to pay. However, the absence of human contact can turn customers off if there is no compensation in the form of lower prices and ease of use.

So What's the Big Deal?

I think by now even the most Old Economy die-hards are facing up to the fact that the Internet has changed the way many companies are doing business. More importantly, it is changing the expectations consumers have of the companies they do business with.

I will never buy another computer in a retail store. In the last 12 months, I have bought two computers online. I got what I wanted at the price I wanted. No insolent 18-year-old sales clerks who are worse than not helpful. No driving to two or three different stores and settling for what they think is important to stock. After taking some time to decide what I wanted and then shopping for prices, the actual sale took less than five minutes each time, and I had my computer in three business days. All that from the comfort of my home.

Internet companies provide the engines that drive the *e-commerce* phenomena that I have just described. They are building the infrastructure of the new "e-economy" much like the railroads and steel companies did for the industrial economy during the early 1900s.

In Chapter 24, we look at specific investment opportunities. Internet companies that are building the e-economy infrastructure will be at the top of our list for consideration.

How would you like to have had the chance to get in on the ground floor of General Electric (ticker symbol: GE; ge.com) or Ford (ticker symbol: F; ford.com)? That's the opportunity in Internet stocks.

> **Speak Up**
>
> **E-commerce** refers to transactions conducted over the Internet, many of which could not be done as well or as efficiently without the Internet. E-economy is the new economy that many believe is being created by Internet companies, based on interaction with and personalization for the customer.

What Makes Them Hot?

During the latter part of the 1990s, Internet stocks and technology stocks were the hottest things on Wall Street. Initial public offerings (IPOs) soared like rockets if the company had anything to do with the Internet and/or technology.

The main push on Internet and technology stocks during this time period was, in a word, greed. It was hard not to be greedy when you looked at technology companies such as Qualcomm (ticker symbol: QCOM; qualcomm.com). Qualcomm makes digital wireless communications systems for cellular phones, satellite communications, and a variety of other products and services. Its technology is considered the runaway leader in the field.

When I checked Qualcomm's stock price in March 2000, its stocks were trading at around $142 per share. However, that was not the most interesting piece of information in the quote. In the previous 52 weeks, the stock had ranged in price from just under $8 per share to $200 per share!

Qualcomm is an extreme example, but huge price changes are common in Internet stocks as well. Consider About.com (ticker symbol: BOUT; about.com), an online news and information portal. This company has more than 700 expert guides on a variety of topics that provide original content and direct people to other prescreened quality sites.

In March 2000, Qualcomm's stock was trading at around $70 per share. The company had gone public in the spring of 1999. In the 52 weeks prior to when I looked up my quote, its stock had ranged in price from $19 $^1/_2$ to $100.

(In the interest of full disclosure, I work as one of the expert guides mentioned previously—check out my book *Investing for Beginners*, at beginnersinvest.about. com, for more details—but I do not own any stock.)

I could give you dozens of other examples, all equally startling. Individual investors and mutual funds pumped billions of dollars into the market during the 1990s, chasing the ultimate "buy low, sell high" prize.

Margin Call

For every legitimate company such as Qualcomm or About.com, there are hundreds of fringe companies claiming to be the next superstar stock. Beware of unsolicited e-mail that recommends a company that you've never heard of and can find no information on. Most of the time, the deals either have a 1-in-1,000 chance of being around next year or are outright scams.

Double Click

Despite all the media hype, IPOs are not always good investments. One study showed that many were trading at or below their original offering price within a year of issue.

Day trading, which has been a part of the market for many years, although practiced by only a handful of mostly professional traders, suddenly became the sexiest job in America (see Chapter 19 "Day Trading for Fun and Profit," for more information on day trading). The media was full of stories about ex-cab drivers making $40,000 a month day trading.

On the day I got the previously mentioned Qualcomm quote, the stock fluctuated almost 10 points during trading. This kind of intraday volatility makes day traders swoon with desire.

I'm sure some investors were getting on the Internet stock train for a long-term investment, but many others were looking for a quick profit, knowing that when you get out of a highly volatile stock is as important as when you get in.

I get more questions from investors—many of them novice investors, at that—about IPOs and Internet stocks than anything else. For many people, the stock market has become a combination lottery and casino.

Other sectors of the market also experience these highs and lows at various times. In the 1980s, oil stocks were hot at one point, and I could cite other groups in similar circumstances. The difference between them and Internet stocks is that the cycles seem to be shorter and more intense with internet stocks. Time will tell if this bears out, but be prepared for some heart-in-your-throat drops as well as some push-you-back-in-your-seat climbs.

If you find yourself irresistibly drawn toward IPOs and Internet and technology stocks in hopes of making a quick killing, I have some advice for you: In the words of a character from my 3-year-old daughter's favorite video, Disney's *The Lion King*, "Lie down before you hurt yourself."

Will They Stay Hot?

Will Internet stocks stay hot? The answer is simple: Yes and no.

Great! More market-babble. True, but within this inconclusive answer is an underlying truth about the stock market in general: Sometimes it's up and sometimes it's down. These are natural cycles in the market's life, and Internet stocks are just as susceptible to them as any other security.

Here is a simplified version of the market cycle:

➤ The stock sector is hot (for whatever reason).

➤ The market bids up the price (with more buyers than sellers).

➤ The market overprices the stock dramatically.

➤ Stockholders get worried and begin taking profits (selling).

➤ The selling effect snowballs (with more sellers than buyers).

➤ The price drops dramatically.

➤ The lower price makes the stock attractive again.

➤ The market renews interest in the stock.

This is a pretty oversimplified version, but it does make the point that a stock's price can rise and fall without anything substantially changing about the company.

In our previous example, Qualcomm had a *price/ earnings ratio (P/E)* of over 311, while the S&P 500 averaged a P/E of 39. Many analysts would say that at 39, the S&P 500 is overpriced. Qualcomm is almost 10 times more expensive than the S&P 500 average!

You need two perspectives on the volatility of Internet stocks.

First, in the short run, Internet stocks will tend to bob up and down like a bottle in rough seas. If you are looking to run in, grab a quick profit, and beat a retreat, you had better keep a close eye on your stock.

Secondly, for the long-term investor (five years or more), be prepared for the same amount of ups and downs until the company adds some maturity. Internet stocks are not for the weak-kneed, as we'll see in the next chapter.

Speak Up

Price/earnings ratio (P/E) is a measure of how expensive the earnings of a company are relative to its stock price. The figure is found by dividing the stock's market price by its earnings per share. The closer the resulting number is to one, the closer the stock is priced to its earnings. A high number (any number over 20) indicates that you are paying a premium for the stock's earnings.

However, if you are willing to do your homework and don't have a queasy stomach, there are plenty of opportunities in Internet stocks for significant returns.

The Least You Need to Know

➤ Internet stocks are not your typical investment.

➤ Internet companies are redefining their relationship with the customer.

➤ Dramatic run-ups in Internet stock prices are often matched by equally dramatic falls.

➤ Internet stocks will swing with market cycles just like other investments, only more quickly.

Chapter 2

Are Internet Stocks for You?

In This Chapter

➤ Where Internet stocks fit in your portfolio

➤ How risky Internet stocks are

➤ Minimize risk, maximize gain

It's 2 A.M. and you have been sleeping like a baby: You sleep for 30 minutes and then wake up and cry for an hour; you sleep 30 minutes, then cry for an hour.

The sweat is pooling up in your belly button, your eyes feel like they have been stapled open, and your tongue is stuck to the roof of your mouth. Was that investment in DigitalKumquats.com really worth all this agony?

If this sounds like you, maybe Internet stocks are not the best idea for your portfolio. However, most concern about investing in Internet stocks can be relieved by good information and realistic expectations. Finding the right spot for them in your portfolio can make a big difference in how you react to falling or rising prices.

As a group, Internet stocks tend to be volatile. Wide swings in stock prices are the norm. Knowing what to expect can go along way toward improving your sleep. You must keep in mind that knowledge and information are the two keys in eliminating much of the fear from investing.

Let's Talk Real World

The first rule for financial advisers and stockbrokers is this: Know your customer. This rule, often lost in online trading, requires the adviser to know the client's complete financial picture before recommending any type of investment.

More importantly, the rule prohibits financial advisers from recommending investments that are inappropriate to the client's financial circumstances.

Margin Call

Investing without all the information you need leads to bad decisions and troubled sleep. Much of your anxiety can be relieved with a simple dose of information.

For example, a financial adviser could get into a lot of trouble for investing a retired widow's life savings in the options market.

I don't have a problem with this system as long as you have all the facts before you begin investing. That's where this book comes in. I am confident you are capable of making informed decisions and that you will find all the information you need—or where to find it—elsewhere in the book.

Investing is not about guaranteed returns with no risk. Investing is about taking a known risk in anticipation of a reward in proportion to the risk.

The trick to insomnia-free investing is knowing the amount of risk that you are willing to take and understanding what you might reasonably expect in terms of profits or losses from the investment.

Internet Stock Myths

For many reasons, some valid, investing in Internet stocks has taken on the reputation of being extremely risky and ultimately foolhardy. Let's shine the light of common sense on some of these myths and see what we find.

For High Rollers Only

Investing in Internet stocks is not just for the wealthy investors. Many average investors can and should have part of their portfolio in Internet stocks.

Internet stocks should probably not be your very first investment, and I wouldn't bet my retirement on a portfolio made up exclusively of "dot.com" stocks.

You should have enough common sense to know that there is a chance that Internet stocks will lose money. They are probably not appropriate for achieving a specific financial goal by a certain date. For example, investing for a child's college expenses needs a more stable and predictable vehicle than Internet stocks.

I Will Lose My Shirt

Yes, there is a chance that you will lose money on a particular stock, but you could say that about almost any investment other than U.S. Treasury bonds.

The same general rules of investing apply to Internet stocks. If there were no risk of loss, there would be no chance of substantial gain.

Your goal is to reduce the risk to the lowest possible level while keeping open the possibility of substantial gain. Stated another way, you want to minimize the downside and maximize the upside. That should be your goal with any investment.

People who invest on whims, feelings, intuition, and the like will almost certainly lose money sooner or later. Casinos get rich on people who believe they have a "feel" for gambling. You won't last long in the stock market if that is how you invest.

Of course, you can also turn the argument that you will lose money investing in Internet stocks around and state it this way: You will lose money by not investing in Internet stocks.

Known as *lost opportunity costs*, this argument says that by not investing in Internet stocks, you are denying yourself the possibility of making money. If you believe as I do that Internet stocks will be great investments over time, you are costing yourself money by not participating.

Speak Up

Lost opportunity costs occur when you fail to act on an opportunity. In most cases, you pass up a chance for profits because fear or the lack of information holds you back.

I Will Get Rich

No, you probably won't get rich investing in Internet stocks—at least, not in the short term. If you could buy a stock at the absolute bottom and sell at the absolute top and repeat that process time and time again, you would become rich.

However, you can't do that. No one can do that, not even seasoned investment professionals. *Timing the market*, as it is known, is an elusive goal. The best you can do is buy low and sell high more times than the reverse.

If you begin investing in Internet stocks with the notion that you are going to get rich right away, you have probably sealed your fate. The market is not very forgiving of greed.

Speak Up

Timing the market is a strategy in which an investor tries to pick a stock's low to buy and a stock's high to sell. No one can consistently do this with any success.

There is a saying in the market: Bulls profit and bears profit, but pigs get slaughtered. Greed and the pursuit of a quick buck will derail your chances of making real money in the market.

IPOs Are Pure Gold

One of the most enduring legends is the myth of the IPO. That myth suggests that all you have to do is buy an IPO on the first day it is offered, and then sit back and watch the stock climb a gazillion percent.

If it were that easy, why wouldn't everyone do it? Granted, IPOs are important to the Internet investor (I devote three chapters to them in this book). However, correct investment decisions are made neither quickly nor easily.

I get more mail about IPOs than just about any other single topic. People with no investing experience and no other investments want to get in on IPOs. I once got an e-mail from a man who wanted to know where he could buy shares of IPO.

It is not my intention to ridicule people, but successful investing in IPOs is a lot more complicated than it looks. It is not so complicated that you can't learn it if you are willing to spend some time with this book and do some research.

Blindly throwing money at IPOs or any other investment is a guarantee for disaster. There have been so many IPOs in the last couple of years that it would be easy to assume that they are an easy road to wealth. As you will see beginning in Chapter 4, "Show Me the Money," not every IPO has proven to be the gold mine that investors hoped it would be.

Finding Them a Home

Where do Internet stocks belong in your portfolio? That depends on your age, risk tolerance, and financial goals. By the end of this book, you will be able to make these decisions for yourself.

For now, let's look at some general guidelines that can be refined later based on your personal financial situation. These guidelines are just that: They're not strict rules etched in stone. Common sense will tell you when it is okay to bend a few here and there.

Time Is on Your Side

I am a strong believer in a long-term investing philosophy. History has shown that if you buy quality stocks and hold them for a long time, you will make money. The more time you have to hold your investments, the more aggressive you can be. For example, if you are under the age of 35, you can take more chances than if you are 65 years old. Because retirement is the biggest expense we will have to fund, it makes sense to start as early as possible.

For example, one bright young woman (Jane) begins investing at age 25 and puts $100 a month in a mutual fund earning 10 percent for 40 years. Her twin brother (John) waits until he is 35 to begin investing. He also puts in $100 per month earning 10 percent for 30 years.

What did those 10 years cost him?

Jane invests for 40 years:	$636,900.44
John invests for 30 years:	$227,737.39
John's loss:	$409,163.06

John had $12,000 to spend those 10 years he wasn't investing. I hope he enjoyed it because not investing those $12,000 cost him over $409,000!

All is not lost for our procrastinating pal, though. If he ups his monthly contribution to around $280 per month, he can finish with approximately the same as his sister.

However, it will cost him a whole lot more.

Jane invests for 40 years:	$48,000
John invests for 30 years:	$100,800
John's extra cost:	$52,000

To achieve the same results, John had to invest $52,000 more than Jane did.

So, what's the point? The longer you have to invest, the more time your money works for you and the more time you have to correct mistakes.

For example, say that Jane made some really bad choices the first 10 years of her investment plan and earned only 5 percent instead of 10 percent. To reach the same goal of $637,000, all she needs to do is increase her monthly investment to around $144.

The point is that even bad investment choices are sometimes better than no action at all. Jane had to add only $44 a month to her plan to reach $637,000 by age 65. John had nothing to build on, so his additional monthly cost is $180 to achieve the same $637,000.

Jane was able to correct her 10 years of bad decisions by making a minor adjustment because she still had 30 years of investing in front of her.

If she were 55 instead of 25, her options would have been limited to fairly safe and predictable investments. If she needed to put all of her investments into retirement, Internet stocks probably would not be a good choice for any large percentage of her investing dollars.

Internet stocks are more volatile than the market as a whole. They are not appropriate for achieving short-term goals that require a target amount by a certain date.

Investing or Speculating?

One of the factors that has fueled the great increases in Internet and technology stocks for the past five years is the amount of money that has poured into the market.

As the late Carl Sagan might have said, billions and billions of dollars from individual investors and mutual funds have acted like squirting gasoline on a fire. It is a fundamental fact of the market that when there are more buyers than sellers, prices go up.

Margin Call

Two of the biggest dangers in the market are fear and greed. Fear is the emotion that prevents you from acting when your head tells you it is the right thing to do. Greed is the emotion that compels you to act even though your head is far from convinced.

But is this investing or speculating? Some of both, no doubt. I get a lot of e-mail from people who have no background in business, finance, or investing asking me how can they quit their job and become professional investors. These folks have been bitten by the market hype that dominates the news. You do not need a background in business, finance, or investing to be successful with your investing. This book will certainly help you do that. However, that is a long way from becoming a professional investor. These folks spend years learning their profession. Don't expect to duplicate their efforts your first week out.

Investing is about identifying quality stocks and sticking with them until there is a reason not to anymore. Speculating is about taking a chance and hoping it works out. Informed speculation can improve the odds that you'll hit a winner.

I don't have a problem with informed speculation, but don't do this with your first investment dollars. Make sure that you are adequately taking care of your retirement needs with a blend of appropriate investment tools.

Diversify or Die (Figuratively, Of Course)

One of the best protections against investing disaster is diversification—that is, not putting all your eggs in one basket. This applies across your whole investment portfolio and applies equally when investing in Internet stocks.

Once you decide what portion of your investing dollars is going into Internet stocks, map out a plan to place investments in several different segments of Internet stocks, such as retailing, portals, and so on.

If you are buying individual stocks, this may take a while to achieve—staying with your plan will minimize the risk. Another way to achieve diversification is by investing in mutual funds that specialize in Internet stocks.

These mutual funds are still fairly young and have yet to prove themselves over the long haul, but this is a simpler way to participate in Internet stocks. Chapter 18, "Mutual Admiration Society," covers Internet mutual funds in detail.

Investors may choose to do both—place some dollars in individual stocks and the rest in mutual funds. This not a bad strategy at all, but be careful that the individual stocks you are buying are not held by the mutual fund.

This is not a bad thing, but it does defeat the diversification protection you are looking for. Also watch out for mutual funds that call themselves Internet funds but that are also invested in other segments of the market, such as technology stocks.

How Much Risk Is There?

So much has been written and said about Internet stocks in the media that it is not surprising that many people are confused about their risk. Unfortunately, this is not an easy question to answer.

What seems risky to me may seem perfectly natural to you. I can't imagine circumstances under which I would go skydiving. However, thousands of people, including former President George Bush, have done it and survived. Chapter 5, "Time for a Risk Check," is devoted to the topic of risk in more detail, although the focus there is on personal risk tolerance.

We can make some specific observations about risk and Internet stocks. Before we do that, though, it might be helpful to put this in a context of the stock market in general.

From a historical perspective, the risk of owning individual stocks diminishes the longer the stocks are held. Stated another way, the shorter the time you hold stocks, the more likely you are to lose money. Investors who buy and hold stocks consistently do well in the stock market. Traders who jump in and out of the market often find skimpy returns over the long haul.

Double Click

Mutual funds have a lot of advantages: professional management, diversification, and liquidity. However, fees, taxes, and expenses can eat a big hole in your return. Focus on funds with low expense ratios for the best protection.

Speak Up

Intraday prices are those that occur within a single trading day. Speculators and day traders follow them closely.

If you examine any consecutive 20-year period in the history of the stock market, an investor owning individual stocks as represented by the S&P 500 would have never lost a penny. This suggests that if you buy quality stocks (Internet or otherwise) and hold them for a substantial period of time, odds are that you will make money.

On the other hand, people who speculate or move in and out of the market over short time periods will see this type of trading working against them. Internet stocks lend themselves to this type of trading. Significant *intraday* moves often occur in

21

Internet stocks, meaning that the stock experiences wide price swings in one trading period.

It is not uncommon to see swings of $7 to $10 per share of a really volatile stock—and when you look at IPOs, the notion of volatility goes through the roof.

Would-be traders see these swings and picture themselves buying at $20 and watching their profits soar. If it were only that simple, I wouldn't have to write books so that my poor children can have their daily bowl of swill. (Buy several copies for friends. They will thank you, and my poor children can have a hard roll with their swill.) In Chapters 16 and 17, I will talk in detail about when to get in and when to get out of IPOs, as well as other hot issues.

In this case, risk is really coming from the investor who is driven by the scent of a quick buck rather than cool-headed analysis. Here's what can happen.

In March 2000, 3Com Corp. (ticker symbol: COMS; 3com.con) spun off its popular Palm Pilot line of personal digital assistants into a separate company, Palm, Inc. (ticker symbol: PALM; palm.com). 3Com issued an IPO for shares in Palm, although the company retained more than 90 percent of the stock.

An underwriter set the price at $38 per share. When the stock opened for public trading the first day, it opened at $145 per share. Any hopes investors had of grabbing it at $38 and riding it up were dashed.

Still, plenty of investors jumped on at $145. At various times during the day, the stock hit a high of $166; at other times, it traded at a low of $93. It closed at a little over $95.

The speculator must ask himself whether the stock still is as attractive at $145 as it might have been at $38. Should he jump on it anyway, figuring that it is going no place but up, or should he wait and see?

Help File

Investors are often confused about opening prices, especially for IPOs. They hear that the underwriter has set a price at one level, only to find that this price may never be available. The price of a share of stock on the open market is determined by how much a buyer is willing to pay for it. The greater the number investors who want to buy a stock, the higher the price will go.

It is easy to see what the proper course of action was when you have the benefit of looking at what has already happened. What will happen tomorrow or next month or five years from now becomes a little more problematic. The self-induced risk here was in forcing an investment decision in a market with 80-point swings.

The "Gee Whiz" Risk Factor

Many Internet companies make or use technology to enhance their business. Companies that rely too heavily on cutting-edge technology face the danger that their technology will not be accepted by the market or will be replaced by something better tomorrow.

Investors must decide what role this "gee whiz" factor plays in a company's success. In a later chapter, I suggest that technology is not really that important. What is more important is the ability to adapt to an ever-changing landscape in which there are few secure leaders.

Qualcomm, the company I mentioned in Chapter 1, "Why Internet Stocks Are Different," is a good example. Qualcomm's communications technology is the accepted standard, which allows different vendors to make communications devices that can talk to one another. Qualcomm's stock, which experienced a 1,400 percent increase in 1999, shot up because the license fees for this technology are almost pure profit. The same situation exists with Microsoft (ticker symbol: MSFT; Microsoft.com) and its Windows operating system. However, things have a way of changing. The technology for telephoning dialing was once the rotary system—every phone had a rotary dial. Neither Qualcomm nor Microsoft has a lock on the future.

Investors in Internet stocks that are solely reliant on their technology are on thin ice for the long run unless evidence suggests that they are willing to replace their own technology with something better.

The Least You Need to Know

➤ Internet stocks have a place in your portfolio; age, risk tolerance, and goals determine where.

➤ Diversification reduces risk by spreading your investments over several industry sectors.

➤ Risk is manageable and predictable with the proper tools and when armed with good information.

Chapter 3

The Internet

In This Chapter

➤ What the Internet is

➤ Why the Internet is important to your investments

➤ The dot.com phenomenon

Imagine that there are only two telephones in the world, as there were in the beginning. That's interesting technology, but of no practical value. Now imagine that there are 500 telephones all connected to each other. That's slightly more interesting, but still of limited value.

Now imagine that there are 500 million telephones, they are all connected in a way that any one telephone can contact another specific telephone located next door or around the world. That is a network. The value of telephones is not their exclusiveness, but their inclusiveness. Every time you add one telephone to the network, you create 499,999,999 new connections.

That is also the Internet. The bigger it gets, the more value it has.

It's Magic

Many years ago, I was working on convincing Advanced Micro Devices (ticker symbol: AMD; amd.com) to locate a microchip facility in San Antonio, Texas. I flew out to corporate headquarters and got a tour of one of the plants.

Microprocessors are made in these space-age rooms under extremely dust-free conditions. Workers are garbed in what looks like space suits, and everything is spotless.

My guide was an engineer who worked in the communications department. He was trying to explain to me how microprocessors work. The blank look on my face cut his explanation short. I told him I needed a simple explanation for my report. He said, "Just tell them it's magic."

He was right. I understand magic, but I don't understand how microprocessors work. The same is true of the Internet. It is not necessary or important to understand the technical details of how messages on the Internet find their way to the right address.

Of course, it is necessary to understand in some broad terms how the Internet is put together. In Chapter 24, "The Big Push," we explore investing opportunities that focus on the infrastructure of the Internet.

How Does It Do That?

The analogy of the telephones is worth following a little further. In nontechnical terms, both the telephone network and the Internet do the same thing: They break up information into small chunks and send it to a destination.

That destination, whether it is a phone number or a Web site's *URL*, is maintained in the system so that it can be found almost instantly.

Speak Up

A **URL,** which stands for universal resource locator, is the equivalent of a street address for a Web site. If you know this, you can find the site.

You may type yahoo.com into the Web browser on your computer, but that is not what your computer sees. If you look at the bottom bar of some Web browsers, you may see a message that looks something like this: "Connecting to site 111.111.111.111." Each site is designated by a series of numbers that are further translated into a computer code. All of this happens almost instantaneously.

Your data request or e-mail is sent through a maze of computers scattered all over the place, yet each one knows what to do with the request when it arrives.

If you are interested in more detail, I am sure that you can find dozens of books on the subject. In this chapter, you'll learn how you can use your knowledge of the Internet to make better investing decisions.

All the Pieces

From an investment perspective, the sum of the Internet's parts is greater than the whole. I can't invest in the Internet because no one owns it. However, I can invest in the parts that make it work.

Part V, "Blue Chips and Micro Chips," deals with some of the major Internet opportunities for investors. Many of those opportunities involve the infrastructure of the Internet, as well as the more obvious Web sites and vendors.

For now, I want to introduce you to these components of the Internet so that you will have a broader picture of what investing in Internet stocks is all about.

I told this story in another book (*Macmillan Teach Yourself Investing in 24 Hours*, but it is worth repeating here.

During the late 1970s and early 1980s, the financial services industry was going through a major deregulation. Two young hot shots were trying to figure out which banks were going to benefit most from deregulation and how they could profit from it. Meanwhile, a retired schoolteacher quietly made a killing in the market.

How did she do it? The former teacher noted that deregulation allowed banks to put automatic teller machines (ATMs) offsite. She concluded that this would be a very popular way for customers to do business with the bank.

While the two hot shots were drawing up complicated investing schemes, the former teacher invested in the company that made the ATMs. Her logic was that it didn't matter which banks did well and which didn't—they all would need the ATMs.

That's the point of this chapter. Everyone who uses it needs these components of the Internet. Each component is an investing opportunity.

➤ **The interface**—Either a computer or some other device.

➤ **The connection**—For most of us, would be an Internet service provider.

➤ **The backbone**—A high-speed, mostly fiber optic connection.

➤ **The software**—General and specialized software that makes the Web work.

Everyone knows about Amazon.com, but many investors don't know about the companies that make Amazon.com and all the other Internet businesses possible. Invest in the obvious, if you want, but with a better understanding of the Internet, you will have an edge on investors who don't want to take the time to learn.

None of what follows is hard or technical. It does set the stage for Chapters 24 to 28, in which I talk about Internet stock opportunities.

The Interface

Not too many more words from the computer age have been more overused and abused than "interface." Fortunately, this term seems to being dying a natural death—it has been some time since anyone has wanted to "interface" with me.

Although some folks have moved on to *access point* and other more modern phrases, "interface" still has meaning in this context. For most current users, the interface to the Internet is through a personal computer, either at home, at work, or both. We know who the major computer manufacturers are (Dell, Compaq, IBM), and we'll look at some of them later in the book.

The really exciting news is how the market for new ways of connecting to the Internet is exploding. Digital phones, personal digital assistants (PDA), e-mail terminals, pagers, and more are all becoming connecting points to the Internet.

Qualcomm's stock, which I mentioned in Chapter 2, "Are Internet Stocks for You?" has exploded because its technology has become the standard for communicating with these devices. Palm, also mentioned in Chapter 2, makes the most popular of the digital assistants, the Palm Pilot. Attach a wireless modem to it, and you have access to the Internet.

Digital phones that can download e-mail and pagers with two-way communication through the Internet are growing markets. There is even a device that appears to be a cross between a PDA and a pager that is designed specifically for doctors. In addition, several models of cars now come with onboard computers and Internet connections. (And you thought people trying to drive and talk on their cell phone at the same time were dangerous.)

One of the hottest areas in personal computing involves networking homes and/or home offices. A growing number of people are working full-time or part-time out of their homes. Sharing Internet access with co-workers and children is one of the main uses for home networks.

We don't have cable television in our house, but we have three computers. Two are connected with a wireless network. I can take my laptop virtually anywhere in the house and connect to the Internet via the wireless network. If I want to print out a document, I no longer have to copy it to a disk and run upstairs to the computer that is connected to the printer. I just hit Print.

It is very convenient to have multiple devices, but one of the problems is keeping them in sync. If you have a PDA with names and addresses, you want your computer to have the same information. If you correct an address on one, you want the other to have the new information.

You can connect the two and update the information, but there should be an easier way. Fortunately, a new technology from Bluetooth (URL: bluetooth.com) will allow devices equipped with a certain chip to automatically update one another when the devices are within a certain physical distance of each other. You'd just walk into your office, and your PDA would automatically update your computer with new client in-formation, and your computer would update your PDA with new addresses and e-mail information.

In the not-too-distant future, instead of asking someone for a business card, each of you will simply instruct your PDA to update the other's PDA. Now you have the con-tact's name, address, phone number, e-mail, Web site, and any other information that person wants to share.

Another interesting device is the e-mail reader. This is not a computer, but it's a de-vice designed specifically to send and read e-mail. Many older adults, who have no interest in surfing the Web but would like to keep in touch with family and friends, may find devices like this very attractive.

Any fan of science fiction or *Star Trek* knows that in the future we will ask the com-puter for what we want. Voice activation has been around for some time, but it requires tremendous computing power to be effective. As personal computers get more powerful, a new generation of voice-activated devices will be the norm. New software makes chatting with the computer more natural than before. Voice-activated devices and the corresponding software have a long way to go, but in the near future many Internet devices may have this capacity.

I haven't covered all the bases here, but hopefully you can see the possibilities. This is a fast-changing market, with new leaders emerging on a regular basis.

We'll look at these opportunities in more detail in Chapters 24–28. By the time we get there, you will have some tools to help you evaluate companies and identify investment opportunities.

The Connection

Most people who use the Internet at home use a dial-up connection over regular telephone lines. They dial in to an Internet service provider (ISP), who is connected by high-speed lines to the Internet.

ISPs may be local or national companies and typically provide e-mail, personal Web pages, and other amenities. Most people pay around $19 to $21 a month for the service, and even less if they are willing to prepay for a quarter or a year in advance.

The fastest speed available in this configuration is 56 kilobytes per second (Kbps)—that is, 56,000 bits of data per second—although the speed depends on the user's modem, which may be slower. The largest ISP in the nation is America Online (ticker symbol: AOL; aol.com), which has more than 20 million accounts nationwide. Obviously, may people find AOL a friendly way to connect to the Internet and like AOL's proprietary content.

For most people who use the Internet for e-mail and casual surfing, 56Kbps is plenty of speed. However, in a media-hungry culture, it becomes a bottleneck. Web site developers have the technology to deliver live video, music, and a variety of other applications, but a 56Kbps connection slows everything to a crawl.

The big push in this area is for broadband delivery to homes. Broadband is a term that describes connections that deliver information at speeds far in excess of 56Kbps—in some cases, thousands of times faster.

The two main technologies right now are DSL and cable. DSL, which stands for Digital Subscriber Line, works over normal telephone lines. Cable uses a portion of the same line that brings cable television into your home.

Margin Call

I am not a big fan of these deals in which you get a big reduction in the cost of a computer or other device in exchange for signing a multiyear contract with an Internet service provider. If you don't like the service, or if another alternative high-speed service becomes available, you are stuck.

Both have their advantages and disadvantages. DSL must be within a certain physical distance of the phone company's central switching equipment. Cable speeds may decrease as users in your neighborhood are added. This technology has been slow to reach the home user. Neither cable nor DSL is widely available. AOL's recent acquisition of Time Warner (ticker symbol: TWX; timewarner.com) bought it some cable capacity, and several of the regional telephone companies are beginning to roll out DSL service. Each of the technologies requires a physical connection to the customer. The sleeper in all this may be wireless technology, which does not require a physical connection.

With the possible exception of smaller ISPs, every participant in the Internet wants broadband service available to the home user at a reasonable cost. Advertisers in particular are hungry for broadband access to the home so that they can deliver more "television-like" ads to computers.

In Part V, we look at this land of investment opportunity in more detail.

The Backbone

The backbone of the Internet is a series of ultra-high-speed, mainly fiber optical, connecting cables that serve as the information expressway.

These cables move data at speeds of more than 13 gigabits per second (Gbps)— 13 billion bits per second. Considering that traffic over the Internet is increasing every month, these cables become even more critical.

As fast as the Internet is growing in the United States, the bigger market may be overseas in Europe and Asia. Many of the companies that provide the facilities are forming alliances with foreign partners. These alliances between foreign communications companies and American players like Sprint and AT&T are well known, but the notion of a wireless backbone of some configuration may present all sorts of new possibilities.

Software and Services

One of the more exciting areas of the Internet is the software and services arena. Changes here could ultimately impact the way we all work and the tools we use to do that work.

Software and services for devices such as PDAs, pagers, and cellular phones are still up for grabs. If technology repeats itself, a leader will emerge and become the standard.

Developing software standards that every developer and manufacturer will agree to has its benefits and faults. At fault is the stifling of competition and new ideas. On the positive side is the rapid expansion of products and services that can talk to and work with each other. You may not remember the early days of personal computers, but every manufacturer had its own operating system. Some of them were compatible, and some were not. Microsoft's Windows became the industry standard, and the number of PC manufacturers and software developers exploded. You now can load a Windows-based piece of software that you have never seen and instantly know something about it because the interface (there's that word again) looks just like your other Windows software. For better or for worse, standards will open the market to a variety of ideas and innovations.

Speak Up

Application service providers are companies that house software on their Web sites and "rent" it to customers.

One of the most talked about new ideas is "renting" software off the Internet. Known as *application service providers* (ASP), these services are already appearing on the market.

Full implementation of ASP assumes that everyone will be connected to the Internet at all times or have easy and convenient access. The software you use to do your work will reside on a Web site, along with your data files. You will not need a "computer" as such to access this hardware or your files; instead, you will use a variety of devices ranging from a "smart" terminal at your desk to PDAs and cellular phones. When you travel, your office travels with you, whether it is across town or around the world. All of your devices will work wherever you are.

A company called NetLedger (ticker symbol: (private); netledger.com) offers an accounting software package that resides completely on the company's Web site. All of your data resides on its servers, and the company assures you of its confidentiality.

The benefits listed include these:

➤ **Low cost**—You pay only $4.95 per month.

➤ **Current software**—Every time you log on, you have the most up-to-date version of the software.

➤ **Easy access**—You can access your software anytime, from anywhere, with any Internet device.

➤ **Multiple users**—With your permission, any number of other users can access and update your files, no matter where they are.

I am not recommending this product—I haven't tried it, but it is a good example of how the world might work in the near future. If you have ever tried to figure out what files you needed to take on a business trip and what backup software you might need in case one of your programs crashes, you will appreciate the idea of having the same access to your work in your client's office as you have in your own.

This will further blur the line between work and home, which may or may not be a good thing. I believe that technology should work for us, not the other way around. When I hear people complain about how the computer and e-mail dominate their lives, I want to remind them that it won't if you don't let it.

The Internet has made things possible in my life that I couldn't have imagined 15 years ago. I live in a small town, but I do business with people all over the United States, many of whom I have never met in person.

I have an agent in New York; an editor in Indiana; another editor in Arizona; business associates in Colorado, Kansas, and Iowa; and a Web site that gets e-mail from all over the United States and numerous foreign countries. I do all of this from my home a few blocks from Lake Michigan in Wisconsin while watching over my 3-year-old daughter.

What the world will be like in 15 years is hard to imagine, but there are some very clear trends that mean investment opportunities for investors with their eyes and minds open to the possibilities. These aren't "pie in the sky" kind of predictions. Ford Motor Co. announced in early 2000 that it was giving all of its employees a personal computer and Internet access. This huge investment by Ford is to make sure its employees keep pace with the future.

As we work through this book, you will gain tools that will help you separate the "gee whiz" from the solid breakthroughs that will lead to new opportunities.

It Will Grow on You

The number of Internet users is growing at a rapid pace, with some 60 million connections in the United States alone. Whether this growth rate will be sustained is a matter of some debate in the Internet community.

Some feel that the easy consumers have been pretty much mined and that future domestic growth will be slower as the Internet tries to reach lower-income households, where the Internet is considered a luxury right now. The push to connect libraries and schools continues, but if the kids come home to an unwired house, they will probably fall behind their wired peers.

The growing concern over the divide between the digital haves and have-nots has raised some serious social issues. As responsible citizens, we can't ignore these concerns. For right now, let's look at how the Internet will continue to grow and in what areas we might find investment opportunities.

Necessity or Luxury?

For many people, the Internet is a form of entertainment and a way to keep in touch with friends and family. These people may check their e-mail once a day or every other day at most.

Others have access at work and use the Internet in their daily business activity, although there is deep concern by management that more time may be spent checking the stock market, visiting pornography sites, or playing games than doing actual work.

If you have access to the Internet that is always on, you know that this facility increases use. High-speed connections at work and the growing number of high-speed connections at home offer glimpses of how the future might develop. The idea of immediate and instant access to the Internet through a variety of devices and independent of location is not as farfetched as you might think.

Those of you old enough to remember the comic strip Dick Tracy (or those of you who saw the movie with Warren Beatty and Madonna) know that its creator saw a time in the future when people had a two-way television on their wrist like a watch. That vision now is a virtual reality (pardon the pun). Cell phones, PDAs, pagers, and other devices access the Internet, offer e-mail, and allow the user to interact with the Internet—and all in a device that will fit in a pocket.

The relatively high cost of accessing the Internet over a wireless system is the only thing holding back these products. Do you see an opportunity here?

Double Click

When picking Internet devices, watch for compatibility issues with existing hardware and software. A device that won't work with anything else may soon be outdated.

Offshore Opportunities

Growth of the Internet overseas may match or pass that of the United States in a very short time. Major telephone services and product companies are already forging alliances with offshore companies to participate in this growth.

In an ironic twist, countries we call "less developed" may leap-frog past us in some areas. For example, countries such as China are developing tremendous wireless telephone systems where there has been little service available in the past. Why? It is easier and cheaper to build cellular telephone transmission towers than it is to string wire to every home and business in remote areas. Infrastructure-type investments may pay off handsomely in the not-too-distant future.

The Dot.Com Thing

An ad for a Web site-hosting service shows a farmer with a pitchfork staring off the page at the reader. The caption reads something like, "He has a Web site. Do you?"

IBM (ticker symbol: IBM; ibm.com) ran a television ad showing an American couple in Italy stopping at a quaint shop that apparently sells olive oil. A little old lady greets them, and the ugly Americans proceed to tell her that they have three stores in Ohio. The woman nods her head knowingly and reveals that she has customers in Ohio. She hands them a business card with her Web site address. They clearly don't have a Web site and are properly humbled.

Everybody and their brother now have a Web site, it seems. This explosion has led to what I call the dot.com phenomenon. The dot.com phenomenon describes the rush to get businesses online, no matter what.

The frantic nature of the Internet's growth has led to a lot of bad decisions, including investing in anything that had dot.com at the end of its name. I have seen this same behavior three other times. Once it was real estate around the new DFW airport, once when oil prices were going through the roof and everyone wanted to be an oil baron, and once during high inflation when gold was bid up out of sight. In each and every case, business reality eventually caused these markets to collapse on themselves. Will that happen to the dot.com economy?

Almost certainly, this market built on incredibly overpriced stocks must retreat some, to one degree or another. This is not necessarily a bad thing, from an investor's perspective. Bringing stock prices down to some realistic level ultimately will benefit everyone. Weak and ill-conceived businesses will need to improve or risk failure.

Internet stocks were super-heated through the 1990s, but it is not realistic to assume that this growth will go on forever. Quality investments in areas likely to produce continued growth will always do well over time.

The Least You Need to Know

➤ The Internet's strength lies in its inclusiveness, meaning that it costs very little to participate, which encourages usage.

➤ Every part of the Internet's infrastructure provides opportunities for investments.

➤ A basic knowledge of the Internet will improve your chances for investing success.

Chapter 4

Show Me the Money

> ## In This Chapter
>
> ➤ What a venture capitalist is
>
> ➤ Where all that money comes from
>
> ➤ IPOs that go for the gold
>
> ➤ How to get in on the deal

The popular image of an Internet company usually involves someone coming up with an idea, and next month they are billionaires.

It doesn't happen quite that fast, although a few companies have literally exploded. The more typical cycle involves a startup company funding itself on the founder's savings, credit cards, and loans from friends and family. Once a certain level of growth is hit, the company catches the eye of venture capitalists or private investors and gets its next shot of funding. At some point, the company is mature enough (for Internet stocks, that can be measured in months), and the company issues its initial public offering (IPO).

Understanding this cycle and the participants will help you make better investing decisions. We'll pick up the cycle with the venture capitalist and move through the IPO, as this is the stage where you can realistically first become involved.

Who Are These People?

If you think that investing in Internet stocks is risky, try being a venture capitalist. Venture capitalists take the biggest risks of all by providing funding for brand new companies with no track record—and, in many cases, no actual product. They still take a chunk of equity when they hand over the cash, but with the market today, they probably aren't getting as much as they did in 1990.

What do venture capitalists have to do with you and your investment plans? First, knowing about venture capitalists will help you understand the IPO process if you see where it starts. Second, there may be some investment opportunities in venture capital firms.

Speak Up

Going public is the process of offering shares of stock of a privately owned company to the public via an initial stock offering on one of the major stock exchanges.

A venture capitalist is the personification of an organization that specializes in funding emerging companies. A venture capitalist's goal is to grow the company until it is ready to *go public*. At this point, the venture capitalist sells all or a part of his holdings—hopefully at a huge profit.

Sounds easy, doesn't it? I'm sure if a young man came to see you five years ago with an idea of selling books through an online bookstore, you would have gladly handed over $50 million. Right?

But wait a minute. This young man has no track record of doing this sort of thing, no one else is doing this, and it may not even be technically feasible. He doesn't have a working model and is not sure how to build a distribution system that will actually get the books to his customers. Still sound like a good idea?

This is the world of the venture capitalist. These investors are swamped with hundreds of ideas, most of which they will toss after a five-minute review. Out of the 1 or 2 percent that get a closer look, most will follow the first batch into the circular file.

When the venture capitalist finds one that looks interesting, he bores into the company and looks at every part of the operation. He assesses management, marketing, and every other aspect. Many times he will require changes such as bringing in experienced managers before he agrees to funding. Venture capitalists who do their homework reduce the risks they are taking dramatically.

However, even the most careful consideration cannot anticipate every possibility. Venture capitalists live with the knowledge that a certain percentage of their investments are going nowhere.

What It Takes to Be a Venture Capitalist

Venture capitalists come from a variety of backgrounds, but they all have strong analytical skills of both the companies and the people behind them. Many have been in business themselves and understand the practical realities of operating a company. It is not unusual for venture capitalist to have advanced business degrees (MBAs, for example) or professional designations (CPAs, for example).

Not too many years ago, most venture capital companies were fairly small and often focused on single industries or market segments (healthcare, for example). However, as the 1990s exploded in the technology sector, venture capitalists often found more deals than they could fund under normal circumstances. This has led to huge funds being formed to participate in the explosive growth of the Internet and technology companies.

A good example was the formation of @Ventures Global Partners, which was the third billion-dollar-plus fund in the past three months. This fund was organized by CMGI (ticker symbol: CMGI; cmgi.com) and includes two other organizations active in venture capital deals: Hicks, Muse, Tate & Furst, and Pacific Century Cyberworks (ticker symbol: traded on Hong Kong exchange; pcg-group.com). The fund will invest $1.5 billion in global Internet opportunities. In a short three months, CMGI has put together funding totaling $3.5 billion.

Some of the other big players in the venture capital market include companies that may have received funding themselves. For example, Microsoft (ticker symbol: MSFT; Microsoft.com), AT&T (ticker symbol: T; att.com), Intel (ticker symbol: INTC; intel.com), and other Internet and technology companies are big players in the venture capital business.

This is not a case of big brother reaching down to help a younger company get on its feet. These Internet and technology giants have their own interests at heart. They can stay on top of leading-edge technology and participate when these companies go public. It isn't unusual for one of these giants to help a company along, only to buy it or a substantial portion of it later.

Where They Find Deals

Venture capitalists usually don't have trouble finding deals: They are offered hundreds of "can't-miss" deals every year. The problem is finding deals that have a chance not only of succeeding, but also of doing very well.

Venture capitalists aren't interested in companies that will do average. They are after a company that is a future market leader or that will be so attractive that it will get snapped up at a premium.

The actual community of venture capitalists that do Internet deals is fairly small and tight-knit. They are in competition for the best deals, but they also bring each other

Double Click

If you have the hottest Internet deal since Microsoft, you may have venture capitalists calling on you. However, it is more likely that you will need an introduction from someone whom the venture capitalist respects.

Speak Up

Incubators are special organizations set up to help startup companies get off the ground. Nonprofit groups run some, private or governmental units run others, and venture capital firms themselves run some.

into deals that are too big or risky for a single firm. They also refer deals to each other, when appropriate. In fact, referrals are the main way deals get to venture capitalists. The old saying "It's not what you know, but who you know" is certainly true with venture capitalists. Venture capitalists often get referrals from banks or accounting firms that they trust. Sometimes individual investors in the venture capital firm will bring in a prospect.

The odds of a venture capital firm funding an unsolicited deal that comes in the mail are slim to none. If you think you have a deal (yours or someone else's), find a banker, accountant, or some other financial professional who will introduce you to the venture capital firm.

Another source of deals is through *incubators*. Incubators provide a variety of services and facilities for startup companies. These services may include office or manufacturing space, professional consulting, and secretarial services.

The idea is to let the company founders concentrate on perfecting their product or service without spending a lot of time worrying about some of the more mundane business items. When the company reaches certain goals, the venture capital firm may fund it for further development or expansion. With the incubator under its wing, the venture capital firm can keep an eye on the companies, noting which ones are the best candidates for further funding.

According to Venture Economics, venture capital firms provided more than $43 billion in financing to companies in 1999, a 150 percent increase over the previous year.

How They Work

Despite the mind-boggling numbers in the earlier sections, most venture capital firms don't raise billions at a whack. They raise money for the deals through *limited partnerships*, many of which are sold to wealthy individuals and other companies. If you are interested in participating in a venture capital firm and have a high net worth and a fairly large sum of free cash, say $250,000 or so, you might ask your banker or investment adviser for contacts with a firm in your community that is accepting outside participants.

Most venture capital companies are small and often join with others in funding a company. They may never take a company public by themselves, but instead participate as part of a group of venture capital firms.

Once a venture capital fund has selected a company for funding, it often provides help in the form of management consulting to the company. A representative of the venture capital fund will sit on the board of directors and will be involved in the growth and development of the company. One of the venture capitalist's major concerns is the depth and quality of management. It is not unusual for a founder of an Internet or technology company to step aside as president in favor of a seasoned manager.

The venture capitalist may provide several rounds of financing to the company based on the achievement of certain goals. Each step of financing is targeted at taking the company to the next-highest level of size or profitability. Some companies reach a point at which it becomes obvious that they will have a hard time surviving as a standalone business. The venture capitalist will help the company find a buyer of either the technology or the company to be operated as a division of a larger parent.

Other companies are deemed ready to go public— that is, proceed with their IPO. These companies enter a whole new world of government regulation and market scrutiny.

Speak Up

A **limited partnership** is a legal entity that is formed for a specific purpose. Venture capital firms act as the general partner, meaning that they have management responsibility while the other partners contribute money to the deal.

Why Go IPO?

The process of issuing an IPO is cumbersome and expensive, as you will see in the next section. A legitimate question is, "Why?"

The obvious answer is money. If successful, issuing stock to the public is a way to raise millions of dollars that don't have to be repaid. This is also the way that the founder and many of the early employees are rewarded for sticking with the company when it was young and struggling. Startups commonly pay employees all or part of their salaries in stock or stock options. Early employees of Microsoft and America Online became millionaires as those companies went public and saw their stock soar.

Another advantage of issuing stock is using that stock to buy other companies. Their stockholders become your stockholders, and little or no money leaves the company.

IPO to Go

The legal and marketing steps of issuing an IPO are fairly complicated and expensive. This is not something a company should undertake lightly.

IPOs must be registered with the Securities and Exchange Commission, which has regulatory oversight of the process. Certain documents must be filed, and a prospectus must be developed. The prospectus is a document that outlines the offering in detail, along with the risks associated with the offering. Anyone who has ever read a prospectus in detail knows that the document makes the investment look like you are throwing your money in the toilet.

Every possible negative is listed in detail. The management team is examined, and anything negative in its background is revealed. You must be given a prospectus if you are buying an IPO from the underwriter.

While the prospectus is being developed, the SEC imposes what is called a "quiet period" prior to the actual public sale of the stock. The quiet period is implemented to prevent the company from hyping its upcoming offering. Strict rules must be followed, and deviation can cause serious consequences. The SEC takes its role in preventing stock fraud very seriously; because it has life or death powers over the offering, companies do their best to follow the rules.

Margin Call

There are tons of "deals" on the market in which a company is attempting to issue an IPO itself. Beware of these deals. There is a reason that these companies didn't go the normal route, and that reason is usually an extra margin of risk in the deal.

Following the stock market crash of 1929, the SEC has worked very hard to eliminate stock fraud from the market. Not only does fraud steal money from unsuspecting investors, but it ultimately undermines confidence in the market, which could lead to another crash. The SEC also recognizes the very risky nature of IPOs and warns investors that they could lose some or all of their money. That warning would have fallen on plenty of deaf ears during 1999, however, when most IPOs were up substantially over their initial offering price.

Certification of a public offering by the SEC does not mean that it is a good deal. The government doesn't guarantee you a profit: It simply tries to guarantee that you won't get ripped off.

However, just because a company jumps through all the government hoops and completes all the necessary paperwork doesn't mean that the SEC is certifying the investment as sound. It simply means that the company has complied with the law.

How Much Does It Cost?

How much does it cost to go public? How long is a piece of string? The answer will depend on a lot of factors, including how many shares are to be offered and how hard or easy the underwriter believes the issue will go.

Aside from the underwriting expense, there are legal fees to lawyers who are specialists in security law. These folks aren't cheap. There are also accountants to prepare the financial statements necessary before the prospectus can be completed. It is possible that a small offering might not cost more than $250,000, while larger offerings often run well in excess of $1 million.

Who Fixes the IPO Price?

A key player in the IPO process is the investment banker the company chooses to underwrite the issue. The investment banker is in effect the wholesaler of the issue.

Investment bankers underwrite, or guarantee, the sale of the securities to the public. The lead investment banker may pull together several other firms, sometimes called underwriters, to help and spread the risk. Investment bankers set the offering price of the stock. This offering price is what retail brokerage houses and large institutional investors will pay. This price is arbitrary, although it's based on considerable research into what other similar IPOs have gone for.

Underlying numbers and projections go into the offering price, but the main factor driving the process is what the underwriter thinks the stock will sell for on the open market.

Help File

How stock prices come about is one of the most misunderstood processes in the market. In the public market, a stock is priced by what someone is willing to pay for it, not what it closed at the night before. For example, let's say that a stock closes Monday at $50 per share. After the market is closed, the president is arrested for stealing the company blind. What do you think the stock will open for the next morning? It won't be $50, because investors likely will try to dump their shares as quickly as possible. When you have more sellers than buyers, the price goes down.

For example, the IPO for Palm, which I mentioned in Chapter 2, "Are Internet Stocks for You?", was set by the underwriter at $38 per share. However, shortly before the IPO was issued, the price was thought to be going for $14 to $16 per share. Just before the stock was made available to the public, the offering price was doubled. This increase was due exclusively to the feeling that the IPO was going to be very popular and that a higher price could be obtained.

It is important to note that the general public could not buy the stock at $38 per share. That price went to big institutional investors who regularly buy IPO stock from the underwriter, and to retail brokerage firms that also move a lot of IPO stock. The retail brokerage companies reserve hot IPOs for their best customers. Most of these are full-service brokerages that have well-heeled customers, and these are the ones who get an opportunity to buy the IPO.

Some online brokerages are getting access to IPOs and are coming up with some creative ways to distribute them (a lottery, for example). Unfortunately, plenty of IPOs out there are too risky or just plain bad ideas. Just because an IPO is offered for sale does not make it a good investment. With all the media hype surrounding IPOs, too many investors believe that any IPO must be a good IPO.

In Chapter 16, "Jumping On the IPO Bandwagon," and Chapter 17, "Jumping Off the IPO Bandwagon," we look at investing in IPOs in detail, including strategies for getting in and getting out. This is still risky business, under any circumstances.

A good rule of thumb is that if you are given the chance to buy an IPO at the offering price and you are not a big customer at the brokerage, the stock probably isn't worth owning because it is too risky for the regular IPO distribution channels.

Where Does the Money Go?

The great thing about IPOs from the company's point of view is that the money raised never has to be repaid—it's theirs to keep.

Following our example of Palm, the stock with an offering price of $38 per share opened for public trading at $145 per share and went up from there. The proceeds from the first sale of each share went to Palm (minus fees and commissions). This is called the *primary market*.

Speak Up

The **primary market** is the first sale of the company's stock. This sale is often made to institutional investors and brokerage houses. Money from this sale goes to the company.

Later in the day, Palm's stock dropped severely in price, which is not unusual for an IPO. What happens is that the institutional investors that bought from the underwriter start selling their shares. This money goes to the institutional investor, who already paid $38 per share for the stock. This is known as flipping.

Institutional investors can get away with it, but if your broker let you buy shares of a hot IPO and you flip them right away, you may not see any more IPOs for a while. Brokers don't want you and other retail customers driving down the price by dumping stock on the market.

As more shares are dumped on the market, the price declines. What happens next depends on a lot of circumstances. Investors may smell a bargain and jump on the stock, driving up the price again, or the stock price may languish.

In many ways, none of this matters to the company: The company has its money. Trading of the stock on the secondary market doesn't bring in any new dollars to the company.

What Changes for a Company?

I knew a man who owned a good size oil and gas company. He took the company public and regretted the decision. Every time I saw him, he would say, "Whatever you do, never take your company public." His regret centered on the goldfish bowl he found himself and his company in. The investment community and the stockholders examined everything he said or did.

Some managers and founders of startup companies can't or don't want to make the transition from entrepreneur to company executive. The smart ones step aside and bring in professional mangers to handle the complicated business of running a publicly traded company. Watch out for startup founders that can't make the transition. They may well ruin the company's chances for success.

For Internet startup companies, the change from a tight-knit group of people with a vision living on pizza and a promise, to a publicly traded company accountable to the investors and the market must be like slamming on the brakes of a speeding car.

When it was a struggling private company, no one cared if the president went out for a beer and complained about not being able to find the kind of talent needed to make the firm go. However, if the president of a publicly traded company hints the same thing, the stock may take a nosedive. Officers and key employees have to be careful about what they say in public because it could cause a sharp change in price.

Here's an example of what the SEC and other regulators look for:

> The chief financial officer of a company hints that earnings are going to double what was predicted. The stock leaps on the good news. And, guess what? The financial officer picks that time to unload some of his stock.

> If the news about earnings is true, the officer may be guilty of insider trading. If the news about earnings was a lie, the officer may be guilty of stock manipulation. In either case, he is toast and could go to jail.

Companies that go public also face pressure to make money. This is not unreasonable—after all, that is why you invest in a company. However, sometimes the long-term goals of the company conflict with short-term profit pressures. This is not an easy juggling act.

Money, and a lot of it, is the fuel that makes Internet companies go. The process begins with the venture capitalist and ends in the stock market. Along the way, entrepreneurs must become financial wizards as well as technical experts.

The Least You Need to Know

➤ Venture capitalists are frequently the source of initial funding for a new company.

➤ The venture capitalists hope to take a company public and make a large profit on the stock they hold.

➤ The IPO process is complicated and expensive.

➤ Publicly held companies are placed under a magnifying glass by investors and the markets.

Part 2
How to Love Internet Stocks

The media is fond of jumping on the latest buzzwords, and the Internet has provided its share and more. The Internet has changed our economy in some fundamental ways, so it is not surprising that we have some new words to throw around.

Old Economy is a phrase coming into great use to describe the world we knew when the Dow and blue chips were the most important influences in the stock market.

New Economy is a phrase used to describe the "dot.com" world of instant millionaires and multibillion-dollar companies barely 12 months old.

These phrases suggest that the two are mutually exclusive, but I don't believe that is the case. There can be no doubt, however, that they are different. I like to draw the distinction this way: The Old Economy is more concerned with things, and the New Economy is more concerned with ideas.

Both have an important role in a "successful economy," and the quicker they learn from one another, the better we will all be.

Chapter 5

Time for a Risk Check

In This Chapter

➤ Risk and reward go hand-in-hand

➤ Finding your risk tolerance zone

➤ Matching your risk tolerance to investments

➤ How to deal with risk aversion

The two experiences we can count on for sure are death and taxes—neither of which is a pleasant prospect.

If we stretch that over to investing, we would need to add risk to the list of certainties. Without risk, there will be no substantial rewards from investing.

The trick is to find how much and what type of risk you are willing to accept and then to make sure that your potential rewards match that level of risk.

If I were to offer you this deal, would you take it? We'll cut the cards and if I win, I get your house; if you win, I will give you $10,000. Most of us would say, "No, thanks." But what if I raised the stakes to $100,000? Or $250,000? Or $1,000,000? There may be some figure that would make the risk of losing your house worth the potential reward.

Safety Nets

Some people are absolutely terrified at the thought—or even the potential—of losing money on an investment. Older Americans who lived through the Great Depression in the late 1920s and 1930s are particularly adverse to risk.

They have good reason to be afraid of risk. Many Americans lost everything during this time, although the actual number of investors in the stock market was a much smaller percentage than it is today.

The stock market crash precipitated the Great Depression, but it was the domino effect on banks and then businesses that really did the most damage. Banks failed, and depositors lost all their money. Businesses went under and closed, leaving employees unemployed. Farms were lost as loans were foreclosed. It was a time of great uncertainty.

Over the past 60 years, the government has worked very hard to put in place fail-safe systems to prevent the kind of cascading effect that took place during the Great Depression. The banking crisis of the 1980s, which was tied to the collapse of the real estate market, caused a large number of financial institutions to go under. Yet, no depositor in any of those institutions protected by Federal Deposit Insurance Corp. (FDIC) lost a penny of their savings.

Help File

The market crash of October 19, 1987, resulted in a 22.6 percent loss of value in the market. That translated to a loss of more than $500 billion dollars. The crash of 1929 saw a 12.8 percent drop and a dollar loss of $14 billion, according to *The Wall Street Journal's Guide to Understanding Money and Investing.*

The stock market crash of 1987 was worse in some ways than the 1929 crash, yet there was no domino effect throughout the economy. Trading procedures were put in place to help prevent another market free-fall. The government and self-regulatory agencies such as the National Association of Securities Dealers (NASD) (www.nasdr.com) are not trying to eliminate risk from the market. They are trying to maintain confidence in the market systems that may prevent a catastrophic loss.

Investors today can have a reasonable amount of confidence that despite the market's ups and downs, there is less chance of "end-of-the-world" scenarios playing out than ever before.

Honest Talk About Risk

There is risk associated with virtually any investment in individual stocks or mutual funds. Historically, the shorter the period you hold a stock, the greater the chance that you will lose money. It is equally true that the longer you hold a stock, the less chance there is that you will lose money.

Internet stocks are not immune to these forces. Because of their volatility, Internet stocks may be held for shorter periods of time than regular stocks. Internet stocks may experience large swings in price even on a daily basis.

Say you own 100 shares of an Internet stock that closed the night before at $125 per share (that's $12,500), and you work in the garden all the next day without hearing any news. After supper, you fire up your computer and log in to your online account only to find that your gem closed the day at $110 (that's $11,000). You lost $1,500 today!

If that kind of volatility keeps you up at night, then you need to be very careful about the investments you pick. Of course, in our example, the loss is on paper until you sell the stock. It wouldn't be unheard of for the stock to be trading at $135 the next week, or $75, for that matter.

Many Internet companies end up on the scrap heap for the same reasons that other small businesses fail. Internet companies are even more at risk. The Internet stock myth is that anything with a dot.com in its name is a gold mine. The ugly truth is that many Internet companies never make it beyond a very early age. They die for many of the same reasons all young companies do: poor management, lack of funds, competition, or a poor business concept.

In addition, young Internet companies face some unique challenges, such as technology made obsolete by a competitor and a lack of market acceptance of their technology, product, or service. It may take a conventional company three or four years to discover that it is not a viable business. Internet companies may face that reality within six months of putting their product or service on the market.

Understanding the relationship between risk and reward and then knowing how you can minimize risk will go a long way toward a peaceful night's sleep.

Enough Gain for the Pain

Three elements exist in a simple investment formula: the amount of money invested, the length of time the investment can mature, and the level of risk you are willing to accept to achieve a goal.

This investment formula predicts the odds for success of an investment (don't worry, no quadratic equations are involved). I use these three elements because they are the ones you have some control over, unlike market conditions and similar considerations.

There is a direct relationship between these elements that will help you figure out what it will take to achieve a certain financial goal.

Amount Invested

Obviously, the more money you invest, the less time you will need and the less risk you will have to take. However, if the amount you have to invest is smaller, you will need more time and will have to take more risk. The longer you hold an investment, the more time it has to mature and achieve market leadership. However, a turkey stock will just become an old turkey stock if you hold it forever.

Length of Time

Stocks do better over a longer period of time. If you can invest for the long term, then you will not need as much money and can reduce the amount of risk.

Conversely, if you have only a short time to achieve your goal, you will have to invest more money and take a greater risk.

Level of Risk

Depending on the length of time and amount you have to invest, you can determine the amount of risk you need to achieve your goal. If you are willing to accept more risk, you may achieve your goal in less time and with less money. If your risk tolerance level is low, it will take more money and more time to achieve your goal.

None of these scenarios guarantees that you will achieve your goal. After all, the very definition of risk is uncertainty.

You may choose to look at these situations in a different way. For example, if you have 40 years to fund your retirement, I would counsel that the early years are a good time to take some chances. You have many years in front of you and your highest income to come. This means that you can recover from mistakes or risks that don't work out.

Of the three elements—risk, time, and money—risk is the dominant concern. Even if you work things out so that risk is always low, it can still work against you. If you have a low risk tolerance (that is, if you are risk-adverse), you should plan your investments to take advantage of time and money and keep risk to a minimum.

There is nothing wrong with this strategy—in fact, it has the greatest odds for success of all the combinations. There are plenty of investment opportunities for these types of investors in Internet stocks, and you don't have to bet the farm every time you invest in Internet stock.

Types of Risk

Investing in the stock market subjects you to certain types of risk, regardless of what kind of stocks you buy. We will look at these risks and how they affect Internet stocks in particular. The three major risks are these: market value risk, inflation risk, and economic risk. All stock market investments face the same set of risks, and Internet stocks are no exception.

Market Value Risk

The concept of market value risk is that the market will ignore or devalue your investment in favor of a hotter sector, or for some other reason.

It is hard to imagine a sector getting any hotter than Internet stocks and technology. However, in the first couple months of 2000, these sectors were hit, and some of their spectacular gains were given back. Leaders such as Microsoft and Cisco Systems (ticker symbol: CSCO; cisco.com) were trading quite a bit below their 52-week highs.

Hopefully this served as a wakeup call to those investors who believe that technology and Internet stocks are bulletproof. They definitely aren't—and it's tough to say whether the downturn was a one-time *correction* or a general dissatisfaction with the overpriced stocks.

One of the best defenses against market value risk is *diversification*. This book is based on the understanding that Internet stocks are not your first investment and that you are addressing major financial goals such as retirement with more stable and reliable investments.

Even so, within the dollars that you are allocating to Internet stocks, you should try to achieve some balance. Later in this chapter in the section titled "The Balancing Act", we look at particular ways to achieve some balance in your Internet stock portfolio and reduce market value risk.

Margin Call

If you have any doubts that Internet stocks can lose money, look up some of the ones you are interested in on Morningstar.com; notice the 52-week highs and lows, and the price at which that stock is currently trading. Someone bought it high and sold it low—maybe a lot of someones.

Speak Up

Correction is a polite term for a full-scale retreat by a market sector or the whole market. It is usually caused by some external event, such as interest rate hikes, and generally lasts for only a short time. **Diversification** is the strategy of spreading out your investments over different types of products that do not move in tandem so that peaks and valleys of performance are leveled out.

Inflation Risk

Inflation has seemed a very distant and ineffective challenge for most of the late 1990s. The Federal Reserve Board (the Fed) has acted swiftly and decisively in raising interest rates to cool the economy when inflation reared its ugly head.

Younger investors may not appreciate how devastating high inflation can be to an economy because a decade has passed without high rates. Double-digit inflation destroys the value of your investments and even your earning power.

Just as its economic effect is severe, high inflation can work its poison on consumer confidence. Consumer confidence plays a major role in our economy—when it is shaken, our economic system shudders.

Here is an example of why high inflation destroys confidence. Assume that inflation is 10 percent and that you have an investment that pays 8 percent. What happens to your investment in this situation?

Amount invested:	$1,000
Interest earned:	$80
Total for year:	$1,080
Minus inflation:	$108
Minus taxes (25 percent)	$20
Total deductions:	$128
Your net:	$952
Your return:	–4.8 percent

Although your bank balance would show $1,060 ($1,080 – $20), your actual purchasing power would be $952 after inflation. Ouch! Talk about one step forward and two steps back. This is no way to make money.

Under these conditions, you could quickly become discouraged and conclude that you are almost better off not investing the money at all. That kind of financial uncertainty doesn't bode well for the stock market.

The Fed uses interest rates to combat inflation. When the economy is overheating and it looks as if inflation is coming back, the Fed raises interest rates. The Fed meets quarterly to discuss interest rates and the general economy. At these meetings, the Fed can raise, lower, or leave untouched key interest rates, depending on whether members believe that the economy needs to be cooled off, heated up, or left to simmer. If interest rates are raised too much or too quickly, this could slow down the economy more than anticipated and create a recession. Sometimes the cure is as bad as the disease.

Past periods of high inflation have seen money flee the market of investments in so-called hard assets, such as gold and real estate. Fewer buyers than sellers always mean that prices are going down.

How do you protect yourself against inflation with your Internet stocks? In truth, there is probably no way you can do it with just your Internet stocks.

Economic Risk

Economic risk is the danger that the economy could turn against your investments. It may seem hard to believe that the economy could turn against Internet stocks, considering how much investors love them. However, previous markets have loved healthcare, biotechnology, real estate, oil and gas, and gold, only to dump them for something else. The market is a fickle lover. Protecting yourself against the whims of the economy is not easy when considering just one market sector.

Your Personal Risk Tolerance

At this point, you need to do a little exercise in self-awareness. Spend some serious time considering your personal tolerance for risk and, if there is a partner in your life, that person's tolerance also.

This is time for some real honesty about where you fall on the risk scale, without considering what others may think or urge you to do. This honesty will help you find those investments that will give you the best chance for success without keeping you awake at night.

Remember also that risk aversion can be a factor in dealing with a good event such as an inheritance or a bonus at work. What you do with these situations will also be instructive in determining your risk tolerance.

Many roads lead to financial success, and most of them do not involve huge amounts of risk. You know you are in the wrong investment in these cases:

➤ You can't sleep at night.

➤ You check the price every 15 minutes.

Double Click

Practicing your trading patterns on paper may turn up some situations in which your risk tolerance comes into play. It may seem like much ado about nothing, but erratic emotions can do more to damage investment plans than just about anything else.

Margin Call

Money—or, at least, worrying about it—can ruin your life. The purpose of investing is to achieve some measure of financial security. If investing becomes a gut-wrenching experience, find someone, such as a fee-based financial planner, to do it for you.

➤ You scour chat rooms looking for encouragement.

➤ You worry when you are away from your computer that something bad is happening.

No investment is worth ruining your life with worry.

You can take several online risk-tolerance tests, but an honest dialogue with yourself and your partner will probably give you the answers you need.

Consider the following scenarios, and assess your reaction to the real or perceived risk. These might be good discussion points with your partner so that you understand each other better.

Example #1: Rich Aunt Helen, the one who always pinched your cheeks, has left you $50,000 in her will. What do you do with it?

1. Pay off your credit cards and then put the rest in a good index mutual fund.

2. Buy a new car and invest the rest in options.

3. Give it back—you never really liked her.

Example #2: The sure-fire, can't miss stock your barber recommended has just dropped 30 percent. What do you do?

1. Sell, and lick your wounds, vowing to pay more attention to the stock you are buying next time.

2. Buy more, because it is sure to go up again.

3. Punch your barber in the nose.

Example #3: Your brother the stockbroker, who just bought the nanny a new BMW, has a stock that you really want to buy, but you are short of cash. What do you do?

1. Take a cash advance on all five credit cards.

2. Say thanks, but I'll let you know when I have some money.

3. Hold up your barber (he owes you, after all).

This is not a quiz with right or wrong answers (although if you picked option 3 more than once, you should consider counseling). The point is to get you thinking and talking about situations that are more relevant to you.

When I hear a little voice in my head saying, "What are you thinking?", I know I am over the line. You will learn to hear that voice or whatever the trigger is when you cross the line with risk aversion is a matter of identifying where the aversion lies and avoiding those situations. You can adjust the investment formula we discussed at the beginning of this chapter to help you reach your goals at a level of risk where you are comfortable.

The less risk you are comfortable taking, the more time and money you are going to need to meet your goal. That is the importance of an honest assessment before you get started. Knowing that you need more time may motivate you to get started on your investment plan sooner.

Some Internet stocks and products built on Internet stocks will fit all but the most risk-adverse investor. This may surprise some people who have assumed that all Internet stocks were a roll of the dice, at best.

In the next section, we begin talking specifically about different types of Internet stock investments; in Chapter 8 "The Basics of Evaluating Internet Stocks," we go over some of the techniques to find and evaluate specific stocks and mutual funds that will meet your financial goals.

The Balancing Act

Balancing risk and reward is the process of balancing your portfolio with products that meet your particular situation. When you are working within a narrow sector such as Internet stocks, balancing becomes a little more problematic because you don't have the diversity of choices like you do in the open market.

A more thorough explanation of balancing risk and reward can be found in my first book, *Macmillan Teach Yourself Investing in 24 Hours*. Another shameless plug.

Different Types

It might be helpful to begin with a discussion of low-, medium-, and high-risk Internet investments. Of course, you should understand that these are general observations, not specific recommendations.

In Chapter 8, I devote a considerable amount of time to evaluating individual investments to reveal that one small Internet stock may be very risky, while another is not nearly so risky.

Low-Risk Investments

It may seem like an oxymoron to talk about *low-risk* Internet investments, but everything is relative. You need to remember that we are talking about only a portion of your portfolio devoted to Internet stocks.

Plenty of investors would like to be in on the Internet stock boom, but they find the double-digit swings in price more than their stomach can handle. An alternative for those folks might be a mutual fund that invests in Internet stocks. As of early

Margin Call

Of course, the term **low risk** is relative: low risk as compared to what? Internet stocks are not low risk in the general context of all investments, such as Treasury bonds, but the risk can be minimized.

2000, these funds haven't exactly set the world on fire, and some of them are as volatile on a percentage basis as some stocks.

I discuss specific situations in Part 4. However, I would like to alert you low-risk investors to a class of mutual funds that invest in Internet stocks and are relatively low risk.

These are mutual funds tied to Internet stock indexes, such as the Dow Jones Composite Internet Index and others. Index funds attempt to mimic the index they follow. They are fairly mechanical to manage and own, and there will soon be a number of these index funds on the market.

A couple that are on the market now are: the Internet 100 (ticker symbol: M$-BDGA) and the Internet.com Index Fund (ticker symbol: GFINX; www.gffunds.com/fundfacts/ icom.html). Index funds are usually fairly conservative, low-risk investments. Because they follow a particular index, they keep you up with the market, but you'll never beat the market. On the other hand, the market as reflected in the index won't beat you, either, meaning your investment will rise or fall with the overall market as opposed to individual stocks.

Speak Up

The **Standard & Poor's (S&P) 500 index** is a weighted index of 500 of the largest stocks. The S&P 500 is the most widely used measure of broad market activity and is often the benchmark to which other investments are compared.

One of the big reasons that index funds for the general market (such as the *S&P 500 index* funds) are successful is that they have a very low expense ratio. The expense ratio is an accurate predictor of a fund's success. The higher the expense ratio, the less likely that the fund will be successful.

On this note, the current crop of funds fails. A good Internet index fund should have expenses below 0.5 percent (that's one half of 1 percent). None of the current funds can match this expense ratio, but I'm sure that one will soon.

A predictor of the success of individual Internet stocks is size. The larger companies will have an easier time riding out the bumpy spots than small companies just barely hanging on. However, don't expect spectacular growth, either. In Chapter 8, I give you some specific tools for evaluating these Internet giants.

Moderate Risk Investments

If you poll investors, most of them will place themselves in the category of moderate risk-takers. They want some of the spectacular gains and are willing to take some risks to get them, but they aren't going to bet the farm.

These folks will be age-sensitive in their investments, realizing that the closer they are to retirement, the fewer risks they can take. The larger gains are typically found in medium to small Internet companies. These are the ones that have about the same potential to explode or implode. A moderate-risk investor will tend more toward the medium-size companies and will spread some of the risk over more established hybrid Internet companies, such as Intel or Microsoft, for stability.

As Internet funds develop, the moderate risk-taker will look at those funds focusing on midsized and smaller companies. The moderate risk taker then will make sure that the rest of her portfolio offsets the risks associated with Internet stocks and funds.

High-Risk Investments

Hold on to your hats! Our high-risk investor is about to take off. If you want spectacular rewards and can live comfortably with a corresponding amount of risk, Internet stocks are the place to be.

Right off the bat, a high-roller will want to speculate with IPOs, using market timing to catch a quick profit (or loss). She may spend most of her time studying and planning her next IPO deal.

Even though she is a high-risk investor, though, she isn't stupid. She does as much research, if not more, than other investors. She knows the odds, but she also knows how to position her trading to take the highest possible reward.

If she has a losing trade (and she will), she learns from her mistakes and moves on without any regret or worry over spilt milk. She may try day trading or options, or foreign Internet stocks. Most importantly, she is able to take all these risks and sleep through the night.

Margin Call

High-risk investments in Internet stocks are right up there with the riskiest of investments. The Internet market is unforgiving, and few companies get a second chance if they stumble.

Risk Is Your Friend

Risk is not something to be avoided at all costs when investing in Internet stocks. If you try to avoid risk, you won't find investments in this market sector.

Look at risk and your reaction to it as a barometer of your investing health. If you can make investments in Internet stocks and sleep well at night, then you are on course. On the other hand, if you toss and turn like a person in need of an exorcism, you probably have passed through your comfort zone and into that area between dusk and dark known as the starch-in-my-shorts zone.

Information and realistic expectations will go a long way toward counteracting the hysteria generated by the media every time the market dips.

The Least You Need to Know

➤ Know your risk tolerance, and investing in Internet stocks will be a more rewarding experience.

➤ Risk and reward cannot be separated because without risk there is no opportunity for reward.

➤ Match your investments to your level of risk tolerance so that you are comfortable with them.

Chapter 6

Doing Your Homework

> ## In This Chapter
>
> ➤ Information sources to keep you on top of Internet happenings
>
> ➤ Finding information on stocks to evaluate
>
> ➤ How to avoid the scams and sales pitches
>
> ➤ Chat rooms, newsgroups, and other traps

My grandfather lived with us for a number of years before he died in his mid-80s. I was about 10 years old when he died, so I had the privilege of knowing him as I was growing up.

Pop was a carpenter before he retired, and even in his waning years, he could put in a full day's work around the house. He let me help him and was patient in teaching me how to use tools correctly and safely.

Pop had a cousin about his age who spent hours in his woodworking shop. Unfortunately, the cousin was not as careful as Pop and was missing the tips of three fingers.

Pop taught me the carpenter's golden rule: Measure twice and cut once. That's good advice for Internet stock investors, or you may find some financial body parts missing.

Information Is Your Best Tool

Perhaps more than any other group, Internet stocks require a considerable amount of homework before you start investing, especially in the smaller companies. That's the bad news.

The good news is that there are plenty of places to find all the information you want and then some.

Now for some more bad news. In addition to the many resources available, you will find a host of fly-by-night sources claiming all sorts of inside information. Most of these are benign, but can be annoying if you end up on their mailing list. Others are outright scams. We'll sort through them in this chapter.

Double Click

Unlike some investments, you can actually try out many of the Internet companies and see how you like them. If you find them awkward or confusing, it is likely that others will also.

How about some more good news? I think you'll find that researching and evaluating Internet stocks is a lot more fun than it is work.

Your Tool Box

The best place to look for information on Internet stocks is the Internet, of course. Some magazines are worth looking at, but your main source of information will be the Internet itself.

This raises an important point: If you are not using the Internet, you really have no business investing in Internet stocks. It is imperative that you know what the Internet is about before you start putting money into it, and you can't get the sense of what it is about unless you experience it.

The Good, the Bad, the Ugly

My high praise for the Internet comes with a stern warning. Like all free exchanges, it is the hunting ground for people who will abuse the access it affords.

These people believe that the Internet is their personal ticket to your pocketbook and will go to any extreme to find a way to separate you from your money. Many are predators in every sense of the word.

However, let's back up a step and look at the other bogus patrons of the Internet. These range from the harmless to the annoying, but they all have one thing in common: They will rob you of your time, if not your money.

Newsletters

Almost any site you visit these days wants you to register. Some will deny you access to parts of the site until you do sign up. If you are visiting reputable sites, including the ones I note in this book, it usually is safe to register.

Some of the fringe sites, however, should be avoided, especially if you have to register. At the very least, they are going to want your name and e-mail address. At the worst, they will want a whole lot more, including personal information such as credit card numbers, Social Security numbers, and so on. A Web site should not need any more information than your name and e-mail address for you to receive a free newsletter. If they ask for personal information, try another site.

Never, ever give out any information of a personal nature unless there is a legal reason to do so. For example, you can't open an online brokerage account without supplying your Social Security number, either online or on a paper document that you mail to the firm.

All legitimate Web sites have a privacy policy posted on their sites. If you have concerns about what they are going to do with the information they collect, read the policy.

The Sting

Because of my work on the Internet, I look at hundreds of sites. Unfortunately, I am registered all over the Internet. If you like to get junk mail, register at about a dozen fringe sites and watch your mailbox fill up. This is the Internet equivalent of writing your name and phone number on a public bathroom's wall.

Although most of what I get is harmless, other than taking up space in my inbox, I do get quite a bit of mail that is far from harmless. These little gems usually start out with a lot of words in all capital letters (the Internet equivalent of shouting) and proceed to tell me they have found an "undiscovered" or "overlooked" or "undervalued" stock that I can't live without. This diamond in the rough is about to be discovered by "the big boys" or has a deal in the works that will make Microsoft look like a mom-and-pop burger joint. And, best of all, the stock is only $1.25 a share.

Double Click

If you find yourself on the mailing list of a newsletter or some other such e-mail publication, look for an "unsubscribe" feature at the end to get your name off the list.

All I have to do is call them, and they can make sure that I'm not left out of another megadeal. I'm sure that you have enough common sense to see through this scam.

Usually one of two things is happening. Either the e-mail is from the company itself and hopes to juice up its stock, or a group of people buy a big chunk and then get on the Internet and plant all sorts of stories and rumors, hoping that the stock will go up. When it does, the crooks dump their holdings for a big profit, and the stock drops like a rock.

Either way, someone is trying to con you. These deals may be fairly easy to spot because they are usually so crude. The really dangerous ones have every appearance of being for real.

Sometimes you will get an e-mail suggesting that someone you know gave the person your name as a savvy investor. This may be followed by a telephone call from a representative of what sounds like a very prestigious brokerage firm. This person will let you know that he has a good deal that you can get in on, if you act quickly.

Several months ago, I got an e-mail from a man who lost $20,000 in a scam similar to this. He was offered a ground-floor opportunity on a hot IPO that was to go public in a few months. He bit. When he hadn't heard anything for a while, he called the salesman back, only to find that the phone was disconnected. The man and the firm he supposedly had worked for had disappeared.

The fellow who lost the $20,000 could have saved his money if he had spent less than five minutes at a site that lists upcoming IPOs. He would have seen that there was no IPO with the name given to him by the salesman.

I don't believe this man was stupid; the moral of the story is to never underestimate how persuasive these con artists can be. Sometimes we want to believe that, for once, something has come our way, and we grab at it without really thinking.

The System

If you are ever up late at night with absolutely nothing else to do, turn on your television and watch some of the program-length infomercials that populate the wee hours of local television. You can buy real estate with no money, catch fish with no effort, lose weight eating pizza, and do just about anything else that will make you rich, healthy, and popular with small children. You might even see a system for making a fortune in the stock market. If you don't see one on television, it won't be long before they will start popping up in your e-mail and snail mail.

The Hook

These pitches all begin to sound alike pretty soon, but here is how they start: "Millionaire Wall Street Tycoon" shares the secret to stock market riches. Usually the story goes that an elderly stock trader tells his young protég[as]e the secret that made him rich. The protégé is now prepared to pass on this secret formula for investing success. Most of these scams use words and phrases such as "secrets revealed," "anyone can learn," "incredible returns," "miracle," and so on. They all let you know that the stock market is impossibly complicated and that the "small guy" doesn't have a chance against the "big guy." For a small (or not so small) fee, they will let you in on their system, which has returns for the past 10 years of 650 percent per year.

The Line

The only thing these folks really possess is the power of persuasion. Even though I know that these schemes don't work, I find myself reading through their material and almost dropping my guard. Their arguments are very convincing. These folks have records showing how their system would have produced spectacular returns over some past period. Satisfied customers provide glowing testimonials from the side of their swimming pool at their new house, which they bought with the profits from their first six months of using the system.

The Sinker

How do they achieve those spectacular results? First, some are outright lies or exaggerations. Second, although it takes some work, it is not difficult to design a system based on historical data. If I know what happened and when, it is not very hard to design a system that is in and out of the market at the right times with the right stocks. This method is called *back testing*, and it produces exactly the results it was designed to produce.

Here is the truth: There are no secret systems. There are no miracle formulas for trading success. No one has a system that will time the market consistently. And, yes, Elvis is dead. Successful investors work hard for their gains, and some use very sophisticated analytical tools. They are successful because they do their homework and keep an open mind. When they make a mistake (and they all do), they cut their losses and move on to the next deal.

> **Speak Up**
>
> **Back testing** is the process of using historical data to construct an investing plan that produces spectacular results, and then suggesting that it will work in the future.

The Rumor Mill

The Internet is a great place to meet and trade ideas. Three of the places this occurs are chat rooms, message boards or forums, and newsgroups. All three of these services provide a place for people with similar interests to meet and trade ideas and thoughts about any subject you can think of. All these places provide easy ways to get investing ideas, but always verify the information from independent sources.

Many of the major sites listed in this book offer one or more of these facilities, most often message boards. Although they differ in format, functionally they are pretty much the same. You log on using an online name, which could be your real name or something you make up. Once on the system, you can talk to whoever is online at that time by typing in your comments or questions and waiting for a reply.

As you might guess, investing is a big topic on the Internet, and you will find lots of message boards and chat rooms in which the ongoing topic is the Internet.

Some of these facilities are "moderated," and some aren't. The purpose of the moderator is to keep the conversation on track and to eliminate annoying posters that are not contributing anything. Moderators also watch out for stock scams and manipulation. However, most of these facilities are not monitored, and anyone can post anything.

The Rip-Off

Several recent cases have surfaced of people arrested for stock fraud who were using the Internet to manipulate the price of a particular stock.

People may pose as company officials or ex-employees, or use some other ruse that seems to give them credibility. The anonymous nature of the Internet makes it easy to claim to be whoever you want to be. Two recent cases involved stock manipulation in a way that has regulators truly worried because they can go undetected long enough to do damage.

The first scheme involved a hacker who broke into a company's Web site and posted a notice that the company was about to merge with a bigger company. The crook then posted notices on message boards all over the Internet with a link back to this story. Investors saw that the story was on the company's Web site and assumed that it was legitimate. As buyers flooded the market, the stock's price rose dramatically.

The company began getting calls about the merger. It was then that officials discovered the bogus story on the site. They killed the story and denied the merger, but the damage was already done. Investors had bid up the price for no reason; when the truth came out, the stock retreated to its original range, but not before the crook dumped a bunch of stock on the market.

The second version of this con is to build a Web site that is a duplicate of some respected financial adviser or broker. The crook posts notices on message boards with links to the bogus site. Investors go to the site thinking that they are looking at the real thing. The bogus site touts a stock, and investors began to bid it up. Eventually, the ruse is spotted and the fake Web site is taken down, but again the damage is done.

Don't believe everything you read on the Internet. Tips, secrets, and rumors should all be taken for what they are worth, which is nothing.

Sorting the Tools

Now that we have covered the danger areas, let's focus on the positive. After all, you are interested in what you can do, not what you can't do.

Your tool box (the Internet) has a variety of tools to help you keep up on Internet news, select stocks to evaluate, and make your investments. They can be broken down into three broad categories: news and information, recommendations, and screenings and evaluations. News and information are in the following sections, the last two areas will be covered in the next chapter.

Some of the Web sites you will be looking at have more than one of these services—in fact, most have more than one function. You will learn fairly quickly which area of a site is strongest and which areas are either weak or thinly disguised sales tools.

Appendix C, "Web Sites," has an extensive section on links to Internet stock sites and other sites that you will find helpful.

General News and Information

News and information sites are abundant on the Internet. Many of the general interest sites have sections on investing and may cover Internet stocks as a subset of technology.

A few of my favorite are these:

➤ The Online New York Times (ticker symbol: NYT; www.nytimes.com/yr/mo/day/)

➤ The Interactive Wall Street Journal (ticker symbol: DJ; interactive.wsj.com/home.html)

➤ CNN (cnn.com)

➤ Microsoft Network Money Central (ticker symbol: MSFT; moneycentral.msn.com/home.asp).

The Online New York Times reports technology and Internet business news from a little different perspective. I find the reporting accurate and comprehensive. Its coverage is often of the "step back and look at the big picture" variety. This site is good about explaining technology and relating it to business or consumers.

Help File

Most information on the Internet is available for free, even if you have to register to enter the site. A few sites offer a combination of free and paid services. Most of the sites that are all subscription or that have "premium" areas will let you try them for free, usually for 30 days. If you think that you might want the premium information, try it for free first.

The Interactive Wall Street Journal is the online version of the well-respected daily newspaper. There is a subscription fee to use the site, but it is fairly inexpensive and is worth the money to have access to these detailed reports.

CNN.com is the online partner of the cable television network. News coverage is comprehensive, and the business and technology sections are very helpful, although the information tends to be more daily news than in-depth articles.

Microsoft Network Money Central is another good general resource, although I would stick to the section that focuses on personal finance, including investing.

Specific News and Information

These sites are focused on the Internet and Internet investments, and should be your first source of information.

CNET.com News (ticker symbol: CNET; www.news.com) is a leader in technology news reporting. This site is rich with content that is interesting to the Internet stockholder. Rankings by different sectors can be sorted a number of different ways. Along with giving news, this site also provides many different subsets of technology information. Not all of it applies to the Internet, per se, but this is one site that you will want to visit frequently.

The Internet Stock Report (ticker symbol: INTM; www.internetstockreport.com) is another site that is devoted to investing in Internet stocks. This site has links to a number of other major Internet sites and also offers its own content. The site covers the markets and major news stories, along with news and listings of IPOs. The site also features news and updates on venture capitalists and which companies are getting funding.

Help File

Red herrings are prospectuses of new companies that are incomplete, meaning that their information may change before it is finalized. The term is also used to describe investments that are risky because all of the details are not known. The "herring" part comes from the use of fish scent to throw off bloodhounds hunting escaped criminals, according to Red Herring Communications. The "red" comes from the red print on the front.

The IPO Monitor (www.ipomonitor.com) offers comprehensive information on the IPO market, including an IPO index. The site reports on all IPOs, not just Internet or technology offerings. Some information is free, but the best stuff is available to paid subscribers only. If you are really interested in the IPO market, the subscription may be worth the money. If not, much of the basic information is free on this site or elsewhere.

The Red Herring (redherring.com) is the online version of the print magazine that is a popular technology observer. This is a rich site that is easy to navigate. The site's focus is on technology, not the Internet exclusively, but you'll find the content well-written and comprehensive. This is another excellent site for staying on top of Internet news.

Internet.com (ticker symbol: INTM; internet.com), as you might guess, is devoted to covering the Internet and its many components. This site covers everything from technology to investments. The site has 12 channels of information, some of which are offsite links to other information providers.

The Standard (thestandard.com) is a comprehensive Internet site that is worth your time. This is the online version of a magazine by the same name. Its focus is on the Internet economy in general, which covers investing and general e-business news. This site includes a number of newsletters covering daily markets, venture capitalists, and others.

The Wall Street Research Network (wsrn.com) is another comprehensive Internet site that covers the Internet like a wet blanket.

Interactive Week Online (ticker symbol: ZD; zdnet.com/intweek/) is one of the online magazines offered by ZD Inc. This site takes a fairly comprehensive look at Internet business and technology. Its strongest suit is that it focuses on the technology behind the Internet, as opposed to investing, although this site does publish an index of Internet stocks. This is a great site to keep up with new products and services.

If you want to follow only one site, I recommend WSRN.com. This site is the most complete, from my perspective. Most of the information is free, but if you want truly detailed information, including company financials, there is a subscription fee.

The Internet is an open market of information. Some of the information is thinly disguised sales pitches or outright lies. However, there is plenty of good, reliable information if you stick with reputable site.

The Least You Need to Know

➤ All the information you need to make investment decisions is available on the Internet, either free or at a very low cost.

➤ If information seems too good to be true, it probably is—always check your sources.

➤ The Internet is fertile ground for stock manipulations and other schemes.

➤ Avoid investing on the basis of unconfirmed rumors and tips you find in chat rooms and on message boards.

Chapter 7

Online Resources

> ## In This Chapter
>
> ➤ Stock screen tools and how to use them
>
> ➤ Buy/hold/sell recommendations
>
> ➤ Online research

My last summer in college, I took a job in a small plastics factory to help pay expenses. The company employed about 10 people, and management let me meet my early morning class before coming to work.

The first day the boss put me to work clipping extra plastic off a part for a helicopter. After seven hours, my hands were covered with blisters. The next day he took pity on me and gave me the job of packaging some small plastic parts. One hundred of these parts would fit in a small paper bag.

Although this was much easier on my hands, I was feeling a little annoyed that as an almost college graduate, this work was beneath me. I had been working for about an hour when the boss stopped in to see how I was doing.

He looked at the several piles of 100 parts I had counted out on the table for a minute, and then went over to a shelf right in front of me and took down a small scale. He put it in front of me and walked out of the room without saying a word.

My ego appropriately deflated, I weighed a pile of 100 pieces, then proceeded to use the scale to weigh out successive 100 piece units. I was finished in no time.

The right tools can make any job easier. In this chapter, we look at some of the tools that will make investigating Internet stocks much easier.

Trolling for Stock

There are hundreds of Internet stocks on the market, and more are being added every week—and these are just a small subset of the nearly 10,000 stocks on the market.

How are you going to find one that is right for you? In this chapter, we look at some of the ways you can reduce your list to a manageable size.

One of the first tools you will learn to use is called a *stock screen*. There are two issues to deal with when using stock screens. The first is how they work and what you can do with them. The second is knowing what characteristics you screen for.

In this chapter, we go over how stock screens work and explore what you can do with them. In Chapter 8, "The Basics of Evaluating Internet Stocks," we focus on what we should be looking for when screening stocks.

Speak Up

As the name implies, a **stock screen** acts as a filter, letting those stocks that meet the criteria pass through and preventing the stocks that don't.

A Quick Look

Stock screens are useful when you are looking for a stock with particular financial and performance characteristics. For example, you could ask the screen to find all the stocks that have a price/earnings ratio (P/E) of 35 or higher and a market capitalization of $50 million or less.

When run through the MSN MoneyCentral custom screen, this reveals 140 that stocks match those parameters. That narrows it down somewhat, but obviously more detail is needed to get the number down to a workable level. As we narrow our search by adding parameters, we get closer to a number of stocks that we can realistically evaluate.

Next we add a screen for revenue growth, comparing the current year-to-date revenue with that of last year, and ask for 20 percent or more. This will eliminate companies that are not experiencing revenue growth over the last year. When we add this screen, the number of companies drops to 38.

Now let's add a screen for stock price. In this example, we want only stocks that have increased in price by 50 percent or more. This screen gets us down to 21 companies.

Our final cut is to zero in on a particular industry classification. In this example, we are looking for manufacturers of scientific and technical instruments. After this screen, we are down to two companies.

➤ Pollution Research and Control Corp. (ticker symbol: PRCC; dasibi.com) makes pollution-sensing and measuring devices. It had sales of $6.3 million and income of $500,000 in the last 12 months.

➤ Image Sensing Systems, Inc. (ticker symbol: ISNS; x), makes traffic-sensing equipment that helps keep traffic moving by providing information on congestion and other factors using video cameras. It had sales of $4.8 million and income of $300,000 in the last 12 months.

Try this exercise yourself, but notice that your results almost certainly will be different from mine. Every day the market is open, numbers and ratios change. The following figure shows the screens used in this exercise. This is the Microsoft Network's MoneyCentral.

This was a fairly unstructured search for demonstration purposes only. If you experiment with stock screens, you will learn to adapt them to your particular needs. Most screens will let you save your search so that you can run them again at future dates.

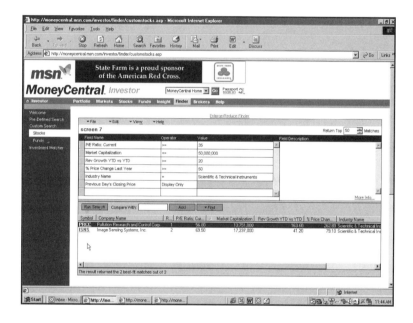

The MSN MoneyCentral finder allows you to make custom searches.

There are a number of stocks screens on the Internet. They all do basically the same thing, but I think you will find some that are easier to use than others.

Most screens have two or three levels of detail. Most also have a basic screen that looks at just a few variables, a preset screen that has a fixed set of variables, and an advanced screen with which you can select the variables you want.

Variables

The "variables" that most screens (they are called "finders" on some sites) offer deal with basic financial information, such as growth in revenues, earnings, dividends, and so on. Some screens offer you the opportunity to use just a handful of variables, while others may have up to 90 or more variables that you can manipulate.

Our example exercise used only five variables, but it narrowed the search to two stocks out of 8,264 the day I did this screen. As a practical matter, you will seldom use more than a handful of variables in any one screen, especially at first. As you become more comfortable with screens and refine your interests, you may want to use more variables.

The other consideration is that it is easy to ask for variables that are normally mutually exclusive. For example, if you asked for dividend yield, a Market Capitalization under $50 million, and a net profit margin of 15 percent, you probably won't get many, if any matches. Small companies don't often have dividends, and many don't have net profit margins close to 15 percent.

In addition to financial variables, some screens offer variables such as the number of employees, an industry description, location, and so on. Market Guide's (marketguide. com) StockQuest system is not that easy to use, but it offers more variables than most of the screens.

StockQuest by Market Guide offers an abundance of selection possibilities.

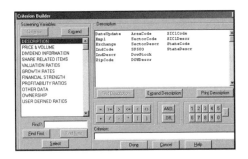

Preset Screens

Most screens offer a number of preset screens that you can run just by clicking on them. These preset screens look for stocks of certain characteristics and have titles such as "Distressed Values," "Tech Titans," and so on.

These are easy to use, and if you happen to be interested in the type of stock they are screening for, they can be very helpful. I have found that the most benefit, however, comes from studying what the screens were looking for and how the sites constructed their screens. By modifying their screens to fit your particular search, you get the benefit of their screening expertise and the customization to your particular concern.

Almost all of the preset screens are free on most sites. Some of the best prescreens are these two: Morningstar.com's stock finder and MSN MoneyCentral investment finder.

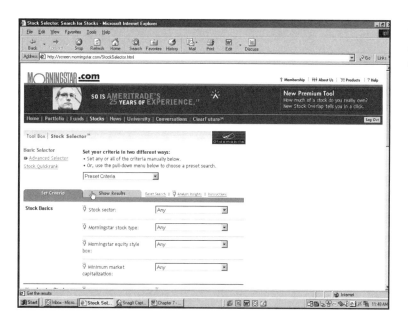

Morningstar.com stock finder is easy to use and free.

Custom Screens

While the preset screens are fine for a quick look at a particular area, you will want more sophisticated screens as you refine the kind of stock you are looking for.

Some sites, such as Morningstar.com, include the advanced screens only as part of their premium service. However, at plenty of sites the advanced screens are free.

One of the most comprehensive stock screens comes from Market Guide. This site offers a screen that works on the site, but the one with the real muscle is StockQuest, a download. The first time you want to use StockQuest, you download it from the Web site, and it becomes a resident program on your hard drive. When you want to update your information, you can go to the Market Guide Web site and download a new database with current quotes and information.

The Market Guide database has just under 10,000 stocks, which makes it more comprehensive than many other screens, which eliminate stocks below $2 per share. Its preset screens are also helpful in constructing your own screens that vary slightly from those offered. However, this site's real powers show through when you use the custom feature and build your own screens.

Speak Up

Beta is a measure of a stock's volatility. The higher the number over 1, the more volatile is the stock. The number 1 represents the market as a whole, so the beta measures how a stock reacts relative to the whole market.

This screen results in 240 stocks that meet the criteria.

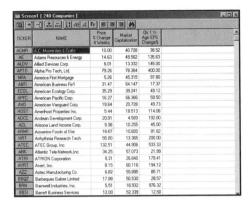

Once you construct your screen, the result looks like the screen in the following figure. You can add variables to the result to provide a more detailed look without changing your screen.

For example, if you want to look at the beta variable to the result, you can do so without changing the screen because that was not a variable used to build the screen. The following figure shows the addition of *beta*. You also can sort or rank the findings by any column. If you wish, you can export the findings to a spreadsheet.

Stock screens are useful tools for narrowing down a large group of stocks. In later chapters, we will use them to do just that.

The addition of the beta figure does not change the screen.

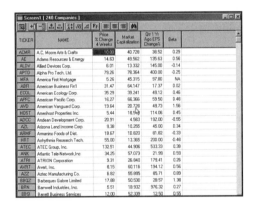

Online Research

Researching Internet stocks is not very complicated because these stocks are in the news so much these days. All the information sources I mentioned in Chapter 6, "Doing Your Homework," are good places to begin your research.

Your research will take two forms. The first is identifying specific companies to research based on the sector it is in or the financial profile you identify (as in the previous screens).

The second is checking out names in the news, or companies that pop up on the information sites that you check on a regular basis. Some may argue that once a company becomes visible because of publicity, the time to buy has passed. If you are a day trader or other short-term speculator, that is probably a fair assessment. However, if you are looking for stocks for a longer holding period, that may not matter so much.

IPOs attract a lot of attention, and you see stocks often zoom to incredible heights. This is clearly not the time to buy. I will talk about IPOs in more detail in Part 4, "IPOs, Mutual Funds, Day Trading, and Options."

Overpriced Stocks

One of the big knocks on Internet stocks is that they are overpriced and should be avoided. I don't disagree that many are overpriced, but by the time you read this book, a major correction may have changed that dramatically.

The problem with protests over high prices for Internet stocks, is that the argument has been going on for a number of years. People who heeded that advice missed out on some spectacular gains that the doomsayers said couldn't happen.

However, investors still face the same problem. Overpriced Internet stocks keep going up and up—at least, that's the popular media hype. The truth is that not all Internet stocks keep going up and up. Some drop like a rock.

Founts of Facts

Web sites that specialize in Internet and Technology news are probably the best source of news and information. However, for conventional financial information, you can rely on some of the top financial sites, such as Morningstar.com, MSN Money Central, SmartMoney.com (smartmoney.com), and others.

What kind of information can you find on these sites? Most information sites offer the same basic financial information, including all the popular ratios and balance sheet items. However, many sites try to distinguish themselves in some way from the others. Let's look at one of my favorite sites, Morningstar.com.

Morningstar.com

Morningstar.com has built a reputation as an authority in mutual funds, but its stock information is just as thorough. Using one of the companies we identified from our screening exercise, Pollution Research and Control Corp., we can look at some of Morningstar's features. The basic screen following the quote is the Snapshot, which gives a brief overview of the company.

Morningstar.com's Snapshot of a company gives you a good overview of what it is about.

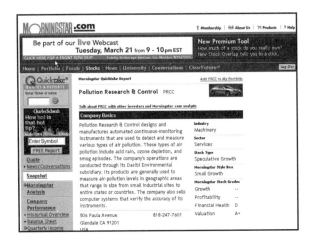

To the right of the narrative are several category listings. Each of these listings places the company in a certain group, allowing easier comparisons with its peers. It is identified in the following categories:

➤ Industry—Machinery

➤ Sector—Services

➤ Stock Type—Speculative Growth

➤ Morningstar Style Box—Small Growth

➤ Morningstar Stock Grades

➤ Growth—NA

➤ Profitability—NA

➤ Financial Health—D

➤ Valuation—A+

These listings tell us that the company is in machinery and that its sector is services (Morningstar.com provides data definitions if you are confused about what a label might mean).

The site classifies the stock as speculative growth, meaning that this stock should be used for that portion of your portfolio in which growth is the primary focus and you are prepared to take some significant risk to meet the goal. Morningstar also uses a label to describe how the stock fits into a matrix that measures stock size and characteristics. In this case, that label is small growth, which can be used to identify other stocks in the same category.

One of Morningstar.com's strengths is that it develops a report card on each company, using growth, profitability, financial health, and valuation as areas to grade.

In this case, the stock is too young to be measured on growth and profitability; it is measured on financial health and valuation. Financial health is a measure of the company's balance sheet and whether the financial condition is improving or declining. The valuation section looks at the company and attempts to come up with a fair market value of the company per share (appraisal ratio) along with traditional valuation tools.

You will notice that on the Morningstar.com menu that appears in the left column, some of the items have + beside them. The + indicates that these reports are available only to premium members; this subscription costs less than $10 a month.

I don't want to go through all the screens on this stock, but they are extensive, even though this stock barely qualifies for inclusion by Morningstar.com. The site's total database, at the time I did these reports, included 7,264 stocks.

MSN MoneyCentral

MSN MoneyCentral features much of the same information as Morningstar.com and adds its own twists.

One of the most notable features is the fyi advisor, as seen in the following figure. The "fyi" appears where significant events have occurred. These might be news stories or unexpected high volume or some other extraordinary event.

MSN MoneyCentral "fyi" sends you to additional information.

Clicking one of these takes you to an alert page where the event is highlighted. These tidbits are very helpful in spotting unusual events in a stock's life, such as heavy trading for no apparent reason.

One of the neatest features of MSN MoneyCentral is the research wizard, which walks you through a fundamental analysis of the company—not some abstract theory, but actual data analysis of the company. See the following figure for an example of the first of several pages.

*MSN MoneyCentral helps
you analyze a stock.*

The research wizard walks through the analysis but does not recommend a course of action—that is up to you. However, some Web sites are more than happy to provide recommendations to buy, hold, or sell shares.

The Tout

One of the hottest and sometimes most controversial areas of the Internet are services that recommend buy, sell, or hold actions for stocks.

These advisory services are largely unregulated, so you may or may not be getting quality information. In Chapter 6, I warned against recommendations from visitors to chat rooms and message boards.

Although there are many reputable advisory services, this is definitely a situation in which the reader should beware. Because most of these services are unregulated, they are pretty much free to say whatever they want.

Constant reference to just a handful of stocks may be a tip that these folks have a hidden agenda. That agenda may include ownership or a short position in the stocks recommended. These stocks also could be advertisers or somehow pay for recommendations. It happens, believe me.

Of course, several of these services I believe are legitimate. However, I would never buy or sell a stock solely on the recommendation of a third party. Still, a change in position can signal that it is time to take another look at the stock.

Zacks.com

One of the better known advisory services is Zacks.com, which offers its advice through the Zacks Advisor. The service offers a buy or sell scale from 1 to 5, with 1 being a strong buy and 5 being a strong sell.

One of the points Zacks is known for is its intense interest in earnings estimates as a predictor of stock price movement. Companies release earnings estimates periodically as a way of suggesting future business strength. Analysts often make their own earnings predictions.

Expressed as earnings per share (EPS), these calculations are important for predicting a stock's movement, according to Zacks. Every day the site reports "positive" surprises when a company has beaten the EPS estimates and "negative" surprises when a company falls short of expected EPS estimates.

Zacks also maintains model portfolios based on several factors. The first is Zacks' number one ranked companies, which are stocks that are expected to move over the next three to six months. The rankings are derived from Zacks research and analysis of the stock.

InvestorPlace.com

InvestorPlace.com is another advisory service, but with a significant difference. Unlike Zacks, InvestorPlace.com is really a clearinghouse for a number of newsletters focused on particular market segments or mutual funds.

The home page maintains some interesting information and is free. It includes several columns written by the newsletter authors and other assorted information. This site is worth visiting to check out its uncompromising comments regarding stocks the experts like and dislike.

The newsletters, however, are a different story. They are fairly pricey (one on Internet stocks is $299 per year), although all claim great track records if you follow their advice. I am wary of high-priced newsletters, but I honestly have never evaluated them. If you think they might help you, give them a try. Philips International owns this site, a major online and offline publisher. This leads me to believe that the newsletters are honest opinions. Whether those opinions are worth $300 a year is something you will have to decide for yourself.

Numerous other online advisory services also exist, some of which are listed in Appendix C, "Web Sites."

The Old-Fashioned Way

While I believe that you can get all the information you need from the Internet, I know that some investors feel more comfortable with traditional paper reports and research.

The best source for detailed research the old-fashioned way is Value Line Investment Survey (valueline.com). This comprehensive research publication covers the market like no other printed report. Its reports are detailed and all organized in the same way so that you can easily compare one stock with another on key points.

Value Line has been at this for more than 70 years, so its research is not only timely, but deep as well. Each company is covered in detail, beginning with a discussion of the business or businesses that the company manages. This is similar to the "snapshot" information found on many online services. You also get a rundown on how much stock is owned by insiders (officers and directors). Here's an investing hint: If none of the officers or directors owns the stock, why should you?

Stock performance in the recent past (for Internet stocks, that won't go too far back, for most) is shown on a graph, and historical financial information is included as well. Although it might be interesting to know what a company looked liked 15 years ago and how its finances have changed, this information is not necessarily helpful in figuring out what that company will do in the future.

More interesting is the current information on key financial ratios, including key balance sheet calculations. Several securities analysts follow most stocks on a regular basis. Their assessment of a company and its stock often make for interesting reading, although you should understand that things change quickly in the Internet economy.

Value Line also offers a rating system of its own regarding the future prospects for the stock. These systems have proven effective over time and with many stocks, but they should not be taken as absolute buy or sell signals. Historically, highly rated stocks have outperformed the market, and stocks with low ratings have underperformed the market more often than not.

Much more is involved with the reports; if you learn better with a written report, Value Line Investment Survey may be right for you. Unfortunately, a subscription is pricey (their Annual Investment Survey is $570), but you can get a trial subscription at a modest price at the Web site. You also might check out the reference section at your library—many libraries carry copies of Value Line.

Addicted computer users, have no fear. Value Line makes a computer version of its reports, and you can find information about it on the Web site.

The best place to research Internet companies is on the Internet itself. There you can find all the financial information you need and actually visit the company's Web site and view its products.

The Least You Need to Know

➤ The Internet has powerful research tools, most for free.

➤ Stock screens can considerably narrow your search for a good stock to buy.

➤ Several services provide detailed information about companies for free, such as Zacks.com, InvestorPlace.com, and Morningstar.com.

Chapter 8

The Basics of Evaluating Internet Stocks

In This Chapter

➤ Evaluation tools for picking winning Internet stocks

➤ How to know what you are buying

➤ What is the future worth?

A lot of clichés have been used to describe investing in the Internet. Some of my favorites are nailing Jell-O to the wall and changing the tire on a moving truck.

Although both of these clichés have a ring of truth to them, neither one of them is entirely accurate. While Internet stocks are often portrayed in the media as wildly gyrating and uncontrollable loose cannons, the truth is that many of the stocks can be evaluated with some degree of accuracy.

In this chapter, we focus on pure Internet stocks because these are the most difficult to evaluate. In Chapter 22, "Mixed Marriages", we look at hybrid Internet stocks, but they are more easily evaluated by conventional methods.

Evaluating pure Internet stocks is part science and part educated guess. The world of Internet stocks is changing at a very rapid pace, but it is not impossible to stay on top of those changes and to explore how you may profit from them.

Unconventional Conventional Wisdom

Conventional wisdom holds that evaluating stocks is a process of analyzing sales, profits, profit margins, and other financial markers. Many of these tools do not work with young companies, however, because they have no track record of success—or even failure, for that matter. By definition, pure Internet companies are young companies and, as such, often behave in the same erratic ways that adolescents do.

While I don't pretend to understand adolescents, despite a close association with a number of them, I do recognize that growing is a lot of work and takes a lot of energy. The same can be said of pure Internet companies, which expend a lot of energy growing and trying to find their place in the world.

Thanks to the media, we have a vision of Internet companies being built by a bunch of people under age 30 and living on pizzas while they put together a company that will be worth several hundred million dollars in six months. Certainly this has happened, but the process is much more serious than that. For every one of the startup companies that makes it to the market, there are hundreds that never do.

The attrition, or failure rate, for small businesses is extremely high, and when you factor in the extra pressure of building a business that has a very short time to prove itself, it is not surprising that so many of these Internet companies never make it out of the garage.

Margin Call

The Internet operates on what some call "Internet time," meaning that everything is accelerated. Internet companies have a very short time to catch the investment community's eye, or they disappear.

So how are investors to decide which stocks will be around in 12 months and will be worth anything? This is a question that we will try to answer in part during this chapter. In addition to developing some understanding of stock evaluation tools, you will need to keep yourself informed about what is going on in this particular area of business.

Reality Check

A note of caution: There are no experts in evaluating Internet stocks. The oldest pure Internet company is barely 6 years old, and that is not nearly enough time to establish any reliable pattern of behavior for a whole market segment.

Almost half of the pure Internet IPOs from 1999 were trading at or below their opening price in early 2000. This does not include the number of companies that never made it to the IPO stage before they folded. Rational stock market observers have been saying for months that Internet stocks were overpriced and could never live up to the values given them by the market. Especially at risk are Internet sites that sell consumer products with low profit margins. These e-commerce sites must generate hundreds of millions in sales to ever live up to the valuation the market gave them.

By way of contrast, one of the hottest new areas of Internet stocks is referred to as business-to-business e-commerce, or B2B. The profit margins in these businesses are very high, and for the most part, their services are not duplicated in the non-Internet world.

What You Are Buying

When you buy an Internet stock, you are basically buying a piece of the future. When you buy conventional stocks, you are buying growth, income, or some combination of both. You assume that the stock's price will appreciate in some relationship to the company's fortunes.

Since mid-1990, the stock market has been treating Internet stocks as if they were making the large profits. If the stock market is willing to overvalue Internet stocks with no history of earnings or potential profits in the immediate future, what will happen when and if those profits materialize?

If an Internet stock is trading at around $100 per share with no profits in sight, does that make it a good buy or not? These are the kind of questions you will need to answer before you can make a logical judgment about whether you want to own a particular stock.

Let's walk through the process of evaluating Internet stocks, which is similar to how you would evaluate a traditional stock, but with some major exceptions.

Double Click

Want to buy an Internet stock, but the $100–plus share price means that you cannot afford a round lot (100 shares)? Keep an eye on the financial news. More Internet stocks are doing splits, which reduces the per share price and increases the number of shares.

Dangerous Numbers

In the Old Economy, evaluating stocks was a process awash in numbers—ratios, indexes, support, resistance, yadda, yadda, yadda. Granted, numbers are helpful in evaluating pure Internet stocks and will be even more valuable when we look at hybrid Internet stocks later. However, there is a real danger in hiding behind numbers to evaluate Internet stocks. The danger is that numbers work best when you can compare a stock to its peers and the market as a whole. The database I have built of Internet stocks is filled with more "NA" entries than anything else, meaning that the numbers aren't there to evaluate.

A few numbers are helpful, but for the most part they serve as warnings instead of beacons. Just be careful of jumping on a number in isolation as a buy or sell signal without looking at the bigger picture.

Using Numbers

This evaluation uses a very basic form of fundamental analysis as its basis because I believe that is the most logical way to proceed. Plenty of technical stock analysts seem to find some measure of success reading their charts, but I don't find technical analysis to be any more helpful in evaluating Internet stocks than reading tea leaves.

To make this evaluation more meaningful, I will use actual stocks to walk through the process. The stocks I have chosen are representative of the companies you'll find on the Internet. They represent three companies in roughly the same category of Internet information providers. The three also represent large, midsize, and small companies, as measured by sales. *Market cap* is another common way to measure the size of a company, but these numbers change every time the stock's price changes.

Market cap doesn't predict stock price (stock price is a part of the market cap calculation), but sales have a much more direct bearing on stock prices. Using three companies of different sizes will let you look at the pluses and minuses of investing in different size companies.

One of the companies is About.com (ticker symbol: BOUT; about.com), and I am familiar with it because I operate one of its guided sites, Investing for Beginners (beginnersinvest.about.com). However, I have no inside knowledge of its financial situation or any other information that you cannot find on the Internet. I am an independent contractor and am not on the company's employee payroll. I also do not own or control any shares or options of About.com stock.

Speak Up

Market cap is short for "market capitalization." It is a way of measuring the size of a company, and is calculated by multiplying the current stock price by the number of outstanding shares. A stock trading at $55 with 10 million outstanding shares would have a market cap of $550 million.

The Biggies

For starters, let's look at stocks from companies classified as information providers. Two of our three example stocks are among the biggest pure Internet companies, America Online and Yahoo!. (I know, in the first chapter I said that America Online was a hybrid stock because of its merger with Time Warner [ticker symbol: TWX; timewarner.com], but that merger will take some time before its effects show up in America Online's financials.)

The first step is to decide what businesses the company is in and whether the company competes effectively and efficiently. We'll have to determine what the financial strengths and weaknesses are and how they impact the stock's price.

The Internet sites that I described in the previous chapter all provide information that will be invaluable in your analysis. Included in this information is a snapshot of the company and what it does. To break this down even further, all businesses are assigned a four-digit code called a *Standard Industrial Classification (SIC)* code. The SIC code for the companies I am looking at in this section is 7375.

Using this code, you can find other businesses that are similarly classified and use them as a basis of comparison. While this provides a good first cut, it is too broad for the only cut. More helpful information would be a comparison of the target stock and peers based on size and other common factors. Fortunately, many of the research services will do this for you.

For example, comparing About.com with America Online is not very meaningful. AOL has a market cap of $139 billion, while About.com's market cap is just $1.6 billion.

Understanding What You Buy

You should be able to understand what a company does by reading the 100-word or so description that is available on many of the Web sites.

For example, About.com is an information provider that is sometimes called a Web directory or portal. It has more than 800 individual sites that focus on single topics and are produced by independent guides.

Speak Up

The **Standard Industrial Classification** is a four-digit code assigned to every business. This classification helps the government and researchers identify companies in a particular line of business. Most businesses will have more than one SIC code, but they are required to have a primary one.

About.com competes with 45 other information providers and makes its money primarily off of advertising that is placed on the various guided sites. Of these 45 sites, About.com is ranked no. 16 based on market capitalization.

In the same category are competitors such as America Online, Yahoo!, and Lycos. It is important to be clear about what the company does—this not only will help us focus on competitors, but it also will help us put the company into the proper context.

Web sites such as Yahoo! and About.com make most of their money off of advertising sales, in much the same way that traditional media does. Ads placed on the sites pay a fee based on the number of page views or unique visitors to the site. They may also pay a fee based on the number of visitors to the site who click on their ads.

Internet companies are quickly conceived, quickly born, and, in some cases, quickly die. However, those companies that can adapt to changing technology or market pressures will be the ones that have a better chance of success. Therefore, although it is important to know what a company does now, it may be more important to have a good sense about what the company is capable of in case market conditions change.

As an example, About.com has positioned itself as information provider in a site that is basically funded by advertising revenue. However, the company has formed several strategic alliances that will allow it to push products off its Web sites. These partnerships allowed About.com to sell books and videotapes directly off the guided sites. For example, one of its cooking sites might offer cookbooks and videotapes about different types of cooking. These are only a few of the possibilities that will help About. com generate revenue in a manner other than advertising sales. In broad terms, the company will be following the same strategy as Amazon.com and other advertising-based sites to diversify revenue sources.

Web sites that depend on just advertising support may be in for difficulties in the future. More competitors are vying for the advertiser's dollar, which may have the effect of keeping a lid on rates.

Like all other Internet companies, About.com has not been around long enough to establish any kind of track record. So, we have to ask ourselves what the chances are that five years from now they will still be around.

What Do the Numbers Say?

After we have identified the company's business, we need to look at what financial information is available. It is unrealistic to expect that young companies in highly competitive markets will be profitable very quickly.

What we do want to see are significant increases in sales and expenses that are appropriate for this growth. Normally, we might look at the PE ratios to decide whether the stock is overpriced relative to the earnings of the company.

However, PE ratios are virtually nonexistent in this (and most) segments of Internet stocks. Of the 45 companies in this segment, only three reported profits in their last reporting periods. Not surprisingly, two of the three—America Online and Yahoo!— are the largest and oldest of the companies in this segment.

In the real world of stock market evaluation, size matters. Larger and older companies tend to be profitable more often than small-cap companies. It is easy to forget that America Online, with a market capitalization of $139 billion is only 8 years old, while Yahoo!, with a market cap of $93 billion, is only 6 years old.

America Online may be a model for what successful Internet companies need to become to survive. However, with a PE of 156 (as of mid-March, 2000), its stock is hardly a bargain. Not surprisingly, a beta of 2.48 puts America Online in the speculative category, and this may be one of the most stable companies on the Internet. Its acquisition of Time Warner will undoubtedly change the financial picture considerably.

When I worked on a ranch as a young man, we often had to work with yearlings that were unaccustomed to being herded by cowboys on horseback. These cows were wild and difficult to control. To help them settle down, we would bring in a dozen or so older cows, put some of them at the front of the herd, and mix the rest in the with the youngsters. This made a world of difference in how we could manage the whole herd.

It may take a marriage with an Old Economy company to make the wild Internet adolescents settle down.

Do You Yahoo!?

And then there is Yahoo!, the no. 2 Internet information provider by market cap, which has grown to $600 million in sales in six years and has made a profit (one of the very few Internet companies in any category) for three years.

However, (there's that word again) Yahoo! is selling at a PE based on earnings estimates that is so high that most reporting services dismiss it as not meaningful. How does a PE of 450 sound? When the S&P 500 is considered overpriced with a PE of 39, what are we to make of 450?

This is a shame, too, because Yahoo! has one of the best business models on the Internet. The company shows low costs and high margins, and is the leader in its particular area of portals.

Yahoo! is clearly a leader and among the largest of Internet portals, but this leadership position is not guaranteed. New challengers are popping up all the time. As Web surfers become more sophisticated with use, the need for handholding is likely to diminish. What other services or products can Yahoo! introduce to keep existing customers coming back and bringing their friends?

Well, it seems that rather than identifying Internet stocks to invest in, we've eliminated at least two. However, that is not necessarily true for every investor. As a long-term buy, both AOL and Yahoo! seem way overpriced. Yet, that is what market observers have been saying for several years about the market in general and Internet stocks in particular. Some investors might want to get on the bandwagon even if the price of admission is steep. Still, by anyone's book, these would be speculative investments, at best.

Margin Call

The stock market often reacts badly when stocks don't behave the way it expects, or it gets nervous about economic worries such as inflation and high interest rates. Such was the scene in mid–March 2000 when the Dow came roaring back with a vengeance and the technology-laden Nasdaq fell like rock. If you are going to have part of your portfolio in Internet stocks, this will be a familiar routine. If you can take the roller-coaster effect, consider hybrid Internet stocks.

It seems likely that both America Online and Yahoo! will survive. Of the two, the nod goes to America Online as the safest bet to be around and in business five years from now because of its acquisition of Time Warner.

The Growth Hurdle

America Online and Yahoo! both face another hurdle: the issue of growth. The larger a company gets, the harder it is to maintain historical growth rates. The Internet is accustomed to triple-digit growth rates, and with small companies, that is not surprising.

America Online had sales for the previous 12 months of $5.7 billion, which represented an increase of 48.6 percent. Yahoo! Had sales of $589 million the previous 12 months, an increase of 154 percent. Meanwhile, About.com had sales of $27 million, a 624 percent increase. It is unrealistic to expect America Online to continue growing at almost 50 percent a year. As the growth rate of new Internet users slows, so will the fortunes of large companies that depend on huge numbers of new customers to keep going.

America Online has about 50 percent of the Internet access business in the United States; it will be expensive to increase its penetration. The company will look to get more revenue out of existing customers through new services and products. This is where the acquisition of Time Warner makes sense. If the two companies can meld their management styles and focus on common goals, good things will happen.

Yahoo! is in a good position also because of its size and sector leadership. Although there are indications that new Internet connections are slowing, strong evidence also suggests that the folks who are already online are putting more faith in the Internet and are using it more than as an entertainment platform. That all bodes well for Yahoo!, but being the leader doesn't make it bulletproof. With close to 400 million page views per day, Yahoo! makes a tempting target.

Big Numbers

About.com, on the other hand, showed a 624 percent increase in sales and will likely post equal or better numbers again. It has a lot of room to grow and can add products and services along the way that will increase and diversify its revenue streams.

Like small companies, About.com is vulnerable to any number of attacks. As its numbers rise in the metrics listings, it will draw more attention from competitors and suitors, welcome or not.

Short-term speculators may want to look at Internet stocks with fairly wide price swings as an opportunity to try their hand at market timing. In the long run, market timing has proven an unsteady investment strategy. Still, if you want to get in on the Internet action but are not ready to commit to a long-term relationship with stocks trading in multiples so high that you need an oxygen mask, short-term speculating may be an answer. More about that comes in Part 4, "IPOs, Mutual Funds, Day Trading, and Options."

One More Reality Check

The notion of picking up a cheap Internet stock is one that you should probably just forget. Even with steep drops in price, most of the leading Internet stocks still will not be cheap.

Just to clear the air, let's make sure that we understand the term "cheap." A cheap stock is one that's price is low relative to some benefit, such as earnings, sales, growth, and so on. Stocks with a low PE are considered cheap. An expensive stock is one in which you pay a premium for those same benefits. Stocks with a high PE are considered expensive.

PE by itself doesn't tell the whole story, but it is a good starting point and can be a handy screening tool. Still, it has some real limitations. My database of more than 255 Internet stocks has only 34 stocks with a PE, meaning that these are the only ones with positive earnings.

One of the traditional tools that *does* have some value in evaluating Internet stocks is the price/sales ratio, which basically tells you what you are paying in the stock's price for sales, based on a per-share price for the stock. An assumption here is that sales have to come before profits. Sales are an important measure of a company's future success. A steady growth in sales with a corresponding smaller growth in expenses is a positive trend to look for when evaluating stocks. We will spend some more time in the next chapter looking at sales in more detail.

Brave New World

If one thing appears certain about the Internet economy, it's that change is mandatory. The same products, the same appearance, and the same content are not recipes for success like they were in the Old Economy, where companies wanted to make the customer experience consistent.

You can walk into any McDonald's restaurant in the United States (and many around the world) and have virtually the same experience. The food is the same, the décor is the same, the uniforms are the same, and, if I'm not mistaken, all the employees are the same. Businesses with multiple locations have sought this consistency with a passion. Every customer in every store is greeted with the same environment. I once went to a Sears store in San Juan, Puerto Rico. Except for some signage in Spanish, I could have been in the Sears in Toledo, Ohio.

Can you imagine walking into a McDonald's in some strange town and being greeted by name and having your favorite combo meal ready by the time you walk to the counter and having your check ready for you to verify? In the New Economy world, this will not only be possible, but it may be a reality inspired by Internet companies that have to make the customer experience fresh everyday.

At the start of this chapter, I said that you are buying the future when you buy Internet stocks. This is more than a literary device. Buying Internet stocks is like investing in the futures market on the Internet. The risks are high, but the rewards are exceptional.

The Least You Should Know

➤ There are no magic answers to evaluating Internet stocks, beyond an open mind and common sense.

➤ Some evaluation tools will work, but most won't.

➤ Change is the only constant in the Internet economy.

Chapter 9

What Are They Selling?

In This Chapter

➤ Sales can be a proxy for future earnings

➤ Evaluating Internet stocks, continued

➤ Sales must come before there can be profits

An accountant friend once shared with me some wisdom about setting up a small business. A business owner came to him very worried about taxes and wanted the optimum corporate structure to take every conceivable tax advantage.

My CPA friend patiently listened to the man's deep and heartfelt concerns about taxes. When the company was structured, the business owner asked again if this was the best tax structure possible. The accountant smiled and told the man, "You have not one client and not a single penny in revenue. You have more important things to worry about than taxes."

For many investors in Internet stocks, this same wisdom could be applied to earnings. There are more important things than earnings, at least in the beginning.

Sales Come First

Like the business owner, many folks steeped in the investing traditions of the Old Economy are desperately looking for Internet stocks that act like the Blue Chips they are familiar with, forgetting that even the conservative Dow is unpredictable. (Remember a 660-point rise in two days in March 2000?)

Don't get me wrong—earnings are important, and if there is not some clear notion that the company is headed in that direction, it might be time to move on to another stock. However, getting a young company off the ground in an environment that expects instant results is difficult enough without being concerned with earnings right away.

Still, our task of coming up with a system to evaluate Internet stocks is not made any easier with most of the companies reporting negative earnings. In this chapter, we look at sales and how tracking them can help in our evaluation process. We also look at the quality, as well as quantity, of sales.

What Are They Selling?

This may seem an odd question because it is unlikely that you would invest in a stock without knowing at least some very fundamental truths about the business behind the stock. I suggest that the answer is not always just about products or services.

Seven years ago, investors in Microsoft had no idea that they eventually would own a piece of one of the biggest Internet players in the game. In fact, Microsoft officials dismissed the Internet as a passing fad, not a place for serious computing.

Double Click

Companies that miss dramatic changes in technology or consumer interest and can't catch up are likely to fall too far behind to catch up in the fast-paced New Economy. Watch for companies that form alliances and partnerships to expand their businesses and market shares. These are the ones who will profit in the New Economy.

The investors couldn't have guessed that not only would Microsoft embrace the Internet, but also that its most ubiquitous Internet product (Web browser, Internet Explorer) would be distributed for free. If they managed to recover from these changes, they must have gone into a serious relapse in early 2000 when company officials wondered aloud about a world without Microsoft products, as we know them today.

Likewise, investors in Cisco Systems thought they were buying stock in a company that provided computers for corporate networks. Now they own a piece of an active, robust company that has been transformed by the Internet into a company that provides solutions for complex Internet back rooms.

The New Economy is more interested in solutions than in the "way we have always done it" mentality. This means alliances, partnerships, and links. Hopefully, we've learned the lessons of previous years that it is better to make partners than enemies.

Make no mistake—this is still a very competitive market, made more so by the short time it takes to conceive and bring to market so many Internet products.

The Joy of Cooperation

Those of you old enough to remember the great Beta versus VHS wars know the value of cooperation. Two technologies fought it out for the consumer's dollars in the video-cassette recorder (VCR) market.

To briefly recap: In the beginning of the VCR craze, there were two competing and incompatible technologies, Beta Max and Video Home System. The Beta was the superior technology, but the owners of the patents refused to license them to other manufacturers. The VHS owners sold licenses to any manufacturer that wanted to manufacture VHS recorders.

As a result, Beta disappeared in a short period of time, and VHS recorders were made and sold by dozens of companies. Did the consumer win? Undoubtedly, in the long run, consumers came out ahead. Competing manufacturers drove down the prices, while improvements in VCRs made the VHS quality equal to or superior to the Beta. A standard format allowed content producers to expand the number of titles dramatically. The market saturation of VCRs now almost equals that of television.

Share the Wealth

Internet companies that work toward standards will participate in a much bigger market than those who want to do their own thing.

The Internet is basically an open system that allows anyone to join with few, if any, restrictions. Although the techies may disagree, the Internet is designed around a set of agreed upon standards.

The two main browsers, Microsoft's Internet Explorer and Netscape Communications Corp.'s Netscape Navigator (netscape.com), which is now owned by America Online, both handle Web sites in pretty much the same way. With some minor exceptions, a Web site runs the same way on either browser. An active community of Internet visionaries want to keep the system open, and the only way to do that is to agree upon some standards.

Connected or Not?

What does all of this have to do with sales and evaluating Internet stocks? One of the areas we will look for in an Internet company is how connected that company is to the community and whether it encourages repositioning of its products or services.

Double Click

The Motley Fool is a well-respected Web site that focuses on investing issues. They have their own way of viewing the investing process, for example they don't like mutual funds. In their world something they call "foolish" is good and "unfoolish" is bad.

Clearly, this doesn't work with all Internet companies. The companies that are infra-structure providers or more technical than commercial companies won't fit this model. Here's an example of what I am talking about. About.com, which I mentioned in the last chapter, has a number of investing-related sites. In addition to providing original content, each of these sites links to other sites on the Internet for additional information. About.com even has a partnership with The Motley Fool (fool.com), which could be considered a competitor, and provides links on its pages to The Fool.com.

In this case, the links provide additional page views to both sites, which increases advertising revenue. Web sites that try to be too self-contained may miss revenue opportunities that a more open structure would allow.

Sales As a Proxy for Earnings

Can you use sales as a proxy for earnings? That is, can you draw some conclusions about a stock from examining its sales and sales growth? The answer is a qualified yes.

It is important to remember that most Internet companies have very brief histories to look at; in the stock market world, this makes for some unpredictable predictions. It is also helpful to keep in mind that Internet stocks cannot be judged solely on the basis of traditional analysis.

However, a few tools may give us some clues about the relative price of a stock. We are not looking for that "magic" number or ratio that is going to give us a clear buy or sell signal. That number doesn't exist. We are looking for some way to relate sales to the stock's price. This relationship will then let us compare the stock to other stocks and to certain market indexes.

One tool that a lot of investors use is the price/sales ratio (PSR). This number gives you an idea of how the market values the stock based on this relationship. You get the PSR by dividing the current market capitalization by the *trailing twelve months* revenue. You can find this number on many Web sites, including Morningstar.com and MSN MoneyCentral.

Companies are often acquired using this formula, so it is a pretty powerful number (of course, there are many other factors to consider, but PSR is a great place to start). The lower the answer, the better. Some investors look for PSRs of less than 1 as potential investments, especially if others in their category have PSRs of substantially more than 1.

Speak Up

Trailing twelve months (TTM) is a way of looking at a company's ongoing activity rather than just what is reported once a year in the annual report. This is simply a way to look at the past 12 months, no matter when the data is collected.

Appearances Can Be Deceiving

One of the Internet stocks in my database with a PSR of less than 1 is Cheap Tickets (ticker symbol: CTIX; cheaptickets.com), a discount airline ticket company. In mid-March 2000, it had a PSR of 0.86, which compares with its industry average of 35 and the S&P 500 average of 3.4.

On the surface, it would appear that the market undervalues Cheap Tickets, especially when you consider that it actually has positive earnings. All the other companies in my database with PSRs of less than 1 are operating at a deficit.

Because PSR is frequently used to evaluate companies with no earnings, let's move on to an example of a company with negative earnings. Consider online retailer Value America (ticker symbol: VUSA; valueline.com). With a PSR of 1.20 as compared to a 27 for its industry, this may be a good candidate. Value America's big problem, however, is that it competes with online retailers that average almost $2 billion in market cap, and it has a market cap of just $252 million.

Although Value America is sitting on a pile of cash, you have to ask yourself what it can do to distinguish itself from its giant competitors. On the other hand, if Value America *does* find that niche, it has nothing holding it down. Value America was trading at $5.625 when this was written in mid-March 2000. Where is it now? Would it have been a good investment?

It is a given that the biggest potential for spectacular growth comes from the small-cap stocks. It is also a given that they are the riskiest. Among the questions facing investors in Internet stocks is the issue of size and how it affects risk and reward. Large-cap stocks can have more stability than small-cap stocks, but you may also give up some potential for growth in the process.

Margin Call

One of the truths of both the Old Economy and the New Economy is that small companies are often eaten for lunch unless they can grow quickly enough to defend themselves.

Size Matters

In the previous chapter, we looked at a couple big Internet stocks. We noted that size alone doesn't make them bulletproof, but it helps. In this chapter, we also have looked at a couple small-cap stocks. We have noted that their size is a real disadvantage when their competitors are many times larger. How does PSR work with mid-cap companies?

Mid-cap companies are those in the $1 billion to $8 billion range. Given the huge premiums many Internet stocks have enjoyed, it shouldn't be hard to find some candidates.

CNET (ticker symbol: CNET; cnet.com) is an Internet information provider that falls in that mid-cap range with a cap of $4.2 billion. This company has an extensive Web site that focuses on Internet and technology news (this site is a must-read for Internet stock investors).

When I looked at this stock, its numbers made an interesting example of the point I have raised several times about relying on one number for guidance. Here are some of the numbers:

Market cap	$4.2 billion
Price	$56.50
Sales	$112.3 million
Sales growth	97 percent
P/E	11.47

On the surface, things look pretty good. A positive P/E tells you that the company is profitable, and a 97 percent increase in sales over the past 12 months is healthy growth in anyone's book.

A P/E of 11.47 seems very low for an Internet stock; when compared to an industry P/E of 150 and an S&P 500 P/E of more than 40, this seems too good to be true.

"Too good to be true" is the operative phrase here. While these numbers are true, they are also incomplete and can leave the investor with a false picture. If you add another bit of information, the picture changes. For example, CNET's PSR is 40.6.

Help File

The Internet is too rich in information resources to not take advantage of them. Never buy or sell on the recommendation of one Web site. Look around, and you will find a variety of opinions about what a single set of numbers means for a particular stock. Make your trade based on what makes the most sense to you.

Ouch! How did that happen? A P/E of 11.47 and a PSR of 40.6 don't sound like they belong to the same stock. What's going on that doesn't show up at first glance?

This is when having access to a quality stock research service really pays off. When I accessed Morningstar.com's premium service, I discovered that CNET's earnings (and thus, its P/E) were dramatically affected by the sale of securities. If you backed that out, the company actually lost $0.32 per share. In addition, CNET has embarked on an ambitious ($100 million) advertising campaign that virtually guarantees no profits for several years.

Does this mean that CNET is a bad investment? Not necessarily. CNET actually has a lot going for it. In addition to its Web site, it has a growing presence in radio and television as a content provider. The point I want to reinforce is that you need to have the whole picture before you start investing.

Now let's look at a stock that may (as of this writing) be undervalued. Network Associates (ticker symbol: NETA; networkassociates.com) is a software company that makes antivirus software for personal computers. It also develops networking software for PCs.

Network Associates is a $4.7 billion company, putting it in the mid-cap range. It has been around for several years and, until recently, posted profits for several years in a row. Here are some of its numbers:

Market cap	$4.7 billion
Price	$32.13
Sales	$684 million
PSR	6.63

Like many Internet companies, Network Associates has had some bumpy rides over the past couple years. It has pursued a path of growth by acquisitions. Integrating these companies and their products is a major challenge.

Morningstar.com puts the forward P/E at around 30, which is not bad for an Internet stock and in line with the larger market. In a traditional view, Network Associates would appear overvalued, but contrasted to some of its Internet peers, it could be seen as a bargain.

Using a Stock Screen

You can use a stock screen to help you look for undervalued Internet stocks. I introduced the stock screen in Chapter 7, "Online Resources," and we will be using them throughout the book to help us identify stocks to evaluate. This will give you some practical examples of how to use a screen and how to identify a screen's strengths and weaknesses.

A major weakness is that, as of this writing, no stock screens have "Internet stock" as one of their screening criteria. This is perfectly understandable, though, because there is no such business as "Internet stock," and screens use type of business as one of their criteria. Some are even broader than that and use industry sectors such as "Technology" for criteria.

How It's Done

Even with this limitation, screens can be helpful in identifying Internet stocks to evaluate. Let's look at two examples, using different screens, and examine how you can adapt them to your needs.

We are working on the PSR in this chapter, so we will make that one of our criteria for the screen. In the real-world stock market, we would want to look for stocks with a PSR at or below 1. This would indicate that the market is undervaluing the company's sales.

The Internet stock market world is a little different. As a group, these companies are almost universally overvalued by traditional standards. So, for this screen, I'm going to set the PSR at 10 or less, which is represented by this *operator*: <= 10.

We have also been looking at mid-cap stocks, so let's set the market cap at <= $8 billion.

MSN MoneyCentral Screen

The first screen I am going to run is the one at MSN MoneyCentral. This particular screen does have a partial Internet industry name category. Under it, you can pick one of the following: Internet Service Providers, Internet Information Providers, Internet Software and Sales. Of these three, we are only likely to find pure Internet companies in the Internet Information Providers category. So, for our first screen, we will use that as the industry name.

Speak Up

Some of the common mathematical **operators** you will find in stock screens are these: >= greater than or equal to; <= less than or equal to; = equal to; and ≠ not equal to.

This screen has returned four possibilities, but VitaminShoppe, Inc. (ticker symbol: VSHP; vitaminshoppe.com), is not a pure Internet company. The other three all match the criteria and are pure Internet stocks. They are:

➤ Salon.com (ticker symbol: SALN; salon.com)

➤ OneSource Information Services (ticker symbol: ONES; onesource.com)

➤ Infonautics (ticker symbol: INFO; infornautics.com)

MSN MoneyCentral screen shows criteria and results.

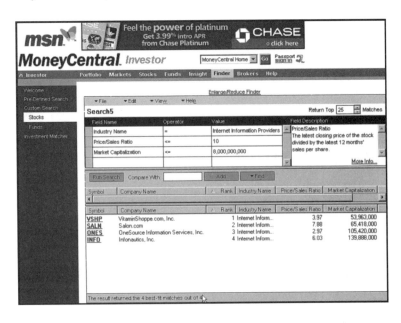

Unfortunately, there are a couple problems with the screen. The first is that although we asked for a market cap of less than $8 billion, we ended up with three very small companies. The largest, Infonautics, has a market cap of less than $140 million. This is way under our target of mid-cap stocks, which should fall in the $1 billion to $8 billion range. To compensate for that, we can add another criteria for market capitalization that sets a floor of $1 billion. The operator for that is >= 1,000,000,000.

However, that is not going to solve the problem because the first screen would have picked up those stocks also. Clearly, no other stocks in the Internet Information Providers category will fit our criteria.

So, the next adjustment is to change the Industry Name criteria to Internet Software and Services. Our new screen looks like the following figure.

The four companies listed in the results fit all the search criteria, but only one, iXL Enterprises, Inc. (ticker symbol: IIXL; ixl.com), is a pure Internet company. This company provides Internet strategy and Internet-based services to its clients.

Double Click

Although it may seem confusing at first, with a little practice you will learn which screens require the input for criteria to be entered in a certain way. For example, some screens want market cap to be entered exactly (one billion = 1000000000). Other screens may want it expressed in millions (one billion = 1000).

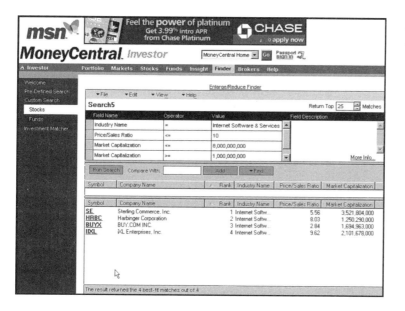

Refining the screen yields some results.

Market Guide Screen

Probably the best site for Internet stock screening is Market Guide (ticker symbol: MLTX; marketguide.com). This site has a very complete Internet analysis section that should be on your must-read list. In the research section is an area called "Internet Analyst," and you can subscribe to the newsletter for free.

You also can read several good articles about screening and analyzing Internet stocks. Each week, Market Guide offers for download in Microsoft Excel format one or more spreadsheets from its database of Internet stocks. When I downloaded a spreadsheet in mid-March 2000, 672 Internet companies were listed. This site also offers downloads for various articles. For example, an article on B2B Internet sites comes with a download of those stocks.

Market Guide's main database on Internet stocks is very comprehensive, but it comes in download form only. While other stocks screens are too vague, Market Guide's may be too specific in the amount of information available on each stock. Because it is in spreadsheet format, it is not as easy to search as regular stock screens. Running screens is a function of sorting the records to get the data in the order you want it. You can then cut and paste the data into a new "workbook" and work with it some more. (If you are not familiar with Excel, I suggest that you pick up a copy of *The Complete Idiot's Guide to Excel* (Macmillan).

Using the cut and paste method of stock screening, I was able to identify 30 stocks with a PSR of 10 or less and a market cap of between $1 billion and $8 billion. This took a little time, but it worked.

The other problem with Market Guide is how this site defines Internet stocks. Basically, if a company does substantial business on the Internet or has a division that does, it is considered an Internet stock. This broad definition may work for most cases, but it makes screening more difficult if you want to stay with stocks that primarily derive their business from the Internet.

Double Click

Just because an Internet tool is free or very inexpensive doesn't mean that it is not powerful. By the same logic, just because a tool or service is very expensive doesn't mean that it is any good.

Power Screen

If you really want to put Market Guide to work for you, the site has a product called StockQuest, which you can download for free. This is a powerful screening tool with some 75 different variables that you can use to construct screens. With the download comes a database on almost 10,000 securities.

As mentioned in Chapter 7, once you have downloaded StockQuest, you can return to the Web site periodically and update your information on every stock in the database by down-loading new data. This process is pretty much automatic and gives you an up-to-date tool for stock analysis.

StockQuest does not have an "Internet stock" screen, but the site does have a portfolio feature that you can use to build your own Internet database. Follow the instructions for creating and importing portfolios, and you can build your own custom database that is updated automatically every time you update StockQuest.

Another neat feature of StockQuest is its capability to add fields of information to your portfolio without running screens. For example, my base portfolio will contain only the ticker and company name. I can then add any of the fields normally used for screening to the report without changing the underlying database.

The following figure shows part of my database of Internet stocks constructed using StockQuest. When I update the entire database of almost 10,000 stocks, my database (portfolio) is also updated.

I have constructed such a database of what I consider pure Internet stocks, and it is a valuable tool for analysis. Not only can you easily sort on a variety of fields, but you also can run screens against your portfolio. Using the StockQuest screens against your portfolio, you can quickly do the screen we worked on previously (PSR 10 or under; market cap between $1 billion and $8 billion). The result of the search reveals 10 companies that match.

TICKER	Primary SIC Code	NAME	Beta	Current Price	Price % Change 52 Weeks	Market Capitalization	TTM Price To Sales Per Share	P/E Excluding Xord Items	Prior TTM Price To Sales P/S
FLWS	5992	1-800-FLOWERS.COM	NA	7.000	NA	432.530	1.06	NM	NA
TFSM	7311	24/7 Media, Inc.	NA	59.000	102.57	1,316.585	13.11	NM	13.53
APLN	8732	@Plan.Inc	NA	9.250	NA	102.361	9.16	NM	NA
BOUT	7375	About.com, Inc.	NA	101.750	NA	1,699.225	39.77	NM	NA
ACRU	7372	Accrue Software, Inc.	NA	45.375	NA	1,217.184	43.12	NM	NA
AGIL	7372	Agile Software Corp.	NA	164.625	NA	3,762.669	66.16	NM	NA
ALLR	7372	Allaire Corporation	NA	157.250	182.06	2,059.032	32.03	NM	8.51
ALOY	5399	Alloy Online, Inc.	NA	18.750	NA	271.313	11.05	NM	NA
AMZN	5942	Amazon.com, Inc.	2.87	65.625	-5.53	22,364.146	13.06	NM	32.50
AOL	7375	America Online Inc.	2.50	61.500	20.59	140,328.734	27.80	151.48	30.79
AMTD	6211	Ameritrade Holding Corp.	2.26	19.250	11.73	3,361.377	8.80	NM	16.06
ATHY	7373	AppliedTheory Corporation	NA	32.766	NA	699.226	16.98	NM	NA
APNT	7389	AppNet, Inc.	NA	48.500	NA	1,576.105	11.56	NM	NA
ARBA	7372	Ariba, Inc.	NA	281.063	NA	27,013.246	301.74	NM	NA
ARTG	7372	Art Technology Group	NA	185.375	NA	6,032.659	108.44	NM	NA
ASFD	5944	Ashford.com, Inc.	NA	8.563	NA	382.132	5.18	NM	NA
ASKJ	7389	Ask Jeeves, Inc.	NA	80.375	NA	2,154.452	80.89	NM	NA
ATHM	7375	At Home Corporation	2.62	29.125	-49.60	11,074.927	27.35	NM	284.14
ADBL	7375	Audible, Inc.	NA	12.500	NA	320.388	113.36	NM	NA

This figure shows part of my database of Internet stocks.

The PSR is a valuable tool in evaluating Internet stocks. It adds a way to compare just about any two Internet stocks because it is not dependent on earnings. Like all tools used in evaluating Internet stocks, it should be used in connection with other analysis, not as a standalone buy or sell indicator.

> ### The Least You Need to Know
>
> ➤ Sales can be used as a proxy for earnings.
>
> ➤ The price/sales ratio is a good tool for finding undervalued Internet stocks.
>
> ➤ Stock screening services on the Internet make identifying stocks for evaluation a simpler process.

Part 3
Playing by the Rules

The great American poet Ogden Nash wrote this poem:

> *In the world of mules,*
> *There are no rules.*

He could have been writing about Internet stocks just as easily. It seems that these stocks operate in a different reality than the rest of the market. Hyper-high valuations and below-zero earnings make finding a good investment seemingly impossible.

All investors are buying a piece of the future. With Internet stocks, that future is just a little more uncertain and farther out.

However, the Internet stock market is not quite as chaotic as it seems, if you understand some of the "different" realities at work. This area is still not for the faint of heart, but there are some rational ways to approach investing in Internet stocks.

Chapter 10

Five Rules You Need to Know

In This Chapter

➤ Why earnings are important, but not urgent

➤ How customers are different than shoppers

➤ Why growth is more important than you think

➤ Why technology is not as important as you think

➤ Why management is more important than anything

I grew up in deep rural southwest Texas. My best friend's father was a veterinarian, and we spent a lot of time at the clinic around the animals. Later, as a teenager, I worked on a ranch in the summer and got to observe even more animal behavior.

You don't have to be too observant to note that animals have their own set of rules for behavior. If rules are broken, there is often a penalty inflicted.

Our two dogs illustrated one of the most important rules in the animal world for me. One dog weighed about 75 pounds, and the other dog weighed about 7 pounds. At suppertime, I would put two bowls of food on the patio.

Even though the bowls were at opposite ends of the patio, the smaller dog would not eat until the big dog had finished. Thus, the rule: Big dogs eat first.

Investing in Internet stocks may seem like a free-for-all with no rules. Make that mistake, however, and you will see what happens when the small dog tries to eat before the big dog.

Earnings Are Not Urgent

Heresy! How can earnings not be urgent? Isn't the whole point of investing to receive a return? Earnings are what drive those returns in the form of dividends and/or share price appreciation.

Folks with backgrounds in the Old Economy may find this hard to accept. They understand that young companies may take a while to get their feet on the ground, but not too long.

Double Click

Earnings are important, but not urgent. If the company can grow rapidly in early years and then convert that growth to earnings, it will be successful.

Earnings are key components in placing a value on a stock. Earnings per share are an integral part of a number of financial calculations. When earnings fall short of where the market thinks they ought to be, the stock is often hammered.

Companies that exhibit steady, predictable earnings growth can expect the market to treat them well. Earnings and earnings expectations are so important that one online advisory service, Zacks.com (zacks.com), believes that they are the major predictor of future stock movement. This service tracks earnings expectations and determines whether a stock delivers earnings as expected or falls short or long. Visit the Web site for a better explanation, if you're interested.

Earnings Estimates

Whether the folks at Zacks are on to something or not doesn't change the fact that earnings and earnings estimates are very important to investors.

Of course, some Old Economy stocks also may not generate profits for many years. Cable television companies and utilities, to name two, often take years to build out their infrastructure before the red ink stops flowing. Not too many new cable television companies are stringing miles of cable, and not too many utilities are building power plants and running electrical lines and gas pipelines. However, the analogy is close to what a lot of Internet companies are doing: building an infrastructure. The Internet infrastructure includes the physical components, which we will discuss in more detail later, and the intellectual and cultural components.

As new Internet companies add functionality to the Web, they increase the value of the whole Internet. The functionality has gone from e-mail and games to shopping, to financial services, to mobile connections for consumers. Just beginning to explode is the B2B side of the Internet, which by its nature will eclipse the consumer Internet quickly in terms of dollar volume.

I Can See Clearly Now

Five years ago, I could see the consumer explosion that *might* happen over the Internet, but there was no certainty that this *would* happen. I had no notion that businesses would be doing millions of dollars in purchases from other businesses.

What has happened in the past five years to take the Internet from a technological novelty to an integral part of our economy and culture? One answer is that consumers accepted it as a legitimate form of communication and commerce. Consumers are also business owners and executives. Once they became comfortable with doing business for their personal use, it was not a long step to integrate the Internet into their businesses.

I am not trying to make a case for giving Internet companies a bye on earnings because they serve some greater social good. However, I am suggesting that quality companies always add more to the economy than they take out. Quality Internet companies will get to positive earnings—some are already there or almost there now.

When you are evaluating Internet stocks, you should definitely pay attention to earnings, but place them in the proper context. That context is the answer to this question: "What are the losses buying?"

By this, I mean that there should be a trade-off for losses. One of those trade-offs should be growth. Amazon.com is an example of what I am talking about. This company has not turned a profit in five years, but it has built a huge customer base. Acquiring 17 million customers was worth losing money for all these years, if the company can convert those customers into profits. Here is the true concern for investors in Internet stocks.

What evidence do you have that the company can convert growth in customers and sales into profits? One place to look for those kinds of clues is the company's income statement. Rather than just look at revenue growth, look at expense growth also. Is $1 of expense buying $2 of growth? $4 of growth? $0.50 of growth?

Cash Flow

Another way to look at this aspect is through cash flow, which is earnings before interest, taxes, depreciation, and amortization (EBITDA). EBITDA is important because it gives you a picture of how the business is doing from operations alone. All of the other terms in EBITDA are "non-operating" expenses or income, which may push the company from a positive position from operations to a loss for accounting purposes or from negative to positive. This figure identifies how much cash is flowing through the company strictly from business operations.

Help File

Cash left over from the IPO can distort a company's financial picture. Some companies report a positive quarter only because of the sale of securities or other noncore business assets.

Many Internet companies are still sitting on a pile of cash from their IPO. There is nothing wrong with this, but interest income from this cash distorts what the company's core business is doing. Likewise, noncash expenses such as amortization and depreciation will make a healthy company look sick. Many stock screens allow you to use cash flow as a screen.

Always look beneath the surface when an Internet company reports a significant gain or loss in one quarter. You may be looking at something other than results of the business.

Customers Are Different

Every business wants customers. Whether that business is the latest whiz-bang Web site or a mom-and-pop grocery, customers are what keep it in business. In many ways, Internet businesses must deal with the same customer service issues that every business faces.

"E-tail," or electronic retail, will live or die based on whether the business can provide a good shopping experience for its customers. It will not do an Internet business any good to have the "latest and greatest" Web site if it can't also figure out how to actually fill a customer's order in a prompt and efficient manner.

Another favorite customer complaint is going through a complicated checkout system only to find when you get to the end that you made a mistake earlier and now have to go back and start over. Most systems require you to establish a user name and password, which is not a bad thing. What irritates me is finishing the process only to be told my user name is already taken, that my password must be at least six characters, or that some other problem occurred that should have been noted immediately.

Internet companies that want to sell you a product should make the sale as easy and as quick as possible. The company also should remember who you are and not ask you again. What's more, the product should ship quickly and correctly.

Speak Up

The term **walking dead** refers to Internet businesses that analysts believe won't survive but that have so much cash from their IPO that they don't know they're dead.

Try It, You'll Like It

One of the best evaluation tools that you can use regarding customer service is to actually try the service yourself. Was your experience positive? Would you come back? Did the site deliver what it promised?

There is little doubt that a major consolidation is coming in the e-tail business. Too many players joined the market with no idea of how to run the practical side of the business. Companies in very narrow vertical niches were given astronomical market caps. Like any ecological system, the stock market has ways of periodically weeding out the weak. Many analysts are calling e-tailing the *walking dead* because the companies have no idea that they are doomed. As cash reserves from the IPO dwindle, many e-tailers will be looking for a partner or a white knight to save them.

Stocks to Avoid

The great thing about the Internet is that it has lowered the entry fee for many businesses. With no expensive real estate to own or rent, and with fewer employees necessary, a company could start selling products almost immediately.

E-tailers that sell other people's products will be particularly vulnerable. This type of business invites plenty of competition, and despite what some thought at first, the Internet is not a big tent with room for everyone. Leaders will emerge and dominate, leaving crumbs for the rest.

Internet companies that sell items with small margins will be hard-pressed to ever achieve profitability. Rising costs and competition will put downward pressure on earnings with no real chance to break free.

Advertising-Based Sites

Sites that depend on advertising revenue use third-party services to measure "page views," or how many people are seeing the advertiser's ad. These statistics are readily available and, like any other growth factor, can be observed over time.

Advertisers pay for numbers of page views, but they also pay for "click-throughs," which are the number of times a customer clicks on the ad and is sent to the site.

How does an Internet company go about encouraging shoppers to become customers? It turns out that the process is not much different from the way any retailer converts shoppers to customers.

Sales, promotions, and marketing are all used to draw shoppers to the site. Many on-line retailers spend as much or more on advertising as their offline competitors. How a Web site draws visitors is more a function of marketing than it is technology.

Ask any offline retailer what the most effective advertising is, and they will tell you that it's word-of-mouth. Testimonials from satisfied customers telling friends and neighbors are the kind of endorsements that gets shoppers to the store with a positive attitude.

One of the areas where the Internet has excelled is in word-of-mouth—or, more correctly, "word-of-mouse"—advertising. The classic story of Hotmail.com (hotmail.com) will probably be taught in Internet marketing classes for years to come.

Here's the story in brief: A couple people came up with the idea of offering free e-mail service to individuals. In exchange for free e-mail, the customer is exposed to advertisements. However, the real killer was a line at the bottom of the screen that invited people to let their friends and family know about Hotmail.com.

Double Click

Converting shoppers to customers still involves providing a good shopping experience followed up by good customer service, when needed.

Double Click

With such a short time limit involved in proving a company's worth, there is tremendous pressure to get to the market as quickly as possible. Sometimes companies come out before they are close to being ready. This usually spells disaster.

The company took root on some college campuses and exploded from nothing to hundreds of thousands of accounts almost overnight, without the company spending any money on marketing. The concept was dubbed "viral marketing" because it spread like a flu virus. Every customer became a salesperson. You don't have to be a math whiz to see how the customer base grew exponentially.

Microsoft eventually bought the company, and the founders became very wealthy. Now everyone wants the next viral marketing product.

Growth Is Not Optional

If investors are willing to wait for earnings in exchange for some other benefit, that benefit will almost always be growth. Strong and consistent growth gets a company to the critical mass necessary for profits.

Old Economy companies often had 5 to 10 years to prove themselves as industry leaders. New Economy companies must do it in months. However, with literally millions of Web sites, how does an Internet company distinguish itself from its competitors and the general competition for surfer's attention?

There is a real premium to getting out first. Amazon. com has retained its leadership position because it was first in the consumer's mind. It also enjoyed the benefit of not having to convert an existing business plan to the Internet, as competitors barnesandnoble.com (ticker symbol: BNBN; bn.com) and Borders (ticker symbol: BRG; borders.com) did. Both these efforts have fallen short of Amazon.com.

How Much Growth?

How much growth should you expect from an Internet stock? That depends on the business of the company. E-tailers should show dramatic and sustained growth, in most cases. In all cases, they should keep pace with their peers.

However, Internet companies have limited histories to draw on for information. Amazon.com is the oldest and biggest of the e-tailers, so market watchers keep it squarely in their sights as a harbinger of things to come for the rest of the e-tailers.

Amazon.com has spent hundreds of millions of dollars building its distribution system and other infrastructure needs. It has branched out from books to a variety of other consumer goods and services—it hopes to become the Wal-Mart of the Internet.

Amazon.com currently has more than 17 million customer accounts, and it makes sense to sell as much to each customer as possible. Research has shown that online shoppers prefer names they know to unknown Internet companies. Management at Amazon.com has said that 2000 will be the year the company stopped the tide of increasing losses and headed toward profitability.

The Internet world is a little messier than that. However, if you use Amazon.com as a model for the growth side of the equation, triple-digit growth should be the absolute rule for e-tailers.

Margin Call

Growth is one of the most important factors to an Internet company's survival. However, a poorly designed business will be just a big poorly designed business with growth but no profits.

Unsustainable Growth

Companies that can't sustain that level of growth must be examined carefully. Does a company have unusually high margins? Are its operating costs unusually low? Where will future growth come from?

Hybrid e-tailers, such as Barnes and Noble, may not need the level of growth that pure Internet companies must have. Some evidence suggests that traditional retailers can leverage their existing physical presence with an Internet site. We will look at this in more detail later in the book.

Internet companies that provide products or services to other Internet companies also may not need the level of growth necessary to sustain e-tailers. Many of their products are intellectual in nature (software, consulting, and so on) and don't need $200 million in development costs to get off the ground. For example, WebTrends (ticker symbol: WEBT; webtrends.com) develops and maintains sophisticated software systems that allow Internet companies to track site traffic patterns, e-commerce, advertising, and a variety of other important management reporting tools. WebTrends' IPO was introduced in February 1999, and the company has been profitable since day one. A little over a year later, its stock was trading at about six times its offering price.

I am not suggesting that WebTrends is a good or bad investment, but I want to point out the extreme difference in business models between what an e-tailer needs to succeed and what a business services company needs. WebTrends has just over 1 percent of Amazon.com's sales, yet it has earned more money than the huge e-tailer in six years.

111

Stocks to Avoid

E-commerce businesses face the same laws of the market that traditional businesses face. If your margins are small, you can make money only on high volume.

A little common sense (in short supply, where Internet stocks are concerned) is often the only tool you will need to drop a stock off your possible investment list. Here are some danger signs to look for when evaluating Internet stocks:

➤ Internet companies that sell other's products at low margins will need exceptional growth to ever have a chance at profitability.

➤ Stocks that are valued in the stratosphere will never live up to valuations if their profitability depends on high volume and if the company can't manage triple-digit growth in the early years.

➤ Internet companies that sell in a very narrow, low-margin niche may not be viable businesses.

Technology Not So Important

Successful Internet companies are less dependent on technology than you might think, and more dependent on integrating technology in the business process.

On the surface, this seems counter-intuitive because it is technology that made the Internet possible. Yet, that has been the history of successful businesses in America for a long time. Back in the days when computers lived in climate-controlled temples and were tended by the faithful, IBM-controlled 70-plus percent of the market. There were many reasons for its dominance, but technological innovation was not one of them.

IBM was successful partly because it took technology, sometimes developed by others, and integrated it in the business to the extent that IBM products became indispensable to customers. The phrase "No one ever got fired for recommending IBM" is a well-earned accolade for the company. Successful Internet companies understand that the online community is moving past the "gee whiz" factor and is more interested in functionality.

Customers will be turned off by a whiz-bang Web site that takes three minutes to load because of all the video, photographs, and so on. If I try to access a Web site and get one of those boxes that say I need to download some 7-megabyte plug-in to view the page, I immediately leave.

The model for efficiency should be Yahoo! Its home page is about as plain as it can get, but it loads quickly and delivers what it says it will.

Good technology makes doing business painless. Bad technology gets in the way.

Pay No Attention to the Man Behind the Curtain

The really important advances in Internet technology are occurring behind the scenes in handling transactions, manipulating databases, and building a personalized interface.

Technology is critical only to those Internet companies that sell technology. Of course, Internet companies can't afford to let competitors adopt technology that makes it easier to do business without answering in kind. I buy a lot of products on the Internet. It takes me less time to buy a customized computer from Dell than it does to buy a book or to order flowers from some Web sites. What does that tell you about Dell's systems?

Internet businesses that are information providers, as opposed to product providers, work hard on improving their *stickiness*, which is the amount of time visitors spend before clicking on to another site. Some people seem to think that stickiness means making it impossible to find what you want. Most of the sites that fail in this area are still mired in the Old Economy, which gives the customer just enough to come in, but makes them pay for everything else.

New Economy sites understand that strength lies in making the site as accessible as possible. A good example of this is Market Guide, where literally tons of information is available in several forms—all for free.

Speak Up

Stickiness is the quality a Web site has that makes viewers want to stay longer and look at more pages.

Stocks to Avoid

If you read just about any Internet trade publication or site, you undoubtedly will find some techie bemoaning the fact that the Internet has been taken over by the marketing department. To that I say, "Good." While some people may want to hold on to the notion that the Internet is just one big community of techies hunched over their computers inventing another way to turn your mouse cursor into a laughing squirrel, it is much more than that.

Marketing people, if they are any good, know that function is what will keep customers coming back, not laughing squirrels. I would avoid these stocks:

➤ Companies that are still stuck in the rut that the Internet is really one big video game and that everything is a game.

➤ Companies that make it hard to do business with them. I signed on to a site to check the price of one of its products. Nowhere could I find a page on their site that would give me a price. That's dumb.

Management Is Most Important

Management is almost always the deciding factor of whether a company is successful. This is true offline and online. It may be even truer for Internet businesses because people founded many of them with little business experience.

The American entrepreneurial dream has always been to develop an idea for a business that succeeds against tremendous odds because you work hard and find a way to build a better mousetrap. The Internet is no different, except that the velocity is hundreds of times faster than Old Economy companies. Instead of taking years to build a business, it takes months. There is little or no time for on-the-job training for the founders.

It is not unusual to see companies flounder just when things seem to be going the best. What you will often find is that the company outgrew the founders' ability to manage it.

Margin Call

It is often not the company that builds the better mousetrap, but the company that makes that mousetrap indispensable to the consumer that succeeds.

The classic reasons small businesses fail are undercapitalization and poor management. Undercapitalization is hardly a problem for many Internet companies, but businesses can't live on cash reserves forever. Poor management manifests itself in any number of ways. For Internet companies, one of the main ways is blindness to business realities. The biggest of these realities is that sooner or later, you must produce a profit.

Logical Profit Plan

Despite my plea earlier for patience, there must be a logical, rational strategy for profits. Management that hangs on to the bitter end with a business model that can't succeed has ruined more companies than any external influence. Internet company founders who understand their limitations and supplement them with experienced managers stand a much better chance of success than those who try to do everything themselves.

It is not surprising that one of the most successful Internet companies, Yahoo!, is commanded by experienced business executives, not the young founders. The young founders showed wisdom beyond their years in turning the day-to-day management of a big company over to experienced managers. For that reason, it is also not surprising that Yahoo! is one of the few profitable Internet companies.

Management is so important that I completely devote Chapter 15, "Management Is the Key to Success," to it. For right now, I want you to be aware of stories in the media about Internet executives. You'll find that the media is pretty quick at pointing out an executive's faults.

Don't be put off by terms such as "eccentric" or "unconventional." The New Economy puts a premium on individual thought and vision. Besides, plenty of Old Economy executives fit these labels as well. Herb Kelleher, CEO of Southwest Airlines (ticker symbol: LUV; iflyswa.com), wears those labels proudly. He built a three-plane fleet with stewardesses in hot pants into one of the most successful airlines in history. Watch instead for founders who routinely fire most of their senior staff or change accounting firms frequently. There is a big difference between bold new plans and foolhardy gambles.

Of course, there is a fine line between visionary and kook. Some people bounce back and forth like a tennis ball at the U.S. Open. You need to worry when the media spends more time detailing an executive's eccentric habits than its business plan.

I would stay away from companies that lose top management people faster than they can recruit them, as well as companies that spend more money on the boss's image than the company's image.

The Least You Need to Know

➤ If losses aren't buying a company growth or other important benefits, it may be time to move on.

➤ Attracting shoppers and converting them to customers is the most important thing that a company can do.

➤ Technology that doesn't improve the shopping or viewing experience is more trouble than it is worth.

➤ Sound management is the key to most business success stories.

Chapter 11

But They Are Broke

In This Chapter

➤ Losing money is easy; making money is harder

➤ How to spot Internet stocks on the way to profits

➤ Estimating a reasonable timeframe to profits

➤ What factors to watch for profit signals in different Internet sectors

---

When Bill Clinton was running for president in 1991, someone on his campaign staff taped a large, hand-drawn poster to the wall with these words on it, "It's the Economy, Stupid." This was to remind the candidate and staff that the economy was a vulnerable point in their favor, so the story goes.

When I need to remind myself why investing in Internet stocks is a good idea, I should make my own poster. It would read, "It's the Future, You Idiot."

That's the point of all investing, after all. Investing is about the future, not the past. The Internet is here to stay. Investors who come to grips with that reality and find a way to make rational investments will participate fully in that future.

A Hole in the Bucket

Why would anyone want to invest in companies that have a track record of swimming in red ink and running through cash like there is no tomorrow?

This is a legitimate question, and one that Internet stocks have not had to answer until recently. Most Internet stocks are overvalued, and this has conventional investors squealing. Pundits are warning of a technology/Internet meltdown any day now.

That meltdown may or may not have occurred by the time you read this book. Certainly, there will be corrections like the one that occurred in the first part of 2000. However, a meltdown has been coming for three years now, according to a number of doomsayers.

Margin Call

Internet stocks are overpriced and overvalued. That is a reality we must deal with. A major correction may drop some prices back closer to where we want them to be, but then again, we may have to live with higher prices.

I have no idea (and neither does anyone else) whether technology/Internet stocks are going to collapse. People who make a living calling market turns are quick to point out the one time they were right, but they usually are quiet about the 10 times they were wrong.

If you believe, as I do, that the Internet in some form is here to stay and will continue to have a profound impact on our business and personal lives, then we need to find a way to make rational investments in this phenomena.

Nobody, except those who got in first, likes the fact that Internet stocks are overvalued. That leaves us with two options:

➤ Sit out of the market until valuations come down

➤ Figure out which stocks are worth some premium and what that premium should be

The first option certainly makes Old Economy sense: Don't buy anything that is not at your price. However, what if it never gets to your price? Could it be that your price is wrong? What if the old models of stock valuation don't work on Internet stocks?

I'm not ready to abandon all the traditional methods of stock valuation, but I do believe that we need new ways of thinking about investing in the future, something that traditional methods don't tell us with any confidence.

This brings us to the second option of identifying those stocks we want to own and that will be around for some time, and then determining how much of a premium they are worth.

Sea of Red Ink

It does get discouraging to look at a vast sea of red ink and wonder whether any of these companies are ever going to make a profit. My database of 253 pure Internet stocks has only 34 companies earning any kind of profits. (That's slightly over 13 percent, for you folks who can't get enough numbers.)

I wish it were simply a matter of taking those 34 and picking the few winners based on reasonable valuations. In an overvalued market, a stock that seems to be trading in reasonable ranges must be approached with caution. Why isn't it overvalued also? A stock that just coasts along in a heated market may have something holding it back.

If we expand our search beyond the pure Internet stocks to the hybrid Internet stocks, the results may feel a lot more comfortable. In Part 5, "Blue Chips and Micro Chips," I will devote considerable time to this marriage of the old and the new.

Investing in pure Internet companies is like investing in a futures market to the extent that we have very little past performance to use as a way to support our picks. The futures market in this context is not the same as the commodities that trade on the Chicago Board of Trade or other exchanges.

The future we are looking for is a vision of which companies will still be playing an important role in the economy three years from now.

Double Click

You can't think about Internet stocks and General Motors the same way. Using the same criteria on Internet stocks will effectively mean that you won't own any of these stocks.

Making Money

Making money is every investor's goal. Speculators are more interested in taking a quick profit than investing for the long term. The result is a bunch of companies that are not economically viable being bid up by speculators.

High market caps are not a validation of a company's business plan, yet investors are often guilty of jumping to this conclusion. A 1-year-old company with a market cap of $5 billion must be worth owning, right? Not necessarily. A $5 billion company may be the result of a stock being bid up beyond a reasonable price by people trying to make a quick buck. This phenomenon is known as the *Bigger Fool Theory*.

The Bigger Fool Theory describes a market in which investors will pay any price for a stock (or any other asset), knowing that a bigger fool will soon come along and pay them more. These speculators do not care what the company does. All they care about is whether they can get in, make a profit, and get out.

At some point, the market runs out of fools and the price collapses. In part, this is the basis for the doomsayers' predictions about Internet stocks. If the Internet stock bubble bursts under this scenario, it will drag down the good with the bad.

It is equally likely that the nonviable companies will collapse on themselves. When they run out of money from the first IPO, companies are likely to seek more through a secondary offering. Many of these walking dead may find the market for their secondary offering less than overwhelming. Of course, a significant downturn in the Internet stock market may mean a wonderful buying opportunity for investors who have identified the quality stocks they want to own.

Remember, though, that the price of a company's stock has little effect on the underlying business and its ability to make a profit. It may become significant if the company wants to make acquisitions with stock, but the core business is not directly affected by the price of its stock. It is not uncommon to hear that company XYZ is in trouble because its stock dropped 20 percent in a short period. Actually, it is the investors who own the stock that are in trouble. The company hasn't lost a single penny. The company may be in trouble, so the stock dropped 20 percent, but it does not work the other way around.

The Herd

The stock market often moves like a herd. If some investors get nervous about a particular stock and sell it off, the whole market or sector may be dragged down.

If Microsoft drops 10 percent in one day, you can bet that the rest of the technology sector will have a bad day. This is a reality in investing in Internet stocks. Some days the whole sector tanks because of one or two stocks.

Once you pick a quality stock, be prepared to ride it through the market ups and downs. Every time the stock is down, ask yourself if anything is fundamentally different that would warrant selling.

Margin Call

Beware the stock wizard who has all the hot stocks nailed down and will gladly let you in on the secret list for a small amount of change. Internet stocks are so new and behave in ways that are so strange that it is impossible to pick winners all the time.

How Long to Wait

Patience is not a virtue widely appreciated in the stock market. Investors are willing to let a growing firm get on its feet, but that shouldn't take any longer than necessary.

It is hard to put an absolute figure on how long to wait for profits because there are so many variables. The answer has to fit your personal style more than any set formula. If you won't feel comfortable until earnings are positive, you might want to look at the hybrid Internet companies discussed in Part 5.

Other investors may feel okay with negative earnings as long as substantive progress toward profits continues. It is clear that the market can be patient, up to a point. Companies that turn in worse quarterly performance than the market feels appropriate may suffer a severe reaction.

Placing more accountability on Internet executives will push companies with ambivalent feelings about profits to reconsider.

How to Pick 'Em

There are no experts in picking Internet stocks, yet the Internet is cluttered with folks who have found the secret and are willing to sell it to you.

I have always wondered why a person whose portfolio is up over 125 percent every year for the past 10 years would waste time writing newsletters and developing Web sites. Let me assure you, my portfolio has not been up 125 percent for the past 10 years, and I don't have any secrets to impart. What I do hope to accomplish is to help you with some tools that you can use—along with your common sense—to make the best investment decisions possible.

You have probably noticed that some themes keep repeating themselves throughout this book. One of these key concepts refers to size, and I don't mean just market cap. As I have indicated, market cap can be a false signal when you look at it in isolation. For instance, speculators may bid up kumquats.com to a huge market cap, but how many people will buy kumquats online? How many kumquats will the company have to sell to become a profitable business?

When speculators are bidding up stocks for a quick buck, they don't care whether it is a viable business. At some point, the business will actually have to make a sale or produce a product—and when stockholders realize that there is no way the company can possibly sell enough kumquats to be profitable, they'll dump the stock like a three-day-old fish.

Before long, the cash from the company's IPO will dry up, and there will be no interest in a secondary offering. The company will disappear into Internet history as another well-funded bad idea.

Things in Common

Internet companies that are worth watching have some things in common. However, there is no such thing as an "Internet company"—there are only companies that do business on the Internet. To work with these companies, we need to divide them further by type of business. The most visible are e-commerce sites and portals, to use two broad categories.

Large market-dominating sites have a tremendous advantage when dealing with consumers, especially in product lines with low *entry barriers*.

Speak Up

Entry barriers are obstacles that companies must overcome to participate in a certain line of business. For example, retail sites that sell other vendors' products have a very low entry barrier because anyone can sell the same or equivalent products.

As we said earlier, Amazon.com has 17 million accounts. Its main competitors, Barnes and Noble and Borders, don't have near that many accounts combined. Amazon offers another advantage as well: When it sells a book, it is not at the expense of a "brick and mortar" sale, as with its competitors.

A nightmare for Barnes and Noble and Borders executives probably involves shoppers coming to the physical stores and looking at books, but then going home and ordering from the Web site. This is called pirating. It costs plenty to build and maintain physical stores, and losing sales to your online counterpart doesn't help either the store or the Web site.

The ultimate nightmare has shoppers strolling through the stores but then going home and ordering from Amazon.com. There may be a way that Barnes and Noble and Borders can leverage their physical bookstores with their Web sites, but it is unlikely that they will overtake Amazon.com in Internet sales.

Whether Amazon.com can translate those accounts into a profitable business remains to be seen. The company was able to achieve such a lead in size partly because it was out there first. We'll see what happens down the road.

Being First

Getting out first is another concept that is important, and America Online is a perfect example of this. The company was operating an online service before there was an Internet as we know it. Despite almost missing the Internet boat, AOL leveraged its existing customer base and now dominates the market with 20 million subscribers. This subscriber base generates a tremendous amount of cash.

Help File

Sectors of Internet stocks don't always fit in neat categories. On some information sites, Yahoo! is a portal; on other sites, it is an information provider. Both may be correct. You may find it helpful to make your own decisions about where a particular stock goes, just to be consistent.

AOL's acquisition of Time Warner is an acknowledgement that AOL is not taking its leadership position for granted. With free Internet access deals popping up all over the Web, AOL knows that its content will keep customers coming back.

Of course, while getting out first is an advantage, it's an advantage only for a little while. If the company doesn't continue to move forward someone will overtake them fairly quickly. It may be harder to grow large consumer-oriented businesses now than it was when the Web was just beginning to expand, but it is not impossible. Companies with more efficient execution will prosper, while older competitors will adapt or disappear. Size and early market entry are two factors to consider when looking at business to consumer Internet companies.

Key Factors

The key factors to look for in portal/information providers are traffic (page views) and revenue growth. Yahoo! is successful because it pays virtually nothing for its content and because it was the first portal on the Internet, giving it a head start that will be hard to catch.

The other interesting thing about Yahoo! and many of the other portals is that they do not have to increase content to attract more traffic. As a practical matter, they do so because it serves a marketing purpose, but there are still enough Internet "newbies" who will respond to marketing promotions that significant growth is possible without an extraordinary increase in content.

The *critical mass* for each portal will be different depending on the portal's particular focus. Yahoo! provides little in the way of original content, so its content acquisition costs are low. About.com, on the other hand, uses a large pool of experts to generate not only original content, but also links to external resources. Its content costs will be higher.

Speak Up

Critical mass is the volume of business necessary to generate profits. This varies from company to company depending on a number of variables, but it is an important goal for every company.

Portals should show significant revenue growth, although large portals such as Yahoo! will not be able to sustain the same growth rates simply because of their size.

Another factor to look for is revenue diversification. Portals live on advertising revenue, but they can also die there. Look for merchandising agreements, referral fees, and other nonadvertising income to reduce dependence on advertising. Most sites that profile stocks, such as Morningstar.com, will provide a breakdown in income sources.

If a company is not the market dominator of its particular sector, then it should be among the growth leaders. Maintaining strong growth in revenue is imperative for Internet stocks. Without revenue growth and without earnings, the company must have some other compelling attribute, such as technology, to put it on the consideration list.

Some of the less visible sectors of the Internet economy are the infrastructure companies that are making the Web easier for businesses to use. These companies provide software and hardware to handle such tasks as customer service, database management, and other back-room functions.

Unless you are a techie, it may be hard to understand what these companies do and how to distinguish one from the other. Here is where some of the Internet news Web sites mentioned in Chapter 6, "Doing Your Homework," and Chapter 7, "Online Resources," will come in handy.

Watch for the same name to keep appearing in news stories and articles, and pay particular attention to notices of clients that the company serves. You can tell a lot about a company by its clients: A company with a stable of top-quality clients is worth looking over more than once.

This will be a tough sector to call if you are not willing to do a lot of homework, but it is also one that is likely to be profitable quicker than most. Intellectual properties such as software and other technology always command high margins.

Entertainment Tonight

The hottest sector on the horizon is entertainment delivered over the Internet. This sector is just starting to form and take shape, so its future direction is far from clear.

What is clear, though, is that entertainment will prove to be tremendously popular, more so than it is now. Music and game sites are probably the formats most people think of first when you mention entertainment on the Internet, along with buying books, music, and so on.

What is classified as entertainment now will look pathetic in five years. What most services classify as entertainment is the equivalent of going to Wal-Mart's movie section and watching the monitors. These services will remain, but movies, short features, more interactive games, and opportunities not currently on the radar will join them.

How will this get into your home? A stumbling block is a bandwidth constraint of dial-up access, currently maxed at 56 Kbps. At this speed, video is jerky and grainy, so the thought of live video or full-motion video at these speeds seems ridiculous. However, by 2003, an estimated 16 million homes will have broadband capability, making them prime targets for rich media programming.

In Part V, we look at the broadband expansion from an investment perspective. Broadband in some form is going to happen: Consumers want it, producers want it, and advertisers want it. We'll look at some investment opportunities in broadband delivery.

Internet Everywhere

Further down the road is the concept of "Internet everywhere," which assumes that we will have access to the Internet through a variety of devices, both wired and wireless. The process of delivering entertainment will have to adapt to the particular device being used.

This is already happening with cellular phones and *personal digital assistants (PDAs)*. With these devices, you can download news, stock quotes, e-mail, and other content. You can also interact because this is two-way communication. Thus, you can trade stocks from your cell phone or your PDA while watching your daughter play soccer.

Internet everywhere will bring entertainment directly into your living room. A box sitting on top or close to the television will receive the Internet signal from some broadband delivery service and display it on your television. No need for a computer.

How will this be different from cable television, you ask? In the first place, it will be a pure digital signal—a move some cable systems haven't made yet—designed for high-definition television. However, it will also be on demand. You could watch a movie when you wanted, not when the cable or local stations decide to run it. In fact, you could watch any movie ever made and a whole bunch of new short film formats produced just for the Internet. You also could play an interactive game with people around the world in which your digital surrogate is a character in the game.

Do you see part of the rationale for the America Online and Time Warner merger? Time Warner has one of the biggest film libraries in the world and one of the largest cable systems (a prime delivery system for broadband Internet service). AOL has 20 million customers. Sounds like a formidable combination to me.

> **Speak Up**
>
> **Personal digital assistants (PDAs)** are new devices that are being used to access the Internet. They have built-in modems and cellular phones to connect with an ISP.

Content Rules

However, the real opportunities are probably in developing new content for Internet entertainment. Simply making movies available over the Internet will be the first step because it is the easiest.

The real power of the Internet is its interactive nature. Entertainment that capitalizes on that strength will be tremendously popular. Companies that develop new content offer great promise for investors. Media-rich content, virtually unconstrained by bandwidth, will become one of the biggest sectors in the Internet economy.

Content will rule the Internet for those sites not in the e-commerce field. News, information, advice, and entertainment will keep people coming back to these sites.

How Will They Make Money?

Entertainment providers will make money in a variety of ways, most patterned after existing Web arrangements and broadcast conventions.

Some vendors, for example, will produce content that will be syndicated in much the same way that television shows are syndicated today. Web sites can buy rights to the content and use it to attract and retain viewers. Other vendors, especially game vendors, will charge per-play or monthly subscriptions. This model already works with games charging a monthly fee for play.

Who Are the Players?

Some of the players are on the ground already and include such names as AOL–Time Warner, Disney Online (ticker symbol: DIS; disney.com), and various game sites.

The new players and where the true innovation will come from are just getting off the ground. Here are some names to keep an eye on, especially for IPOs:

➤ AtomFilms (atomfilms.com)

➤ Atomic Pop (atomicpop.com)

➤ Brilliant Digital (ticker symbol: BDE; brilliantdigital.com)

➤ Electronic Arts (ticker symbol: ERTS; ea.com)

➤ iFilm (ifilm.com)

➤ Launch Media (ticker symbol: LAUN; launch.com)

This is not a complete list, by any means. If you keep an eye on some of the news and information sites mentioned earlier, you will pick up even more to watch.

The Least You Need to Know

➤ Negative earnings are part of investing in Internet stocks.

➤ Growth rate and size are good predictors of future profitability.

➤ Business-to-consumer sites need high volume and good margins to be successful.

Chapter 12

What's a Customer Worth?

In This Chapter

➤ How reliable customer figures are

➤ How you place a value on customers

➤ Why investors are interested in future sales, not past performance

➤ Why customers are kings and queens

In the rural area where I grew up there was a small general store. The counter where you paid was at the rear of the store (you don't see that anymore). On the wall behind the counter was a sign that read: "We cheat every third customer and pass the savings on to you!"

I've never quite made up my mind whether that was the best customer service slogan I have ever read or the worst. My suspicion is that the storeowner, with tongue in cheek, was trying to let the customers know how much their business was appreciated.

Internet customers, whether they are interested in a site's content or products, are the toughest in the world. Tick them off, and, click, they're out of there. To make matters worse, they will probably stop at some forum and let the whole world know just how screwed up your site is.

On the other hand, Internet companies that take care of customers are on the right track to profits. You won't have to worry about evaluating companies that don't take care of customers.

Counting Heads

The honeymoon between the Internet and its customers is officially over. Actually, it has been over for some time, but I want to make it official. (In this context, a customer is someone visiting an e-tailer, viewing content, playing a game, or doing whatever a particular site is about.)

Gone are the days when Web surfers put up with slow page downloads, clumsy forms, and goofy navigation. Customers want to get the information they need quickly and then get out.

Shopping malls became popular because they made it convenient for the customer to shop many stores on a single trip. The Internet has taken that concept and made it possible to visit as many sites as you want with almost no effort.

A common complaint about Internet shopping is the lack of a "human touch." If by that, they mean you don't have to put up with snotty clerks or store personnel that would rather be doing anything else but helping you, I'm all for it.

The Internet equivalent of the bored and rude clerk is a site that is difficult to navigate and takes forever to execute.

There is little incentive to put up with bad Web sites, so customers need to have a good experience each and every time they visit a site. The race to attract and keep customers is where Internet companies will rise or fall.

Counting heads—or, more appropriately, eyes—is of major importance to Internet companies. These counts tell them how much to charge advertisers and whether they are reaching enough customers to sustain an e-commerce site.

The most important count is of *unique visitors*, which means that the customer visited the site at least once during the month. If that customer visits the site more than once in a month, he is still counted only once. Unique visitor statistics are the ones that really matter because an independent party produces them. Customer numbers released by companies can be misleading and may be inflated to make the company look good.

The leading counter is Media Metrix (ticker symbol: MMXI; mediametrix.com). Advertisers, e-commerce sites, and others who have an interest in Web traffic use this service. Obviously, most of the reports are for sale, but you can visit the Media Matrix site and get a look at the top rankings in a variety of categories.

Sites that live on advertising revenue base their rates on how many unique views the site received during the month. E-commerce sites track sales with traffic to determine how much traffic they need to sustain the business.

Speak Up

A **unique visitor** to an Internet site is a count of each visitor to a site during the month. Each unique visitor is counted only once, no matter how often that visitor comes back during the month.

There is some debate among advertisers about the accuracy of these measurements, but they are done by an objective, third party and will stand until something better comes along.

Customer or Not?

Unique views and customers are not the same. E-tailers are more interested in counting customers than shoppers. Unfortunately, most of the customer information available comes from the company, which makes it somewhat suspect in some cases.

Some e-commerce sites are fairly open about their customer numbers, while others are tight-lipped. This makes comparisons difficult at best and impossible in most cases.

Amazon.com is fairly open about its customer counts, placing them at around 17 million. When I looked at Media Metrix's unique visitor count for Amazon.com in March 2000, they numbered about 14.5 million. Does that mean that 14.5 million of the 17 million customers visited the previous month? Unfortunately, it does not tell us that at all. Of the 14.5 million unique visitors to the site, some visitors may have just been browsing, while others could have come to buy.

Why This Is Important

We will struggle throughout this book with ways to place values on Internet stocks and to design tools to compare one stock with another. Knowing the unique visitors to a site provides us with a way to place a value on those visitors.

This measurement works with companies in the same sector, but it falls apart when you try to compare stocks from different sectors. An e-tailer may not be able to translate a visitor to a customer—a sale must occur for that to happen.

However, sites that work on advertising sales can be measured using the unique visitors because these are the equivalent of a sale. (Advertisers pay a fee based on the number of times their ad is seen on the site, so a visitor counts as a sale.)

The calculation we are going to use is the market/viewer value (MVV). This number will tell us how much the market values each viewer to a site. We will divide the market cap by the number of unique visitors to give us a dollar figure to put on each viewer.

Computing Value

The following table shows some Internet companies grouped with some of their peers. As you can see, there is a wide spread in how the market values the traffic that different sites generate.

A higher stock price (one part of the market capitalization formula) will reflect a higher MVV. A high MVV may indicate that the stock is overpriced.

Comparison of Market/Viewer Values (MVV) for Leading Internet Companies

Company	Unique Visitors*	Market Cap**	MVV
ZDNet	9,535	$ 2,142	$ 225
About.com	9,339	$ 1,699	$ 182
CNET.com	8,280	$ 4,151	$ 501
Go2Net.com	5,301	$ 2,407	$ 454
iVillage	5,002	$ 771	$ 154
Amazon.com	13,609	$22,364	$1,643
eBay.com	11,791	$27,290	$2,314
CDNow.com	5,690	$ 211	$ 37
Barnes&Noble.com	5,176	$ 1,216	$ 235
MyPoints.com	4,875	$ 1,619	$ 332
eGreetings.com	4,161	$ 254	$ 61
Yahoo.com	44,698	$88,843	$1,988
Lycos.com	27,121	$ 7,859	$ 290
Go.com	19,487	$ 1,020	$ 52
Goto.com	7,208	$ 2,424	$ 336

* Thousands   *** Millions*
Unique visitors from Media Metrix

That assessment certainly works with Yahoo!—its MVV is a sky-high $1,988, and its P/E is so high that most services won't even report it. Stated another way, the market is willing to pay $1,988 for every unique visitor to the Yahoo! site.

Margin Call

Companies like to throw around numbers that make them look good, but the numbers that really matter are the ones reported in audited financial statements.

eBay.com also puts up a huge number, with an MVV of $2,314. The market is willing to pay $2,314 per unique visitor. That is a large premium for visitors to the site—is the company worth it?

What about those stocks with a relatively low MVV? CDNow.com has a MVV of $37, suggesting that the market thinks CDNow.com's unique visitors are worth about $37 of market cap each. The stock also has a price to sales ratio of 1.31, a very respectable number for an Internet company. The company has sales growth for the past 12 months of 161 percent; total sales for the trailing 12 months was $147 million. On the surface, CDNow.com looks pretty inexpensive compared to some of the other stocks in the table.

Sales Per Visitor

What would happen if we related unique visitors to sales in a way that showed us what the average unique visitor means in terms of sales? Here's our table using sales instead of market cap.

For this table, we divide the sales for the trailing 12 months by the unique visitors to get a sales-per-visitor number. This will tell us how much revenue each unique visitor brings to the company.

Comparison of Sales/Unique Visitors for Leading Internet Companies

Company	UniqueVisitors*	Sales TTM 12 Months*	Sales per Visitor
ZDNet	9,535	$ 104,000	$ 10.91
About.com	9,339	$ 26,960	$ 2.89
CNET.com	8,280	$ 112,340	$ 13.57
Go2Net.com	5,301	$ 26,810	$ 5.06
iVillage	5,002	$ 44,560	$ 8.91
Amazon.com	13,609	$1,639,840	$120.50
eBay.com	11,791	$ 224,720	$ 19.06
CDNow.com	5,690	$ 147,190	$ 25.87
Barnes&Noble.com	5,176	$ 202,570	$ 39.14
MyPoints.com	4,875	$ 24,140	$ 4.95
eGreetings.com	4,161	$ 3,000	$ 0.72
Yahoo.com	44,698	$ 588,610	$ 13.17
Lycos.com	27,121	$ 204,790	$ 7.55
Go.com	19,487	$ 26,810	$ 1.38
Goto.com	7,208	$ 33,830	$ 4.69

* *Thousands*
Unique visitors from Media Metrix

This table presents a different picture. What are visitors contributing in the way of revenue to the company? Remember eBay and its sky-high $2,314 MVV? When you relate the unique visitors to sales, you see that they are generating only $19.06 in revenues each. Less than 1 percent of the premium the market pays for unique visitors is returned in revenues.

One figure jumps off the table at me: the $120.50 in revenues that each visitor returned to Amazon.com. Despite a high MVV, Amazon.com is getting a reasonable amount of revenue from the visitors. Assuming that it can maintain or increase the amount of revenue and the number of visitors, Amazon.com may move toward profitability.

Combination Plate

Let's combine the results of the two tables and see what, if anything, this new table tells us.

Comparison of Market/Viewer Value to Sales/Unique Visitors

Company	Unique Visitors*	Sales/MVV	Visitor
ZDNet	9,535	$ 225	$ 10.91
About.com	9,339	$ 182	$ 2.89
CNET.com	8,280	$ 501	$ 13.57
Go2Net.com	5,301	$ 454	$ 5.06
iVillage	5,002	$ 154	$ 8.91
Amazon.com	13,609	$1,643	$120.50
eBay.com	11,791	$2,314	$ 19.06
CDNow.com	5,690	$ 37	$ 25.87
Barnes&Noble.com	5,176	$ 235	$ 39.14
MyPoints.com	4,875	$ 332	$ 4.95
eGreetings.com	4,161	$ 61	$ 0.72
Yahoo.com	44,698	$1,988	$ 13.17
Lycos.com	27,121	$ 290	$ 7.55
Go.com	19,487	$ 52	$ 1.38
Goto.com	7,208	$ 336	$ 4.69

* Thousands
Unique visitors from Media Metrix

Help File

Investors are always looking for ways to compare two or more companies. Because Internet companies are young, they often don't fall into traditional equations for evaluations, so you sometimes have to improvise.

The MVV tells us what premium the market is placing on the unique visitors, while the sales per visitor figure tells us how much revenue the visitors are bringing into the company. One would hope that if the visitors carried a high premium (MVV), they also would generate substantial revenues.

One weakness of this table is that it makes no distinction between businesses in terms of what a target amount of sales per visitor should be. Should a portal such as Yahoo! generate more or less in sales per visitor than a bookstore?

However, this table is a good way to look at comparable sites. For example, the last grouping of four sites are all related, yet look at the differences between Yahoo.com and Go.com. There are no obvious patterns in any of the groupings.

Playing the Percentages

One final table takes a look at what percentage of the premium is actually converted to sales. We get this by dividing the sale per visitor by the MVV. The result is a percentage of the MVV.

Comparison of (Sales/Unique Visitors)/(MVV)

Company	Unique Visitors*	Sales/MVV	Percent Premium Visitor	To Sales
ZDNet	9,535	$ 225	$ 10.91	4.85%
About.com	9,339	$ 182	$ 2.89	1.59%
CNET.com	8,280	$ 501	$ 13.57	2.71%
Go2Net.com	5,301	$ 454	$ 5.06	1.11%
iVillage	5,002	$ 154	$ 8.91	5.79%
Amazon.com	13,609	$1,643	$120.50	7.33%
eBay.com	11,791	$2,314	$ 19.06	0.82%
CDNow.com	5,690	$ 37	$ 25.87	69.92%
Barnes&Noble.com	5,176	$ 235	$ 39.14	16.66%
MyPoints.com	4,875	$ 332	$ 4.95	1.49%
eGreetings.com	4,161	$ 61	$ 0.72	1.18%
Yahoo.com	44,698	$1,988	$ 13.17	0.66%
Lycos.com	27,121	$ 290	$ 7.55	2.60%
Go.com	19,487	$ 52	$ 1.38	2.65%
Goto.com	7,208	$ 336	$ 4.69	1.40%

* Thousands
Unique visitors from Media Metrix

Amazon.com is up there with a very high MVV of $1,643, but its unique visitors are generating $120.50 in revenues, or 7.3 percent. That's not great, but it's a lot better than eBay.

However, when compared with rival Barnes and Noble, Amazon.com is not nearly as efficient. Of course, Barnes and Noble doesn't command the respect or premium that Amazon does, so its performance looks better on a percentage basis.

What of the low-priced (relatively) CDNow? Its unique visitors cost $37 each but bring in $25.87 in revenue. Almost 70 percent of the premium paid for the visitors is returned in revenue.

Conclusions

What conclusions can we draw from these exercises?

➤ Expensive (high market cap) stocks are not efficient in converting unique visitors into revenue.

➤ These tables are interesting but not conclusive. They do give you an idea of how customers (viewers) relate to the stock's market cap and sales.

➤ The number of unique visitors is an important figure in the evaluation of a company, but it is not very important unless those visitors can be converted into sufficient revenue to make the company profitable.

➤ None of these tables is a predictor of profitability. Yahoo!, with the worse conversion of premium to sales (0.66 percent), is one of two profitable stocks in the tables.

Margin Call

One of the purposes of comparing companies when doing stock evaluation is to see if any fall outside the general pattern of their peers. When a stock does, that may be an occasion to celebrate the discovery of an overlooked gem. It may also be a red flag that something is amiss and that more digging is needed.

Note that in the previous tables, CDNow.com seemed to be the most fairly priced of all the listed stocks: The company converted most of the premium for visitors into revenue. However, by the time you read this, CDNow.com may be out of business or may have merged with another company. In late March 2000, the company's auditors said that it had about 30 days of cash left and brought into question the continued viability of the company.

Customers are worth a great deal to Internet stock investors in many cases. It is impossible for stocks to post positive earnings without strong growth in customers. Equally important, however, is converting those customers to sufficient revenue.

Hard Sell

Earlier, I talked about how hard it was for e-tailers to make money selling other companies' products, especially where the barriers to entering the market are low.

CDNow.com is a good example of a business that almost anyone can get into with relatively little money. How do you distinguish your business from another site selling music?

If you lower prices and increase selection, you have structured a business model almost certain to fail. There are some economies of scale that volume can achieve.

When you are selling a $15 item with $7.50 of product costs, it is unlikely that you can hold down all other expenses such as advertising, inventory, and so on so there is any profit left.

The middle grouping of stocks represents e-tailers of various stripes. Not one of them is close to profitability. The e-tailers that are truly successful are hybrid companies such as Dell that sell their own high-ticket, high-margin items. We will spend a lot more time in Part 5, "Blue Chips and Micro Chips," looking at Dell's business models.

The Internet may be heading toward a period in which only a handful of very large e-tailers will survive selling general merchandise, while companies of various sizes will survive selling proprietary products.

Margin Call

A major shakeup of e-tailers seems probable, but those predictions have been around for a couple of years. By the time you read this book, the shakeup may have already occurred. If so, look for some bargains.

Mom and Pop

This is not unlike the retail experience in the Old Economy. While many people express the desire to shop in small mom-and-pop stores, the reality is that these stores are an endangered species.

Years ago I had a friend who owned a small hardware store in a large city. Her father had operated it for many years and had passed it on to her in his will. She tried to keep it going, but times change. I once went to her store to buy an electric drill, but her prices were 20 percent over what the large chain stores were charging. She noticed my concern and said that it would be okay if I bought the drill at the big store. She told me that the big store sold the same drill for less than she paid for it wholesale.

There are not many ways to compete in that environment. I fear that many e-tailers will find themselves in the same boat.

Ironically, those Old Economy retailers that have established an Internet presence may be in a better position, than the pure Internet players. Earlier, I said almost the opposite, but I believe that both may be true for different companies.

Three Examples

Three major bookstores are present on the Web:

➤ **Amazon.com**—A pure Internet play

➤ **Barnesandnoble.com**—A hybrid, spun off from the brick-and-mortar parent

➤ **Borders.com**—An Old World retailer with an Internet presence

Each has advantages and weaknesses.

135

Amazon.com has the advantage of being out there first, with no existing model to slow it down. Its weakness is that it carries a huge inventory of low-margin items that anyone can sell. The company has addressed part of this weakness by offering other products.

This is a good example of leveraging those 13.6 million unique visitors and 17 million accounts—this is something to look for in online e-tailers. Can the company not only *cross-sell* customers, but also establish itself in different product lines? This is when the value of customers becomes evident.

Barnesandnoble.com, operating as an independent company from the parent, has great name recognition—branding, as they say. This may be tied too tightly to the parent's culture to make it as a pure Internet company. For those of us who live in small towns with no easy access to a Barnes and Noble store, the Web site may prove a real benefit.

Borders.com has remained part of the corporate fold, for better or for worse. If the company uses the Web site as a marketing tool for the physical stores, it may have lower expectations than other companies for growth.

The importance of growth, which I will discuss in more detail in the next chapter, is illustrated by noting several stocks approaching profitability, ZDNet.com among them. These stocks have announced major advertising campaigns that will push profits away for a while longer. Companies can do this with some confidence that investors will understand because future sales interest investors, not past performance. Investors understand that growth in customers and revenue is more important now than earnings.

However, there will be little tolerance for companies with low growth rates. You snooze, you lose!

Customer Service Rules

Internet companies that treat customers as anything less than kings and queens will soon become lonely peasants. There can be no substitute for excellent customer service. Old Economy retailers have known this forever, even if some of them seem to have forgotten it. How many times have you gone into a store and either been treated like an intrusion or ignored completely?

Speak Up

Cross-selling is a way to offer customers who have just bought some merchandise the opportunity to buy something else. An Old Economy example would be offering socks to a man who had just bought a pair of shoes.

Double Click

Customer service is one of the most overworked terms in business. It is included in every mission statement and is often contained in the company slogan. It is also a way of doing business that some Internet companies get and some don't. You'll know which is which very quickly.

Years ago, when I wore suits to work instead of blue jeans, I used to shop at a downtown men's clothing store that had been around 50 years. It was small compared to its mall counterparts, but the store carried very high-quality clothing.

Mr. K was the first person to wait on me, and I bought several thousands of dollars of clothing from him over the years. I always went back to that store because Mr. K called me by name when I came in the door. He remembered my size and knew that I liked all-wool suits and all-cotton shirts. He remembered what he had sold me, so he never showed me the same suit or a similar suit again. He was always pleasant, but he knew I was always in a hurry, so there was no aimless chitchat.

Every Web site you do business with should treat you the same way that Mr. K treated me.

The Least You Need to Know

➤ Customers are worth a great deal to Internet companies.

➤ You can place a value on customers and compare this value to that of other stocks.

➤ Lots of customers may not be enough to save some online businesses.

➤ Converting Web site visitors to customers is the goal of every e-commerce Internet company.

➤ Internet customers expect a high level of personalization and functionality. Treat them like Kings and Queens and they will come back for more.

Chapter 13

What Price Growth?

In This Chapter

➤ How much growth can you expect?

➤ Why some Internet companies have to be huge or die

➤ Paying for growth with earnings

➤ Forecasting future growth

Growth is what Internet stocks are all about. That's a broad generalization, to be sure, but it is worth focusing more attention on in light of our previous discussions on earnings and customers.

In 1967, Dustin Hoffman starred in a movie titled *The Graduate*, in which he played a recent graduate who had returned home after college with no plans for the future and was struggling with his identity. In the film, a man takes Hoffman aside for some manly advice at a party. The advice turns out to be one word: plastics. The man clearly believes that there is a great future for bright young men in the plastics industry. Hoffman decides that it is more fun to fool around with Anne Bancroft and her daughter, Katharine Ross.

Investors have to be concerned with a lot of factors besides growth, but without growth in revenues and customers, most of the other stuff isn't important.

The Great Growth Rush

We have become worshipers of growth, and with good reason—at least, in a secular sense. We have seen many companies, not just one or two, go from nothing to market caps of several billion dollars in half the time it takes most people to finish college.

As strange as it may seem to some young investors, there was growth before the Internet. In fact, there was some spectacular growth, but it was spotty and tended to be in very traditional venues such as real estate and oil.

The rush to technology began in earnest in the early 1990s. Back in the good old days of 1995 you could buy 100 shares of Microsoft for around $1,000, not counting commissions. Barely five years later, thanks to three splits, you would own 800 shares worth around $90,000 as of March 2000.

Microsoft went from a one-idea wonder to the largest or second largest (depending on when you measure) company in America. However, it took a number of years to get there.

Those Amazing Young Rockets

Yahoo!, Exodus Communications (ticker symbol: EXDS; exodus.net), Ariba (ticker symbol: ARBA; ariba.com), eBay.com (ticker symbol: EBAY; ebay.com), and Amazon.com are all too young to go to school, but each is worth over $25 billion in market capitalization.

During this time frame, the Dow Jones Industrial Average went from in the 3,000s to the 11,000 mark, and the NASDAQ Composite Index passed the 5,000 barrier. Did the technology and Internet stocks fuel this explosive growth, or was it the other way around?

Without spending a lot of time in market theory, most observers would agree that there was some "push me–pull you" going on between the technology and Internet stocks and a market on fire with new money.

A strong economy and shifts away from defined benefit plans (which were managed for employees) to defined contribution plans (in which employees took greater control of their retirement investing) all conspired to attract a lot of money into the market. Concurrently, technology and Internet stocks exploded as investors poured billions of dollars into the market. All this is interesting, but what does this have to do with anything?

I'm glad you asked. The point is that in any market in which there are more buyers than sellers, prices will rise. These rising prices in technology and Internet stocks became a lure for more money to be invested in this sector, at the expense of other market sectors.

Double Click

A strong economy, low unemployment, and a surging stock market worked together to drive up stock prices in the 1990s.

Skyrocketing stock prices encouraged venture capitalists to fund more technology and Internet plays. Any business plan with a "dot.com" in the first paragraph had a good chance of being funded. IPOs went through the roof the first day out, and more millionaires were made.

Toward the end of the 1990s, red flags began to go up from market observers who saw a huge bubble about to burst. They figured that there was no way these new companies could ever live up to their huge valuations. Sooner or later, investors would come to their senses, and all of these high-flying Internet stocks would come crashing down.

Growth High

Growth is a powerful narcotic. It is addictive because of all the good things that can come from it, such as earnings, dividends, and higher stock prices. The danger is that growth can mask a fatally flawed business plan when unearned cash fuels it.

This is the dark side of growth. Internet companies sitting on piles of cash from their IPOs convince themselves that nothing is wrong. How can anything be wrong with $50 million sitting in the bank and a market cap in the billions?

With no real earnings pressure, Internet companies can fund their growth with all sorts of market expansion deals, including acquisition (which is often done with stock) and astronomical marketing budgets. There's nothing wrong with this approach. Investors buy future earnings and continued growth. This is the way to move toward those targets. The problem is that many of these Internet companies never should have been funded in the first place. Because investors and venture capitalists wanted in on this modern gold rush, many bad or half-baked ideas had tons of money thrown at them. And a bad idea with lots of money is just a well-funded bad idea.

The market shakeup that the doomsayers have been predicting will probably occur when these poorly conceived businesses run out of money. By the time you read this, maybe a dozen or so companies will have met this fate or sold themselves off to prevent it.

Barron's ran a study in the early part of 2000 listing the Internet companies that were about to run out of money at their current rate of spending. The list was long and littered with e-tailers. As the cash starts running out, the ugly truth begins to shine through: The more these companies grew, the more money they lost.

What Can You Expect?

How much growth can you expect from Internet stocks? How long is a piece of string?

The short answer is this: Expect a lot—in fact, insist on it. Two of your major screens for Internet stocks should be sales growth and customer growth. As we've discussed in Chapters 9, "What Are They Selling?" and 12, "What's a Customer Worth?" these are numbers that you can track. Watch them closely.

141

In most cases, sales growth should outpace customer growth. This indicates repeat sales and bigger sales. For example, in the last chapter, we saw that Amazon.com generates about $120 in sales from the unique visitors to its site. Tracking that over time should show an increase in that number that is greater than the increase in unique visitors.

It is also important to note that when you are looking at large companies such as Amazon.com and Yahoo!, their percentage increases will not look as robust as those of smaller companies. Some math gets in the way. For instance, Amazon.com has 17 million customer accounts. To show a 10 percent increase, that company must add 1.7 million customer accounts. A company with 2 million customers, on the other hand, has to add only 200,000 customers to achieve the same 10 percent growth.

The simple table that follows illustrates this point. For Amazon.com to hit its 10 percent growth target, it must capture 5.15 percent of the available market. The smaller company needs to capture only 0.42 percent of the available market to achieve the same percentage growth.

Internet Market	Amazon.com	Small.com
Total Internet Market*	50	50
Minus current customers*	–17	–2
Prospective customers*	33	48
Growth needed*	1.7	0.2
% of prospective customers	5.15 %	0.42 %

Millions

The numbers here are for illustration only, but the point is still valid. Large companies have a harder time achieving nosebleed growth rates than smaller companies just because of the math.

This model assumes a static universe of Internet users, which, of course, is not the case. Amazon.com's strategy has to be threefold at least:

➤ First, it needs to retain existing customers and convince them to buy more.

➤ Second, it needs to expand its market share of the existing universe of Internet users.

➤ Third, it needs to capture as many "newbies" as possible as they go online.

Right now, investors will be looking for some movement toward positive earnings. However, if Amazon.com can continue its growth in customers and sales, most investors will be happy.

Handling Growth

One of the most important factors you need to consider when looking at an Internet company is its ability to "scale" the business.

This concept is of critical importance because it will tell you what it will cost to increase the business. Scalable businesses can flex with growth by increasing capacity without excessive costs. For example, Yahoo! doesn't have to add additional content to increase its number of visitors. It is constantly adding and updating to maintain a level of freshness, but it can add a million new customers without adding any content. It would need additional back-room systems (servers, high-speed connections, support, and so on), but that is what being scalable is about.

Help File

Although the Internet keeps growing and adding users, many people expect the growth to slow in coming years. Some observers feel that the folks with the money and interest are almost all on by now. Much of the rest of the population may find the price too expensive.

On the other hand, consider an online grocery provider such as Peapod.com (ticker symbol: PPOD; peapod.com). Adding a significant number of customers means lining up suppliers and delivery services. This type of business may be doomed by its own success. Adding new customers or new markets is an expensive proposition for this type of business, unlike the Yahoo! model.

Sucking Cash

Too much growth will suck all the cash out of a company, and, according to the Barron's article mentioned earlier, Peapod will be one of the first casualties. There are many problems with the concept of online grocery shopping, not the least of which is a traditional profit margin in the food business of 1–3 percent.

Even with a hefty service charge and some concessions from suppliers, there can't be much of a margin in this business. How much are people willing to pay for the convenience?

This also brings up a problem with an online business that relies on actual human contact with the customer to complete the sale. How many deliveries can one person make during the day? If the clients are spread out geographically or are on the other side of town from distribution points, a significant amount of time will be spent driving back and forth.

It is not clear whether an online business that requires a human contact to complete the transaction makes any sense. Most e-tailers rely on commercial delivery services such as UPS (ticker symbol: UPS; ups.com) or one of the other services. Once the online e-tailer has "picked and packed" the order, that company is finished with the transaction. Some companies even outsource this part of the process.

Get On the Scale

Let's get back to the scale issue. Companies that can absorb large increases in customers and sales for relatively little cost stand the best chance of success. Most of the time, a little common sense will tell you whether a business is scalable.

Let's look at a couple of examples. Internet consulting firms seem to have hit it big with the valuations. However, they are definitely not scalable. Consulting companies depend on consultants to generate revenue. If a firm wants to add new business, it will have to hire more consultants or, more likely, contract with independent consultants. These folks don't come cheap, either for the customer or for the company.

Just for illustration's sake, let's assume that the consultant and associated costs eat up 80 percent of the fee the company charges the client. If the company adds another customer, it must add another consultant, and it still makes only 20 percent. The company may be able to achieve some economies in the home office related to the support people and the facilities that the consultants need, but not enough to offset the 80 percent gross costs. Add a client, add a consultant, and you still only make 20 percent. Add 10 clients, add 10 consultants, and you still only make 20 percent.

Double Click

Scalable businesses all have the ability to accommodate more business without significant investment.

Now let's look at a scalable Internet company. NetObjects (ticker symbol: NETO; netobjects.com) is a software company that makes products for Web site development. It can sell to as many clients as its site can handle. Heavy sales volume may require adjustments in distribution and back-room activities, but 1 customer or 100,000 customers will not change the fundamental costs.

Many software companies and online stores are encouraging people to download software directly from the Web rather than getting the programs in a box. Some are beginning to discount prices for this form of delivery. We may be approaching the day when most software will be sold and installed this way. The online method of delivery is closer to the true power and benefit of the Internet because it eliminates not only a retail store, but also a warehouse and shipping functions.

Fractured Infrastructure

The concerns I have raised about delivery problems and such bring up another issue about growth for your consideration: whether the infrastructure (internal or external) the company depends on is capable of economically supporting more growth or even the existing business.

It is one thing to ship a 40-pound, $2,000 computer, but the same weight of dog food costs roughly the same to ship. (I assume that the firm wouldn't insure the dog food.) Can you see a problem with this scenario?

Assuming that the firm passes on the shipping cost to the customer, it still makes a big difference when your shipping costs are as much or more than the product you ship. I know that Americans are goofy about their pets, but how many will want to buy pet supplies at this premium? Nevertheless, several companies are vying for that online business.

A more familiar example happened to a couple of online brokers during 1999, when turbulence in the market saw a large number of customers trying to log on at the same time. Several of the brokerages went down for periods of time as their servers were overwhelmed. Some customers could not log on to their accounts, and others got disconnected in midtransaction. The firms didn't have an adequate backup plan, and there were a lot of angry clients.

Time-critical transactions such as stock trades are at risk of infrastructure problems— and sometimes the problem isn't even with the brokerage, but it's somewhere between them and the client. The client's ISP could go down, or power could be lost.

From a growth perspective, time-sensitive businesses (such as brokers and a growing number of other financial services companies) need extra capacity on demand to handle peak situations. It might be frustrating to not be able to log on to Dilbert.com (URL: dilbert.com) for your daily fix, but it could be disaster if you can't get to your brokerage account.

I would be wary of Internet companies that rely on ponderous delivery schemes or shaky partners to make them work. There are too many good Internet companies to chase the dogs.

Earning Your Way

In Chapter 10, "Five Rules You Need to Know," we discussed growth as a substitute for earnings. Few investors would argue that young companies should grow first and worry about earnings later. The questions are these: How much later, and what did it buy you?

Despite what the media may think, all Internet companies are not equal. A fair number shouldn't be in business and won't be for long. Others will ride out any and all corrections and still will be around when the dust settles.

It would be easy to dismiss all Internet stocks as "black holes" for money, but this would be wrong. Amazon.com has lost millions over the years, but it has also bought 17 million customers. Can those customers and more be converted into enough cash to make it profitable? Maybe or maybe not, but this company has a chance, which is more than a lot of Internet companies can say.

There are smart ways to lose money, and there are dumb ways to lose money. The smart ways buy the company something of value other than profits. This something is almost always growth, or market share for the more precise.

The next step is converting that market share into profits. Doing step one doesn't guarantee success in step two. However, if the company can't do step one (growth), step two won't happen.

Some Warning Signs

With no long track records to consult for comfort, Internet investors are always at a disadvantage over their Old Economy chums. So if there is no comfort in history and the future is still to be written, what are Internet stock investors to do?

Here are some warning signs that an Internet company may be losing money the dumb way:

➤ **Copycat business plans**—There is usually room for two or maybe three leaders in most markets, but every entry after that will be fighting for crumbs. There is a tremendous advantage to getting out first. Copycats piggyback on the attention of the leaders, but very few will knock off the leader.

➤ **Flat growth rates**—This one should be obvious. Ever see a canoe at a dead stop in a rushing river? It is hung up on something. Internet companies that are stalled should be abandoned. If the company isn't going forward, it is fatally flawed. This is why it is important to know which metrics are important to a particular business. Metrics can be found for most Internet companies on services such as Morningstar.com.

➤ **Trading at low valuations**—As odd as it might seem, an Internet stock with low valuations may not be a bargain, but a turkey. If the stock has a price/sales valuation significantly lower than its peers, it may be that the market has no respect for the company.

➤ **Declining sales**—This goes along with the other growth indicators. Watch the quarter-to-quarter sales for slippage. Slowing growth is a warning sign, but declining sales is the kiss of death.

➤ **Broken piggy bank**—Rapidly shrinking cash reserves indicate that the company is burning money faster than sales can keep up. A company in the third or fourth year after its IPO should have put the brakes on cash losses. You should see the cash flow from operations increasing and the cash draining from reserves at an ever-slowing rate.

➤ **Parachutes Everywhere**—When key executives begin to bail out, this is a sign that things may be coming unhinged. Many Internet companies try to lock in top executives with deals that reward them for sticking around. If the executives are willing to walk away from some big bucks down the road, maybe they know there won't be any bucks down the road.

Positive Signs

You can also look for some positive signs that may signal an Internet company that is here to stay. These signs are not guarantees, but they do offer encouragement:

➤ **Cash in the bank**—When all is said and done cash in the bank makes the difference between a survivor and "what was their name." This sign is the opposite of the previous warning about cash, and it warms investor's hearts to see plenty of cash riding into positive earnings.

➤ **Fat numbers**—Regardless of which metric is important, leaders lead. Look for top-of-the-chart numbers on a consistent basis. Market leaders are in tremendous positions of power and are worth paying a premium for.

➤ **A company that works**—Internet companies to watch do what they say, and do it better and faster than anyone else. They don't push half-baked ideas on the market, and what they do put out works. The market is very unforgiving of amateurs pretending to be leaders. Sooner or later, the leaders rise, and the rest are left behind.

➤ **Smart management**—Leaders attract and retain the best and the brightest. Whether they are technology leaders, marketing leaders, or financial leaders, these companies attract them like flies.

➤ **Constant refining**—Leading Internet companies are constantly refining and redefining themselves. They find ways to do business not thought of before and to make money doing so. When you hear a company's business plan and you want to slap your forehead because it is so obvious and so smart, that's a leader.

➤ **The hunter, not the prey**—Leading companies acquire others for their technology or market, or both. These are the companies doing the buying. Five years ago, who would have thought that America Online would be buying Time Warner?

Always look at the cash. Is it growing? Is it declining? By how much and why? Answer these questions, and they will tell you a lot about the company and its future.

Forecasting Growth

Forecasting growth of Internet stocks is as easy or as hard as you want to make it. Most investing Web sites, such as MSN MoneyCentral and Morningstar.com, have forecasts built into their reports. Often these are earnings forecasts, but some discuss revenue growth.

You can make your own forecasts if you are into that sort of thing. You will need growth numbers for the past couple of years, if possible, and some idea of the universe of potential customers. Remember our earlier discussion about Amazon.com having 17 million customers? Knowing the company's historical growth rate, you can extrapolate using decreasing growth factors because of the large numbers.

Your best bet may be to keep an eye on the news. Growth figures are routinely reported, especially for the leading Internet companies.

The Least You Need to Know

➤ Growth is incredibly important because without growth there can never be profits.

➤ Companies that aren't growing are dying because they are losing market share to an emerging leader, or the market has decided we can all live without their products.

➤ Watch for the danger signs that the company is about to drop off the radar screen.

➤ Growing Internet businesses can scale operations to accommodate new customers.

Chapter 14

Technology Is Not the Answer

> ## In This Chapter
>
> ➤ Why technology is meaningless unless it enhances or makes possible a viable business plan
>
> ➤ Why Internet companies stumble over low-tech problems
>
> ➤ Where can you find analysis of new technology?
>
> ➤ How to tell the difference between fads and facts

When I was younger and not nearly as wise as I am now, I fancied myself building elegant furniture in my spare time. On weekends and after work, I would retire to my workshop and produce heirloom pieces. At least, that's what I daydreamed about.

After many years of not building elegant furniture, I am forced to admit that I probably never will. What I really enjoyed was buying tools, always with the excuse that it was really an investment because of all the money not spent on furniture.

I think that the makers of tools have known this for years because lots of men buy tools but never actually build anything. Oh, I have built some things—playscapes for the kids, a patio cover, and stuff like that. If I had had that one additional tool, I'm sure that furniture would have flowed from my workshop.

Technology is a lot like the tools in my workshop. They are nice to look at, but they're not of much practical value unless you actually do something with them. Internet companies that rely on technology too heavily often do so at the expense of more important parts of their business.

Selling the Sizzle

Anyone in sales will tell you to "sell the sizzle" if you want to be successful. Sizzle for Internet companies means different things, but too often it is simply some technological gimmick that raises the prospect's eyebrows in that "gee whiz" expression.

The early days of the Internet were wonder years of "gee whiz." I can remember the first time I realized that I could communicate with millions of people all around the world by e-mail.

Flaming logos, cursors that became bouncing squirrels, pages that took forever to load because of all the graphics, and other dumb ideas best remain in history. It didn't take the Internet community long to tire of these silly games, although it seems that some Web sites and banner ads have not learned any lessons.

It Does What It Says

One of the true Internet pioneers, Yahoo!, kept its technology behind the scenes. Its utilitarian design and lack of graphics give it one of the best response times on the Internet.

More importantly, the site did what it advertised. I can remember being awed at the amount of information available at the touch of a couple of buttons. Although Yahoo! is often called a search engine, it is actually an indexer of Web sites, so you don't get everything on the Web when you do a search.

Yahoo! was ahead of its time with this service, although some wondered in the early years whether Yahoo! shouldn't become a true search engine. Unfortunately, with the explosion of Web sites, it is possible to get hundreds of thousands of hits on common phrases or words using a true search engine.

For example, using Yahoo! and two search engines, here are the results for a search on the word *sex*:

Yahoo!	3,333
Google	1,210,000
Alta Vista	3,545,424

Sure, some people might think that 3.5 million hits on the word *sex* sounds just about right, but what normal person needs or wants to wade through that much information?

The Personal Touch

In the Internet's recent past, sites have moved toward personalization as a way to attract and retain customers. While this was cute a couple of years ago, it is now expected. Web sites that can't remember who you are or other pertinent information are considered frustrating and not user-friendly.

This illustrates why it is dangerous for a company to pin its hopes on technology to set it apart from its peers. Internet companies that come up with some new marketing trick based on technology will soon find 50 other sites doing something similar or better.

Although it doesn't happen as much as it used to, I hate sites that pop up one of those annoying windows saying that I need to download some plug-in or the other in order to view the site. This is the Old Economy equivalent of putting a guard in the door and demanding that your customers put on a tie before shopping at your store. I don't even stop at sites that require this kind of assistance from me to do business.

Margin Call

Sites that require obscure plug-ins to run are frustrating and ultimately self-defeating in an economy that values openness.

Selling the Steak

Internet leaders come up with ways to use technology that enhances their products or services. The most useful technology doesn't get in the way of the Web site's purpose; it stays behind the scenes either until needed or forever, depending on the application.

Amazon.com remembers who I am. It remembers where on the site I like to shop and what I have recently bought. Techies know that this is not rocket science, especially in today's market, but it is something that I expect every time I shop now.

Dell pioneered the customization process for ordering a computer. Its innovative ordering process makes buying exactly the computer you want, for a price you want, an easy process. I can't imagine walking into a retail store and ordering my computer with this level of efficiency.

The Internet is not just business as usual. It has profoundly changed the ways companies can interact with customers—and, more recently, suppliers. Leaders find ways to use technology that takes advantage of the Internet's strengths and minimizes its weaknesses.

Change of Clothes

One of the hallmarks of the Internet is change. Leaders initiate change; they don't wait for it to happen. When the Internet was in its infancy, a lot of people (including me) couldn't imagine how people were going to pay for anything.

One company thought it had solved the problem by having people call when they were ready to buy and use a credit card. People are funny. They wouldn't enter their credit card number for fear that it might be misused, but somehow picking up the phone and giving it to a total stranger was okay.

Many years ago, I read an article relating that all clothing in the future would be custom-fit to each person. Your measurements would be entered into a database, and then whenever you wanted clothes, they would be made to perfectly fit you. At that time, the technology was in the cutting and sewing of custom clothes at off-the-rack prices. A computer would guide a laser to cut a pattern to your specifications, and some robot would sew the cloth together.

Double Click

Web sites that encourage inter-activity with viewers are typically more successful than ones that customers passively view.

Margin Call

For all its bells and whistles, the Internet is still about a business interacting with a customer. If the customer is treated rudely, whether by a salesperson or a Web site, that customer is not likely to return.

Although, I am sure that the technology is available to do this, it hasn't become economically feasible. However, one Web site has taken a step in that direction. Land's End (ticker symbol: LE; landsend.com) has a neat idea on its Web site. You enter your measurements (if you are a woman), which the site shows you how to take, and it constructs a clothing dummy for you. Once you have done this, you can see how you will look in one of Lands End's outfits. You can mix and match various pieces of clothing to see how they will look together and on you.

I am not sure how successful this process is, but it is a neat idea and represents the type of technology that makes the Internet so popular. I like it for these reasons:

➤ Although it has some "gee whiz" to it, ultimately it is very practical.

➤ This service is voluntary. Visitors can choose whether to use it with no other site considerations.

➤ It builds on an Internet strength: the ability to personalize the service and interact with the customer.

Lands End went through some rough times in the late 1990s, and its first crack at the Web still needs some work. Whether the clothing dummy is ultimately successful, the company is to be applauded for the effort.

Compounding Mistakes

Sometimes Internet companies can magnify minor technology flaws with terrible customer service. The most frequent offenders are the forms you fill out when buying something. After putting in your name, address, phone number, and DNA, you are told to click the Submit button.

Immediately, ugly pages pop up informing you that you made one or more egregious errors and are to return to the form. More often than not, in addition to fixing the offending entry, you may have to re-enter previously correct information that has disappeared.

Frequently, the "mistake" involved something as silly as not formatting a date the way the site wanted it entered, even though there were no instructions on the right way.

Technology Slaves

Ever since the computer became an important part of business, companies have fallen slave to technology. Whole businesses have been changed to accommodate technology.

My father was a wholesale drug salesman. He called on drug stores and hospitals in a large rural area of deep southwest Texas. Even though his territory was arguably one of the poorest in the district, he was consistently near or at the top of every sales contest the company held.

Then the company converted its order entry to a computerized process, and my father spent the next two years apologizing to his customers because their orders were consistently screwed up. I am convinced that it was the customers' respect for my father that helped keep us from losing everything. This opinion was confirmed when my father retired some years later and his customers threw him a surprise retirement party. Many of them had to drive 80 to 100 miles to attend.

In the early years (and, unfortunately, it continues), companies thought that an on-line presence meant reproducing their brochures on a Web site. Many wrote off the Internet when this process didn't produce much in the way of results.

Others took another approach. They threw up (almost literally) everything they could think of on a Web site. Flaming logos, bouncing squirrels, and so on, and that didn't work, either.

It was only when someone thoughtfully combined content with technology that Web sites began to work. When technology enhances content and the viewer's experience, it is doing its job.

Old Problems

Unfortunately, it is often not new technology, but old technology that trips up Internet companies. E-tailers in particular are in great danger. They may have a wonderful front-end system that guides the viewer through the sale, only to have the whole process come unhinged because some 18-year-old in the warehouse is paying more attention to his favorite CD than whether he is putting the right order in the right box with the right label. Thus, a $50 million system is rendered impotent by an $8-an-hour whiz.

153

Help File

The best customer service that a Web site can offer is to eliminate as many requirements for customer service as possible. That means making the site easy to use and fulfilling the customer's expectations completely.

This is one of the reasons why management is so important to Internet companies, as we will discuss in detail in the next chapter. Experienced management is the key to putting in place all the systems, both high-tech and low-tech, that make a company work.

During the 1999 holiday season, some e-tailers suffered almost systemic meltdown when sites were overloaded with traffic and either crashed or were so slow that customers went elsewhere. In addition to access problems, some e-tailers reported that up to 20 percent of the orders were shipped wrong.

This relates back to a previous point: E-tailers that sell commodity (that is, nonproprietary) products face a difficult task achieving profitability. Under the best of circumstances, most of them will fail. When they chase customers away with stupid mistakes, however, they are sealing their fates.

Technology That Is Important

Unless a company is selling technology, it will not make the difference between success and failure. Many more steps must be executed to achieve success besides having snappy technology.

However, one of the hottest sectors of the Internet economy is actually technology. We will talk more about emerging technology in Part 6, "Is That a Good Idea?"

Unless you are a techie and/or a scientist, it can be hard to get a handle on Internet companies that focus their products and services on providing technology to other Internet and related companies.

Fad or Fact?

How do you tell the difference between technological fads and legitimate advances? If you aren't a techie—and I'm not—the best way is to follow the news.

It is fairly important that you come up with a way that works for you, because pure technology companies (that is, companies whose business is technology) are making up an increasing number of new Internet stocks.

However, a quick look at recent and upcoming IPOs in March 2000 showed that most of them were related to Internet services. The companies ranged from those producing software to better integrate a company's Web site and other computer systems to companies that facilitate Internet advertising.

Most of the companies covered in this limited time frame were companies offering services or products to other Internet companies. For example, consider this blurb from WSRN: Radiant Systems, Inc. (ticker symbol: RADS; rads.com):

> RADS provides enterprise-wide technology solutions to businesses that serve the consumer. The company offers fully integrated retail automation solutions, including point-of-sale systems, headquarters-based management systems, and Web-enabled decision support systems. The company's products provide integrated, end-to-end solutions that span from the consumer to the supply chain. Radiant's products enable retailers to interact electronically with consumers, capture data at the point of sale, manage site operations, analyze data, communicate electronically with their sites, and interact with vendors through electronic data interchange and Web-based marketplaces.

Sounds great, doesn't it? But how do you know if it is great? Maybe the company threw together some existing code and is selling an inferior product. I can understand what the system does, but I don't know at a technical level how it works.

How do I decide whether this company's system is any better than another company's system? I can't test them both and compare the results. I need another way to get some direction regarding the relative value of this company's product.

One of the surest indicators of whether an Internet technology stock will do well is its list of clients. Even the youngest technology companies should have a product to deliver. If not, you are really taking a huge risk. Those types of risks aren't unprecedented in the Internet economy, but I believe that they will become fewer as investors become more sophisticated and the fever of the market cools.

A technology company with market-leading clients is worth a second look. This is not a foolproof strategy—even big companies make mistakes—but it sure is a good sign. RADS lists some top-notch companies as clients. Most of the companies that compete with RADS are behind-the-scenes players as far as consumers are concerned. The company will not likely interact with the public directly.

Other companies with technology that is applicable to the consumer market are usually a little easier to research and understand. Spotting these leaders is not always easy, however, because in many markets there is no clear leader at this point.

A Popular Network

Home and home office networking is very popular these days. As the number of home offices and the number of homes with multiple computers and peripherals indicates, the home networking market is growing rapidly.

Four different technologies are at work:

➤ Traditional Ethernet systems use hubs and cables to connect all the elements on the network.

➤ Phone lines are used by several systems to create a home network.

➤ The existing electrical system is used by at least one vendor to create the network.

➤ One of the most popular home networking concepts is a wireless system made by several vendors.

All of these systems have their advantages and disadvantages. There is no clear leader at this point, and how the market may shake out is still undecided. There is no standard that all vendors can work with to help the market expand. Of course, every company wants its technology to be adopted as the standard.

Standards help the market grow and clear the way for greater acceptance by the consumers. Qualcomm, which I mentioned in Chapter 1, "Why Internet Stocks Are Different," developed the technology that eventually was adopted as the standard for how wireless devices communicate with each other. Its stock has soared on the news, but more importantly, manufacturers can now develop products without fear that they will be rejected by a public nervous about compatibility.

If nobody else cares about a technology, you can assume that it is a fad and won't last for long.

The Least You Need to Know

➤ Technology is not the factor that makes an Internet company successful unless that is what the company is selling.

➤ Flashy technology is often a mask for deeper problems.

➤ Doing your homework will help you separate fads from really useful technology.

Chapter 15

Management Is the Key to Success

In This Chapter

➤ Where to find information on a company's management

➤ Who the rising stars are and where you find them

➤ When it is time for company founders to step aside

➤ How to evaluate stocks based on management

Back in the days when I had more money than sense, I used to love to go to horse races. I lived in a state with no racetracks, so when business took me to a city with horse racing, I would find a way to go.

I was strictly a small-time gambler, and my miserable record proved it. I enjoyed watching the horses run more than the gambling, but having some money on the race made it more interesting.

Once at a racetrack in Chicago, I heard some people sitting near me talking about their winnings that day. What I discovered was that these folks didn't bet on the horse; they bet on the jockey. They followed horse racing enough to know that better jockeys got the better horses, and better jockeys on better horses meant more wins.

This same philosophy has been used for years by mutual fund investors. The track record of the fund manager is one of the most important considerations in picking a fund for some investors.

When you are looking at a sea of unknowns regarding Internet stocks, look for a jockey with a history of winning, and you may find a company worth a closer look.

Why Management Is So Important

There are no expert Internet company managers. A handful have done very well with their companies, but none has any lengthy track record. The Internet economy is still so young that it hasn't had time to produce managers with lengthy track records.

Margin Call

Too much money can make even an ill-conceived company look good—until the money runs out. Be careful of companies that are burning more of their IPO cash every quarter than they did in the last quarter.

What about Amazon.com and Yahoo!, two sites that garner a lot of respect? The problem is that the Internet companies have operated in only one economic environment. Capital was virtually unlimited. Stock prices and valuations soared while the stock market couldn't seem to get enough "dot.com" to satisfy its hunger. The economy was on a historic and unprecedented expansion, and interest rates were still relatively low. Everyone and their brother wanted a piece of the Internet dream.

The danger is that this euphoric bubble hid some really bad companies. Too much money in a market usually has the effect of making every deal look good. When the shakeout comes, the companies left standing will be in a position to solidify market leadership.

Shameless Hustlers

In the pre-Internet days, when venture capitalists weren't shameless hustlers, companies didn't often come to the market half-baked. Those that did receive venture capital had to survive rigorous scrutiny before any money got put on the table.

One of the key components in that scrutiny was the quality and depth of management. More than one company founder walked away from the venture capital table with the money in one hand and a new president of the company. Venture capitalists used to know that company founders aren't always the best choice to take the firm public. They are frequently *idea* people with little or no experience in management and getting things done through other people.

Despite the fact that people with little or no management experience head a number of IPOs, there were some exceptions. One of the encouraging trends in Internet companies is that a number of seasoned executives are leaving their careers to join or start a dot.com. This bodes well for an industry that has yet to suffer any major setbacks.

What the Internet economy desperately needs is some respect from Wall Street and the established investment community. This doesn't mean that every dot.com should try to transform itself into a Dow stock, but more seasoned managers would go a long way toward calming fears of sky-high valuations.

Over 30 Need Not Apply

A certain mystique about Internet companies has suggested that any Old Economy knowledge and experience was almost a negative when looking for managers. In the early days, that was probably true. The Internet was heavily influenced by 20-something techies who looked down their noses at capitalism and what it would do to the Internet.

Like the hippies of the 1960s who are now investment bankers, Web pioneers realized that if the Internet was going to become something other than a large toy, things would have to change.

With all the money to be made in Internet companies that are successful (*successful* being defined as hitting it big with an IPO), it is small wonder that seasoned managers have begun gravitating toward leadership positions in startup companies or have started their own companies. One of the severe problems of the Internet economy is with this definition of success. The goal was to come up with a semi-inspired idea with a truly inspired name and throw together a business plan, get some venture capital, slap a product or service together, and go public as quickly as possible.

Help File

Unfortunately, with all the money being thrown at dot.com anythings, the notion of building a company for the future got lost for a lot of folks involved in the Internet economy.

Seasoned managers could see the risk in this system, but they also saw the potential to grow a business a lot quicker than was possible in the Old Economy.

Finding Information

Information about Internet executives is pretty easy to find. Most of the Web sites listed throughout this book that provide information on the Internet economy also cover top executives.

One of the richest sources of information on Internet executives is TheStandard.com. This Web site publishes regular articles on executives that are shaping their companies and the Internet. The site includes a "network" area in which you can find an alphabetical listing of the people profiled in the site's weekly newsletter and in the magazine. The profiles are short and to the point, but they contain links to the person's Web site and other helpful information. You can also search for a person by name or look at profiles by company.

For example, Alex Kam, director of New Media for Major League Baseball (majorleaguebaseball.com), is responsible for turning the sport's online presence into a powerhouse Web site. Before joining Major League Baseball, Kam worked for entertainment giant HBO and investment bankers Salmon Brothers and Kidder, Peabody. He is a graduate of the University of Pennsylvania and Yale.

How is this information helpful? It is clear that Kam is well qualified to undertake the reconstruction of the organization's Web site. He also understands the economics of e-commerce from his experience with the investment banking firms. Although you can't invest in Major League Baseball, its selection of Kam would seem to be a good one and serves as a nice example of moving someone into a position to build on his strengths. If Kam moves on from Major League Baseball, it might be worth keeping an eye on where he lights.

Even in the "real-time" Internet environment, it is hard to stay on top of the comings and goings of top managers. The listings at TheStandard.com are as complete and up-to-date as I have found, but they are still hard-pressed to stay current. I found a couple of listings that were out of date, so double-check the company's Web site or another information provider.

Another place you can find information about a company's management is on stock information Web sites, such as Morningstar.com. This site and others often mention key executives in their analysis.

Government-required documents are other sources of information on company management. The Securities and Exchange Commission's (SEC) required reports, such as a *10-K* and a *10-Q*, are available on many companies' sites, or you can find them at Edgar On-Line (ticker symbol: EDGR; edgaronline.com).

Help File

One of the big problems in using the Internet for gathering information is that sometimes you have too much, not too little information. Web sites that can condense data into information are a tremendous help. Take a look at 123Jump (123jump.com) and RedHerring.com (redherring.com) as two examples of information sites.

Speak Up

10-K is an annual document companies are required to file. It is very similar to the annual report, but without the slick cover and pretty pictures. It is strictly business and the place savvy investors look for information. **10-Q** is the quarterly version of the 10-K. It focuses on the previous quarter as opposed to the previous year. Both documents contain information about key management personnel. A **prospectus** is a legal document required before a company can do an initial public offering. The prospectus states the nature of the business and outlines the risks associated with the investment.

IPOs must have a *prospectus*, which is often available online from the investment bankers or the company itself. The prospectus contains information about key executives, including anything the government thinks you ought to know (such as the CEO being convicted of stock fraud).

Finally, you can check out the company's Web site for current information about key executives. Unless the information comes from an SEC-required report, you may be reading what the company's public relations department wants you to know.

Stepping Down or Aside

One of the most challenging decisions that a company and its founder have to make is lining up management to take it to the next level. Sometimes this is the founder—Bill Gates has surrounded himself with great management talent and appears in no hurry or need to step aside.

Frequently, a company's founder will have talent focused in one area but has no broad base of management experience to direct a rapidly growing company. There may be no better example of when stepping aside means the difference between just another dot.com and a market leader than what happened at Yahoo! Jerry Yang and David Filo, both graduate students at Stanford in 1994, founded the company in April 1995. They had the supreme advantage of being out first with what they call a Web guide.

Both Yang and Filo have been instrumental in making Yahoo! the most highly trafficked Web site in the world. In mid-1995, they brought two seasoned managers onboard in the two top leadership positions. Yang and Filo now carry the title of Chief Yahoo!, with Yang also serving as a member of the board of directors. They remain actively involved in the development of Yahoo!, but they wisely chose to turn the day-to-day management of the company over to people who had much more experience. The combination has proved formidable.

Only in the new economy could a native of Taiwan and a native of Moss Bluff, Louisiana combine to create the most successful Internet company in its short history.

I think that it is very instructive that the cofounders of Yahoo! brought in top-notch help as soon as Yahoo! began to take shape, not when the company was in a management crisis. There is no question that the two founders continue to play important roles in the company's success. Could they have played those roles if they had been saddled with the day-to-day management issues? Neither had any experience running any company, much less one growing as fast as Yahoo!

Examples of situations in which the founder didn't step down or was forced out are numerous; unfortunately, most of these companies are not in business anymore. It is not hard to find these situations because the media and analysts are usually more than willing to point out the difference between eccentric and arrogant.

If you look at a founder's resume and find nothing indicating that this person could run a large corporation, look for a strong management team—or expect trouble if the founder tries to hold on too long. Looking at a company's management as part of an evaluation process is a valid and necessary step. Fortunately, many of the information services on the Web report on management as well as financial data.

However, small- to mid-cap companies frequently do not get the full treatment from these services, and you may need to do your own research. A lot of information can be found on the company's Web site and in the government-required documents mentioned earlier.

Doing searches on the company using services such as Google, The Wall Street Directory (wallstreetdirectory.com), and the Dow Jones Business Directory (business-directory.dowjones.com) will turn up even more information.

The Least You Need to Know

➤ Information on company executives is usually not hard to find and is worth looking at.

➤ Some of the brightest stars come from nonbusiness backgrounds, but most of the senior management of successful companies have been successful elsewhere.

➤ Making the transition from startup to operating company sometimes requires founders to step aside or to bring in seasoned managers.

Part 4

IPOs, Mutual Funds, Day Trading, and Options

The older I get, the more I appreciate the befuddlement of my parents at the music and culture of the late 1960s. Long hair and free love must have seemed like another world to them.

How they must have winced at the likes of Janis Joplin, the Rolling Stones, and the Doors—drugs, sex, and violence.

I admit having similar reactions to the tattooed and pierced young people of today. Why can't they be more "normal"?

This is what many traditional investors and media types keep asking Internet stocks: Why can't they be more "normal"?

In this part, we look at Internet stocks through the lens of some very traditional stock market institutions, such as initial public offerings, mutual funds, day trading, and options, to see how they refuse to be "normal."

Chapter 16

Jumping On the IPO Bandwagon

In This Chapter

➤ Why prices sometimes skyrocket

➤ Who gets the good IPO deals

➤ What you have to do to get in early

➤ How risky an early IPO position is

Do you know what one thing has made more millionaires than anything else? Gold? Oil? Real estate? The Internet? The stock market?

The answer is: none of the above.

From personal experience, I am convinced that the one thing that has made more people rich than anything else is the spreadsheet. You know, those computer programs that duplicate the accountant's columnar pads.

With this tool, I have become wealthy beyond imagination—at least, that's what the spreadsheet said. The great thing about these programs is that you can set up a spreadsheet to see how much money an investment will make if certain variables are lined up correctly.

If the investment doesn't return enough the first time, just adjust the variables. The problem is that in real life, we seldom have control over all (or any) variables. The results are often disastrous.

Investing in Internet IPOs is best done with both feet on the ground. In this chapter and the next, you'll look at the IPO process and learn how to keep your feet on the ground while you're considering an investment.

Rocket's Red Glare

My candidates for the most annoying people of the new millennium are the ones who can't wait to tell you about an IPO they got in on for $5 per share that's now worth $800 per share—plus, it split 26 for 1. Their $500 investment is now worth more than Rhode Island.

Unfortunately, a lot of people out there think that the truth is not that far from this tongue-in-cheek example. The fever over IPOs is one of the main factors in the obscenely high valuations floating through the Internet market. The huge amount of money dumped into Internet IPOs the last two years of the 1990s and continuing into 2000 has made everyone associated with them a little (or a lot) crazy. Investors snap them up as quickly as they come out, in most cases. Venture capitalists rush companies to market before they are ready, afraid that if they don't, they'll miss the last chance before people come to their senses.

Margin Call

Greed is a powerful motivator. Companies seem to be born with one purpose: to do an IPO. These types of companies seldom last long in the real world.

Businesses seem to start up with but one purpose: cashing out through an IPO. This is no way to run an economy. In late March and early April 2000, the Internet and Technology stocks took a beating. From highs of more than 5000, the Nasdaq composite index dropped to almost 4000 in a few dizzying days and kept dropping to almost 3000.

Some observers say the ruling that Microsoft was a monopoly precipitated the drop. It was unclear what the ruling would actually mean to Microsoft, but the Internet and technology sectors dove for cover. Unfortunately, you can run but you can't hide from Microsoft. When Bill Gates sneezes, the Internet and tech market get a cold.

Everyone knew that a correction was coming, but few expected it to be so deep and so quick. It is amazing how we humans can convince ourselves of anything we want to believe. Many Internet and technology stocks were up by triple-digit increases, yet when some of the wind got knocked out of their sails, it was a big deal.

A Note of Caution

Before we go any further, I need to warn you that investing in IPOs is not for everybody—in fact, it's not for many.

Despite the popular myths to the contrary, IPOs are very risky investments; if the IPO is for an Internet company, you can double the risk. IPOs are risky because, in many cases, you are buying a complete unknown. The company may or may not have an actual product or service—and if it does, it hasn't been around for long. This is not true of all IPOs, of course. For example, United Parcel Service, UPS, had an IPO in

1999. UPS has been in business for 90 years, so investors know something about the company.

Most Internet IPOs, however, are almost always virtual unknowns simply because the Internet is so young. Still, in the face of logic, many Internet IPOs have gone through the roof.

You couldn't pick up a newspaper or log on to a Web site in the late 1990s without learning about another Internet IPO that had just tripled (or more) in value. Every time this happened, I would get e-mails from people who have never invested in anything in their life wanting to get in on the action.

I don't like to pop people's balloons, but folks who think they want to "get in on the action" end up getting trampled by earlier investors on their way to the exit. The popular media seldom reports when an IPO tanks unless it is a particularly high-profile company.

Why So High?

How did IPOs get to be such sought-after items—the adult equivalent of Beanie Babies? The sad truth is that probably most investors couldn't tell you.

At least, they couldn't get beyond the notion that IPOs are easy ways to get rich. I think it is wonderful that so much money has poured into Internet stocks. This has given a real boost to the Internet economy, but at the same time, it has created an *expectation bubble* that had to pop sooner or later.

The expectation bubble is that Internet stocks were a hot new way to make a lot of money in a very short time. For some, that was certainly true. For most investors, the expectation bubble looked too attractive to pass up.

Remember my opening about spreadsheets and how you can adjust the results by adjusting the variables? The problem is that many inexperienced investors do not know when to buy in and when to sell out of a stock or a market. Actually, many professionals don't know that, either.

Speak Up

An **expectation bubble** is the value added to a market or a stock by investors who expect growth to continue on a straight line up. They are willing to pay a premium for this future benefit, even if the benefit is in their imagination.

To the casual observer, it must seem like Internet stocks were on an escalator up, and it didn't matter too much where you got on, because it was still just going up. One of the basic rules of the stock market, however, is that when there are more buyers than sellers, the price of stock goes up. That was never truer than for Internet stocks and their IPOs.

A Quick Review

It might help to stop for a quick review of how prices are set in the stock market. The short answer is that they aren't set.

By this, I mean that there are no fixed prices for stocks. A stock is worth what someone is willing to pay for it and what someone else is willing to sell it for. When these two prices are the same, a trade occurs.

For example, if XYZ is at $100 per share when the market closes on Monday, its first trade on Tuesday may be for $100, or $95, or $105, or $50 per share. The fact that it closed at one price the night before is no guarantee that it will open at or close to that price the next day. Many factors may affect the price of a stock, but ultimately it is the meeting of a buyer and a seller that sets the price.

A major source of confusion on IPOs is the "offering" price that is often quoted in the media. We'll talk about this in more detail a little later, but understand that 99.9 percent of the investors in a hot IPO will never pay this price on opening day. Using an earlier example, Palm had an offering price of $38 per share, but it opened on the market at $145. Investors who hoped to get in on this deal at $38 per share were in for a rude awakening.

This is not an unusual example of what happens to Internet IPOs. Everyone wanted in on this stock, and more buyers than sellers equals big price hikes.

Margin Call

Investors who blindly think that any IPO is a guaranteed money-maker are in for a rude awakening and will find their recklessness rewarded when the market eats their lunch.

Rocket Fuel

Internet IPOs (and others also) are the end result of a long and complicated process of preparing a company to raise a significant sum of money to fund future growth.

Despite its flaws, IPOs are a marvelous way for young companies to grow to the next stage in their development without incurring a large amount of debt. Money raised through an IPO does not have to be repaid. If companies had to borrow all the money they needed to grow, few would survive.

We have already discussed the IPO process in Chapter 5, "Time for a Risk Check," from the company's point of view. In this chapter and the following chapter, I talk about IPOs as an investment opportunity. You might be asking yourself at this point why I'm so negative on one hand, yet recommending IPOs on the other? I am not recommending that you invest in IPOs. I would simply like to suggest that if you want to be a part of this investment scene, you should be armed with the facts and some strategy to give yourself a fighting chance.

IPO Myths

First, let's clear the air of some popular IPO myths:

➤ The odds are slim to none that you will buy an IPO at the offering price.

➤ The truth is that by the time you have a shot at an IPO stock, it already has several sets of fingerprints on it.

➤ IPOs don't always go up in price. The truth is that many IPOs retreat from first-day highs fairly quickly.

Let's look at these individually.

Offering Price

As we discussed in Chapter 5, the investment banker handling the IPO sets the offering price. The price is determined by what the bankers believe the potential of the company is and how similar IPOs have been priced. However, the real determining factor is how high they believe they can push the price and still move all the stock.

The investment bankers then form a syndicate of retail brokers who will sell the stock to the public. They may also sell large blocks to institutional investors or other companies with an interest in the IPO company. It should be noted that buyers of large chunks might pay less than the offering price. This is a negotiated price.

Once the retail brokerages have their allocation, they may offer a few of their largest and best customers the opportunity to buy at or near the offering price before the stock is sold to the general public.

In the past, the big, full-service brokerages have had almost exclusive access to IPOs. This is changing, however, as online brokers take more of the retail business, and some of them are getting access to IPOs. We will look at how they decide who gets the IPO early in the section, "Getting In On the Deal," later in this chapter.

Help File

Some critics have said that IPOs indulge in legalized price fixing, and not without some merit. As long as there are investors who think they can play the game better than investment bankers, there will always be disappointed investors.

Fingerprints

By now, hopefully you are getting the picture that it is highly unlikely that you will be the first one to purchase the IPO. It may be the initial public offering, but it has already gone through several hands before it gets to the general public.

Once the day actually comes when the stock is available to the public, it is dribbled out in such a manner to ensure that the price goes up. Buy orders will already be placed by investors hoping to get in before the price skys.

Double Click

If you want to buy an IPO on the first day of public trading (or any time the market is very volatile), always use a limit order, which sets a specific price that you are willing to pay, and no more.

The truth is that it is unlikely to happen that way. Remember, you can place a buy order at any price. That order is only filled when a seller at that price is located. The folks holding the stock can set a selling price anywhere they want. If an IPO's offering price is $25 per share, there is nothing to prevent a holder from entering a sell order at $100 per share and waiting until the market comes to that price. If enough sellers do this, the price will get there very quickly.

Historically, Internet IPOs have gotten high in a hurry. Enter a market order, which will be filled at the best price possible, and instead of buying the stock at $30 per share, you may find that you have bought it at $100 per share.

Sound Retreat

One of the enduring myths of Internet IPOs is that they go up and stay up. I know that this is a myth because too many investors keep paying top dollar, especially on the opening day.

While it is not unusual for an IPO to soar during the first day, it is also not unusual for it to back off before the close. Here's a scary statistic: For the 62 Internet IPOs introduced from January 1, 2000, to March 24, 2000, only 14 closed higher on March 24 than they closed on their first day of trading. Said another way, more than 77 percent of the stocks closed lower on March 24 than on their first day of trading. And this was before the big correction that came a week later.

So much for the myth that Internet IPOs can only go up.

Getting In on the Deal

Although it is unlikely that you will get in on an IPO at or near the offering price (unless the stock is a real turkey), online brokers are attempting to make the process more open.

Many have designed systems that are less dependent on you being a big hitter. For example, E*Trade (ticker symbol: EGRP; etrade.com) uses an allocation system based on several factors. Here's how it works: You must have an account with E*Trade (makes sense doesn't it?) and meet the company's suitability requirements. You won't find out much about these requirements until you start filling out the online suitability form.

This is because IPOs are considered speculative investments and are not suited for all investors. The firm is required by law to qualify you for the investment. Among the things the questionnaire will ask are these:

➤ How long have you been investing?

➤ What is your net worth?

➤ Do you consider yourself a sophisticated investor?

These and other questions seek to identify your ability to judge the speculative nature of IPOs. If they score your responses as meeting the requirements, you move to the next step.

The second step of the process is to confirm that you have received and read the preliminary prospectus, which is available for download from the E*Trade Web site. This is a regulatory requirement. The preliminary prospectus is the document on file with the Securities and Exchange Commission before the IPO has been cleared for sale. Once the SEC clears the registration, a final prospectus is issued. It may or may not contain changes made by the SEC.

The third step of E*Trade's process is to place a conditional offer to buy a specified number of shares, along with the highest price you are willing to pay. You can change or withdraw your conditional offer up to the time of allocation. Sometimes an offering price will change at the last minute, so E*Trade requires you to reconfirm your conditional offer. Placing a conditional offer does not guarantee that you will receive any shares. Other factors affecting allocation include holding periods for previous issues.

Help File

Securities regulations require brokers to qualify investors for certain investment products to make sure that the products are appropriate for that particular individual. For example, if an elderly widow on a fixed income with no significant savings wanted to invest in IPOs, a broker would be required to say no.

Double Click

If you plan to invest in IPOs at any stage, be prepared to do a lot of homework. Also stay on top of the market because things happen quickly: If you don't react in time, you may lose an opportunity.

Retail brokers frown on selling IPO stocks soon after investors receive them. This is known as flipping, and the investment bankers will reduce future allocations to retail brokers whose clients flip IPO stock. This is because the investment banker is responsible for supporting the IPO once it begins trading on the exchanges. This means that the banker might buy back shares or short shares to stabilize stock prices (that is, keep them from dropping like a rock).

Retail clients who flip IPO shares cause turbulence in the market, so retail brokers often impose penalties on clients who engage in flipping. E*Trade asks retail clients not to sell IPO shares for 30 days after they are issued.

Can you see a potential problem in this scenario? Inexperienced investors might think that they can buy a pre-public IPO from a broker for $35 per share and sell it the first day after it climbs to $100 per share. There is nothing to prevent them from doing this, but they probably won't see any more IPO issues.

Retail brokers can't prevent you from flipping stock, but you may find yourself cut off from future issues if you do. E*Trade and most retail brokers make that very clear up front.

Because IPOs are very dynamic up to the minute they are offered to the public, you must be prepared to stay on top of late-breaking events. E*Trade maintains a bulletin board area on its Web site to keep clients up to date on current offerings.

Consult E*Trade's Web site for complete information and any changes that the company may institute. Several other online brokers offer IPO programs with different guidelines, but research them all thoroughly before making a choice.

Alternative Sources

A fairly large number of amateur investors seem to believe that you don't need to go through all the previously discussed hoops when there are IPOs offered directly to investors through the Internet.

My grandfather would call this penny-wise and pound-foolish. There may be some decent opportunities in these offerings, but I would approach them with extreme caution. Most of the direct offerings are highly speculative even for Internet IPOs.

I put these in the same category as penny stocks, unregulated and riddled with fraud. America has produced some truly great entrepreneurs—unfortunately, some of them are crooks. They capitalize on the IPO craze by passing off inferior offerings as an opportunity for "the little guy." Give me a break.

If you are considering investing in an IPO, look at the front of the prospectus for the underwriter. The name should be familiar to you—Merrill Lynch, Goldman Sachs, or Morgan Stanley Dean Witter. Avoid small offerings (under $50 million or so) and banks that sell only to individual investors.

Margin Call

The truth about investing in IPOs is the same for all investments: If it seems too good to be true, it more than likely *isn't* true.

How Risky Is an Early Position?

The desire to be first is almost as American as apple pie and motherhood (or fatherhood, to be fair). In many business deals, being first is a tremendous advantage.

We have already talked about the importance, especially to e-tailers, of getting out first to build brand recognition. However, when it comes to IPOs, early may not be better. If you can acquire some of the IPO allocation from your broker, that is probably a good thing, but because of the required holding period, you may find being first was not a great advantage.

Once the IPO hits the open market, watch out. If you want to play day trader, you can try to buy on the way up and sell back quickly for a small profit. If you have looked at the company and found that it seems like something you want to own for the long term, then patience is required.

It might be worth your time to sit back and watch for the right opportunity. You should establish a target price that you want to pay and then hold off until you can buy at that point. However, what do you do if, like some Internet stocks, the IPO you want zooms up and never comes too far back? At some point, you have to ask yourself if you really want to own this stock, even if it is selling for 100 times forward earnings.

The Least You Need to Know

➤ IPO prices sometimes rise for no real reason other than that investors are just crazy to own them.

➤ It is unlikely that you will get an IPO at the offering price, but you have a better chance today than in the past.

➤ Retail brokers are required to verify that you are a "sophisticated" investor with a high net worth before selling you an IPO at the initial offering price.

➤ Individual investors who do manage to get in on an initial offering price are often expected to hold the stock for up to six months. Flipping, as selling early is called, may mean you won't be in on any more initial offerings.

➤ IPOs can be bought in the after market, but you may have to pay a high premium.

Chapter 17

Jumping Off the IPO Bandwagon

In This Chapter

➤ Looking beyond the hype

➤ Buying quality for long-term success

➤ Waiting for a second-chance investment

➤ Finding out whether a company is here to stay

A song made popular by singer Kenny Rogers suggests that you need to "know when to hold 'em—know when to fold 'em."

For you non-card players, the reference is to when you should stay with the hand you were dealt or take yourself out of the game by throwing in your cards. The song used this phrase as a metaphor for dealing with life and relationships, which is probably a lot more than you wanted to know about poker and Kenny Rogers.

However, the same metaphor can be applied to investing in Internet IPOs. It is important to know when to get in and sit tight, and it is just as important to have an exit strategy.

In the last chapter, we looked at some of the ways you can become involved in Internet IPOs, and we continue that discussion in this chapter. In addition, we look at how and when to get out.

I Can See Clearly Now

Probably no other area of investing is more obfuscated than initial public offerings. (Isn't *obfuscate* a great word? It means "to darken, bewilder, or confuse," and as soon as you use it, you've done it.)

One of the major problems with IPOs is the misleading way the financial press reports their activity. We have all heard about the 300 percent increases in one day of some hot IPO, but is that number accurate? The answer is yes and no.

Yes, it accurately reflects the percent increase between the stock's offering price and the closing price on the first day. In that sense, the number is accurate. However, it is also misleading because almost none of the investors who bought the stock on the first day got in at the offering price. They bought somewhere between the opening price and the closing price. These prices are often quite different from the offering price.

For example, let's continue with the story of Palm, Inc., and its IPO in early 2000. The stock's offering price was $38 per share. It closed the first day of trading at $88 per share—a nice 231 percent gain. Right?

Wrong. Most investors didn't get in at $38 per share. The first public trade was for $145 per share. During the day, the stock went as high as $165 per share before dropping to $88 per share at the market close. I didn't capture the *intraday* activity, so I don't know if it traded below $88 at any time during the day.

Assuming that Palm never traded for below $88, it is unlikely that you came out of that deal in one piece. If you got in on the opening trades and grabbed a handful at $145 per share, you closed that first day trading down about 39 percent. Ouch! Under the worse scenario, you bought at the high that first day, which was $165 per share, making your first day's loss 47 percent.

Incidentally, as I am writing this, Palm is trading $42 per share, which is up from a low of $32 per share. If you want to do the math, go ahead. I find it too painful, even though I don't own any of the stock.

Speak Up

Intraday activity or trading refers to a stock's activity between the opening and closing bells of the market. Some Internet and tech stocks can experience wild swings during this period.

Overconfidence

Palm may have been a victim of any number of blunders by the investment bankers and the market in general. The company makes a marketing-leading product and should have been a winner. The point is that Palm was riding a wave of IPO mania that swept the market in the last days of 1999. However, a minor correction in the Internet and technology stocks in January may have cooled all but the most rabid of IPO nuts.

Early 2000 IPO figures may reflect some of that cooling. Of the 36 IPOs issued through February 24th, 17 finished lower 30 days after the issue than on the first day of trading. In other words, almost half of the IPOs finished like the example of Palm. If you bought the stock at the closing price on the first day of trading and sold it 30 days later, you lost money. None tanked as badly as Palm did, but quite a few had highs way above the 30-day close.

What does this tell us? It restates the observation made in the last chapter that if you don't get in at the offering price, be very careful about jumping in early on an IPO. You will probably be paying a high premium for the hype that often surrounds IPOs.

A Dilemma

This poses a dilemma for the investor. What if you see a quality company you would like to own, but not at the hyperinflated IPO prices? Unfortunately, the IPO tsunami carries with it good stocks as well as bad stocks.

It is safe to say that sooner or later the market will deal with the weak stocks. That may be one of the benefits of corrections such as the April 2000 event. In the meantime, it may make buying a quality stock more difficult because these stocks are not as likely to drop from their IPO highs as quickly as weak stocks.

As we have discussed in previous chapters, valuations of Internet stocks can be problematic at best. Buying a quality stock in the Internet economy may mean paying a higher premium than normal stock valuations would suggest.

Traditional stock analysts would counsel investors to wait until the stock's valuations are more in line with normal parameters. This means waiting until there are earnings and the stock's price is more in line with the earnings (a relatively low P/E for example). This is certainly wise counsel, but I'm not sure that things will happen the way these experts want it to. Other than momentary dips during corrections, I have doubts that quality Internet stocks are going to retreat in price very much.

The Future

Some of the attention that Internet stocks have received may wane. However, if you think that all Internet companies are just like the rest, you will be sadly mistaken.

Predicting the future is a game for fools, but, hey, that never stopped me. As the year 2000 began, Microsoft and Cisco Systems were the no. 1 and no. 2 largest companies in the market. I predict that by the year 2005, another company will be bigger than either of these—and that company may not even exist in the year 2000.

A significant amount of this book is spent answering the same general question in several different ways. How do you identify a quality stock that you want to hold for the long term, and what do you pay for it? This question is doubly hard for Internet IPOs because the market is putting such a premium on just about any dot.com that hits the street.

We have talked about tools that can provide some help in answering this question. They come from a traditional school of fundamental analysis or have been modified to fit the circumstances of Internet stocks. If you are looking for that one tool, one number, or one ratio that will tell you to buy or sell, I'm afraid you are in for a long wait.

It might be that we need to redefine some terms in the context of the New Economy and Internet stocks and IPOs. The Internet has changed the way we think about business and its relationship to customers. It has also changed the way we think of time and product cycles.

Rethinking Our Definition

How do you identify a quality stock that you want to hold for the long term, and what do you pay for it? Three ideas in our definition need to be rethought: quality stock, long-term, and what you pay. As the question is now, it is equally applicable to Old Economy stocks and New Economy stocks, and that is the problem. Amazon.com is not General Motors. Yahoo! is not Boeing.

When we approach Internet IPOs the same way we approach the 30 Dow Jones Industrial Average stocks, we will become frustrated and will conclude that no Internet stock is now—or probably ever will be—worth owning.

Quality Stock

In traditional terms, a quality stock is one that has consistently rising earnings, shows a strong balance sheet, and is considered a market leader.

Although there is some indication that the market for Internet IPOs is cooling off, the really hot stocks are still going to command a premium. Internet stocks in general are becoming more mature as time passes, and investors are realizing that these stocks are not all alike. It is entirely possible that most of the Internet IPOs of the late 1990s will never see a fifth birthday. Competitors or another company seeking market position will buy them or they will simply go out of business.

We have seen that the same scale used to judge more traditional stocks in particular cannot be used to judge Internet stocks and IPOs. In almost all cases, they don't have positive earnings, although many have a strong balance sheet flush with IPO cash.

One of the criteria we can use is market leadership potential. Especially with IPOs, the issue of potential is most important. Is this the kind of company that can grow to a leadership role in its particular market?

Double Click

Trying to judge Internet IPOs by the same standards as traditional stocks may be trying to fit a square peg in a round hole.

Let's look at an example using Microsoft. If ever there were an 800-pound gorilla, Bill Gates and friends are it, right? If we still lived in a personal computer world, that would be true. Microsoft has dominated and directed much of what has happened in the PC world, for a number of years. The company continues to roll out upgrades to operating systems that will guarantee more billions in cash for its already-overflowing coffers.

Microsoft owes its dominance in large part to blunders by Apple Computer (ticker symbol: AAPL; apple.com) and IBM. Both of those companies had a chance to become the dominant player in personal computers, but they failed to seize the moment.

Embarrassingly, Microsoft found itself committing the same blunder as the Internet began to take off. Only by exercising its tremendous muscle was the company able to catch Netscape (netscape.com) in the browser war. Though, as of the end of 1999, Microsoft had almost $18 billion in cash and no long-term debt. You don't get much stronger than that.

There is a strong sense that the next wave of innovation will leave the PC behind and will center on Internet appliances or devices. These will be a combination of hardware and software that takes advantage of an "Internet everywhere" environment in which your applications and data reside on the Internet, not a PC.

This system will give you access to the tools and data you need when you need them and where you need them. Users will access the Internet through a variety of devices ranging from cell phones to personal digital assistants, to portable terminals similar to laptop computers, to digital tablets, to desktop terminals, and so on. The point is that you will not have to take your computing power with you—it will reside on the Internet, available whenever you want it.

Where does that leave Microsoft? It leaves the company with the opportunity to adapt or slowly die as the number of PC users declines. Microsoft has already acknowledged a vision of a world without PCs.

When we look at Internet companies with market-leading potential, we need to consider that leadership may be defined as the ability to change, adapt, and cooperate rather than dominate and destroy. How can you spot that in an IPO? Well, you probably can't, but you can look for those leadership qualities in management that is willing to consider new ways of doing business and whole new businesses.

Be cautious of a company or management that is so locked-in to its vision of the world that it is

Double Click

Management is still the key to an Internet company's success or failure. Look for leaders who are quick to seize an opportunity and who aren't so fond of their own ideas that they won't change course when needed.

blind to other possibilities. This single-mindedness used to be an attribute, but it cost IBM and Apple big-time, and it almost cost Microsoft.

Long-Term Holding

I am a strong advocate of the benefits of buying and holding quality stocks for the long term. Your retirement account should be full of quality stocks or mutual funds.

Generally, I would consider five to seven years a minimum holding period for quality stocks. In many cases, that could be extended to 20-plus years. This is historically where you will get the best return on your investment.

However, "long term" in Internet time may not fall in these same ranges for every stock. Traditional business philosophy holds that the purpose of creating a company is to build something permanent—something that will last beyond the founder.

In the Internet economy, that may not be a reality for some companies. It is possible that some companies will be created around a single piece of technology or market niche, and then at some stage of maturity, be bought out by a competitor or be absorbed into a larger structure that provides a context for the company. This will all happen by design when the company is created. Investors in these IPOs will never expect earnings or dividends. They will expect a level of achievement in technology, sales, or some other predetermined measure. The company's stock will be valued on how well the company meets these goals.

To a certain extent, this has already happened with stocks such as Amazon.com and Yahoo! It is not unreasonable for investors to pay for 17 million customers of Amazon.com with the expectation that the company can convert those customers into profits at some point. Although Yahoo! has some profits (miniscule by traditional standards), it also has the most traffic of any site on the Internet. It would not be unreasonable to see either or both of these companies buy a partner or merge with another company that could leverage their existing assets.

America Online's purchase of Time Warner may be the model of the way the Internet will build itself out in the future. As few as five years ago, it would have been inconceivable that an Internet company would ever take over a huge, traditional media giant such as Time Warner.

How all this will work out is still not clear. We do know that small Internet companies can grow very rapidly, not only in market cap, but also in customer base or other metrics. This action of "getting into position" quickly is a definite advantage in the new economy.

Margin Call

There is little doubt that Internet stocks are entering a period of consolidation and correction. Look for a number of strategic partnerships that strengthen both companies. Avoid marriages in which there doesn't seem to be any way one can benefit the other.

It could be, however, that this rapid growth precludes building a management and support structure for the long run. It makes sense that a company may look for that structure and support from an existing, established partner.

The Internet economy places a high value on ideas and innovation. These attributes typically grow best in the small, uncluttered environment of startups. However, Internet IPOs that target a consolidation at some prescribed point in the future may offer the growth that potential investors seek with the assurance that the company will have the resources to continue as an ongoing business or part of another business.

What Do You Pay?

We have already discussed the pricing of Internet IPOs in Chapter 16, "Jumping On the IPO Bandwagon." However, the extreme mania surrounding Internet IPOs has only served to support companies with no real chance to succeed and to drive up prices for all.

We need to restate our expectations for Internet IPOs to focus on market share, revenue growth, or some other measure besides earnings. We also need to remove or reduce the hysteria factor from the pricing. Good luck.

Like the song says, "Everything old is new again." Oddly enough, this is all old stuff to the market. Whether it was railroads, automobiles, electricity, electronics, or computers, every new breakthrough generated the expectation bubble I talked about earlier. In every case, the bubble broke and the playing field was dramatically reduced.

Help File

Investing history is full of stories of markets becoming hyperinflated and subsequently crashing. It is doubtful that this market will crash, but it certainly is in for some continued wild rides. This is part of the cleansing process necessary from time-to-time for market health.

Exit Strategy

If you feel that you just have to get in on some IPO action, make sure that you aren't betting the farm. You can take some short-term speculative positions with Internet IPOs that can be profitable (if you are not greedy).

We talked earlier about how many Internet IPOs were below the close on the first day after 30 days of trading. If you go back and look at intraday trading on that first day, you will notice that many—not all, but many—stocks open higher than their offering price and may or may not soar to heights. Once up there, a stock can stay at or about that level, or prices can retreat.

In most cases, the price will come back some or a lot, depending on the stock and what investors think of it. Internet stocks as a group and IPOs in particular are a volatile lot. You can take advantage of those swings if you have a high tolerance for risk. This is known as market timing, and as an investment strategy, it is risky. Still, if you are willing to speculate a bit and keep an eye on the market, you'll probably find some opportunities.

There are two basic ways to go: *long* and *short*.

Long refers to buying the IPO and selling at, hopefully, a higher price. Short refers to selling the stock with the hope that prices will fall and that you can buy it back at a lower price and pocket the difference.

Speak Up

Long in stock market lingo means to buy or to own a stock. You are "long IBM" if you own shares of IBM. **Short** is the opposite of long (now there's a revelation) and refers to selling a stock. If you're "short IBM," you have sold it.

Going Long

This is a traditional way of buying stock that you are probably familiar with. The idea is to buy low and sell high. Keep your eyes open for an upcoming IPO that looks like it might attract a lot of attention.

You can judge the interest by the amount of press the company is receiving. By watching the Web sites I have been talking about in previous chapters, you might get a clue about where the offering price should be. If the company is really hot, the offering price might be raised at the last minute.

We know that the offering price and the opening price on the exchanges are two different items. Hot IPOs will almost always open over the offering price. Remember our example of Palm from earlier? Its offering price was $38 per share, while the opening price on the exchanges was $145 per share. Admittedly, this was high even for Internet/technology stocks. Nevertheless, it points out the nature of the hot IPO. Your strategy will be to get in early, even at a high price. There are two ways to do this.

The first is to give your broker a *market order* before trading begins. This is the same as handing the market a blank check, but you stand a good chance of getting it filled quickly.

Set a goal, preferably a dollar amount, that once achieved is your signal to sell the stock back. One of the ways to do this is to enter a *limit order* to sell at the goal price—do this as soon as your buy order is filled. This strategy may cut you out of some profits if the stock keeps rising, but don't get greedy. Shoot for a nice profit, but not an obscene one.

The second way to do this is a little more conservative. Instead of issuing a market order to get into the stock, enter a limit order to buy at a certain price. This price should be high enough over the offering price to be attractive. The danger is that you will misread the amount of bump the IPO will get when it hits the open market. You could end up paying a lot more for it than if you had stuck with the first plan, although that is not likely to happen.

You can use the same method of limit orders to put a floor under your position, in case the stock heads south. Another way to use limit sell orders is to use *rolling orders*. This pretty much means that you need access to real-time quotes and an online broker.

A rolling order moves the limit orders up as the price of the stock rises. For example …

Price of Stock	Limit Sell Order
$100	$85
$110	$95
$105	$90

The idea here is that $85 per share is the lowest price you want. However, to take advantage of upward movement of the stock, you raise your sell order accordingly. This locks in your profit and lets you earn more, but once the stock retreats 15 points, you get out.

Unless you are willing to sit at your computer for several days, I would make this a one-day exercise. Market timing is a risky strategy, as I have said before. If you feel like rolling the dice, this is one way to do it. Just don't bet anything you can't afford to lose.

Going Short

Another strategy for getting in on IPO fluctuations is to bet on the stock going up and coming down. This is known as shorting and is a common, although somewhat risky, strategy.

Speak Up

A **market order** is an order you place that says you want to buy or sell a stock at the best price available when the order is placed. Market orders are processed first, so if you want your order processed and don't care about the exact price, this is the way to go. A **limit order** is an order to buy or sell a stock when a specific price point is reached. If the stock never hits that point, your order may not be filled.

Speak Up

Rolling orders are sell limit orders that follow a stock's price up to protect a profit. For example, if you own the stock at $75 per share and have a profit, you could put a sell limit order in for $70 so if the stock falls in price you can still sell for a profit. If the stock rises to $80 per share, you can move your sell order up to $75, and so on.

Basically, the way it works is that you "borrow" some of the stock through your broker and sell it when you think the price is near the top during the day. If the stock falls in price, you buy it on the market at a lower price and return it to the owner. Your profit is the difference. For example:

Your Position	Stock Price	Number of Shares	Proceeds
Sell	$100	100	$10,000
Buy	$85	100	($8,500)
Profit			$1,500

This is a great strategy *if* the price of the stock goes down. If the price of the stock goes up, you will be forced to buy the stock at a higher price than you sold it and take a loss.

As you can see, there is some risk in all of these strategies. If you can't stand the thought of losing money, you should probably stay away from these techniques.

The Least You Need to Know

➤ Looking beyond the hype of Internet IPOs requires some discipline.

➤ Identifying quality stocks that will be around for the long run is difficult.

➤ There are ways to profit from an Internet's volatility, but be aware of the risks.

Chapter 18

Mutual Admiration Society

In This Chapter

➤ What an Internet stock mutual fund is

➤ Advantages and disadvantages of Internet funds

➤ How Internet funds have fared so far

➤ Who should invest in these funds

"Wise men say, only fools rush in ...."

That's investment advice from Elvis Presley. Well, if he was seen standing in line at K-Mart, why not as an analyst for Merrill Lynch?

Investing in Internet stocks is not foolish, unless you do so with your eyes wide shut hoping to pick a winner. However, a large number of investors of all types have neither the time nor the interest to pick individual stocks.

They rely on mutual fund managers to do the work for them. This strategy meets with varying degrees of success, but with billions of dollars from IRAs, 401(k) plans, pension plans, and individual investors pouring into the market, there is no arguing with their popularity.

If you find the thought of selecting individual stocks a little unnerving, then Internet mutual funds may be the answer. Like all investments in the Internet, however, these should not be your first or only investments.

What Is an Internet Mutual Fund?

The huge run-ups in Internet stocks were too attractive for mutual fund managers to pass up, and a whole new investment sector was born. By early 2000, there were 28 Internet mutual funds, with more on the way.

For many investors, mutual funds offer an attractive and convenient way to invest. They can be bought without a broker and, if you are careful, at fairly low cost. Mutual funds offer the convenience of low initial deposits (especially compared to the big buy-ins many Internet stocks command) and the ease of making periodic deposits in just about any amount you want.

Speak Up

Actively managed mutual funds employ a manager who buys and sells stocks in an attempt to take advantage of market swings. The expense ratios for these funds tend to be higher than those of index funds.

One of the main attractions of Internet funds is having a professional manager do the buying and selling for you. Remember, though, that there are no experts in picking Internet stocks, so the advantage here may be in having someone else (the fund manager) to blame when things go wrong.

Internet mutual funds come in a variety of flavors, ranging from *actively managed* funds to index funds. There is no indication at this early stage in the Internet mutual fund industry whether one is preferable to the other. Right now, it's a matter of personal choice.

Some of the funds are general funds covering a broad selection of Internet stocks, while others zero in on more defined areas of the Internet economy. Index funds track the market sector as a whole.

A Quick Review

Let's go over some of the major attributes of mutual funds in general and then see how the Internet mutual funds stack up with the rest of the industry. I have already touched on some of these briefly, so now let's expand those ideas and tie Internet funds into that framework.

Diversification

Diversification is difficult to achieve in Internet stocks because there are only a small number to choose from when compared to the broad market. Diversification is one of the major attributes and strengths of mutual funds. By spreading investments over a number of stocks, mutual funds seek to avoid dramatic swings in value that are common with individual stocks.

Diversification also protects investors against economic pressures on particular industries. For example, the housing industry is fairly sensitive to interest rates. When mortgage rates and construction loan costs rise, fewer new houses are built. Investors who hold housing-related stocks might be hurt by rising interest rates, whereas a mutual fund would have investments in a number of different sectors, some less sensitive to interest rate hikes. The result is that one sector's downturn doesn't necessarily signal a loss for the whole fund.

The downside of diversification is that with its investments spread out over many stocks, a mutual fund doesn't enjoy the same big increases when a stock or a group of stocks soars.

The same pressure that keeps a mutual fund from dropping too far when some investments go south keeps the fund from rising too far when other investments post big increases.

Internet funds may or may not benefit from diversification, depending on their direction. In truth, most of the general Internet funds are not pure Internet plays. Most of them invest heavily in the technology sector as well.

There is nothing wrong with funds investing in technology stocks along with Internet stocks—in fact, it makes a lot of sense to add some companies with real earnings to the mix. Just make sure that's what you want.

Another concern is duplicating existing investments with Internet/technology mutual funds. If you own an aggressive growth mutual fund, you probably are already heavily invested in the technology sector. If the Internet fund is just duplicating what you already own, you will be better off increasing your investment in the existing fund.

While general Internet mutual funds may achieve some diversification through a broad ownership in many stocks, they're still tied to the Internet/technology sectors and subject to their same fates. In the general world of mutual funds, most Internet funds would be considered "focused" funds because they are not diversified outside their sector.

Professional Manager

Professional management is a hallmark of mutual funds. One of the major selling points is that professional managers are better at making buy and sell decisions than the average investor.

While that is true up to a point, the sad reality is that there are far more mutual funds (10,000-plus) than there are good managers. For a good part of the 1990s, index funds such as those tracking the S&P 500 did better than most actively managed mutual funds.

When it comes to Internet funds, the picture on managers becomes fairly bleak. As I have said before, there are no experts at picking Internet stocks. Only a handful of

187

the existing funds have been around more than three years. What's more, some people who manage funds have no real experience managing a mutual fund. Always check the prospectus or Web site or Morningstar.com for background on the manager.

A good manager is becoming more important as the Internet matures, and there is no clear vision where these managers will come from. However, you may still feel that someone who spends all day studying the market has a better shot than you do in picking winners.

Internet Index Funds

Index mutual funds are very popular in the open market because they have performed very well. Index funds seek to mimic a particular stock index by buying the equivalent holdings.

Many people are familiar with index funds such as the S&P 500 and the NASDAQ Composite. These funds—and there are a bunch of them—are "automatic pilot" funds. That is, once the fund has bought a representative selection of stocks that make up the index, there is not much management to the funds.

One of the reasons index funds have performed so well is their low expenses. Expense ratio is an accurate predictor of a fund's success: The lower the expense ratio, the better chance the fund has for superior performance.

Index funds have an average expense ratio of .44 percent, with some index funds near .25 percent, according to Morningstar.com. Internet index funds, on the other hand, have expense ratios of more than 1 percent and up to 1.65 percent. Even with triple-digit growth, those expense ratios will eat into your return—and when growth cools off, this will be even more important.

The indexes tracked by these index funds are not as well known as those in the broader market. They are: Dow Jones Composite Internet, Goldman Sachs E-commerce, Internet 100, and ISDEX. Although these are not household terms just yet, they are gaining acceptance in the investment community.

Margin Call

Internet mutual funds are popping up all over the place. Many are out of existing fund companies, but others seem to come from nowhere. An Internet mutual fund that is part of a bigger family of funds probably has better resources to draw on funds that exist in isolation.

Speak Up

Index funds try to match the performance of a specific index by matching the underlying stocks. If an index has Microsoft as 4 percent of its total, the mutual fund will have the same ratio.

Dow Jones Composite Internet

It says a lot about the growth and acceptance of the Internet that the venerable Dow Jones (ticker symbol: DJ; dowjones.com) has assembled an index to follow the Internet stocks.

Although it is not widely reported, the Dow Jones Composite Internet will gain more popularity as it completes the process of selecting the appropriate stocks. The composite is composed of two indexes: the Commerce Index and the Services Index.

This index's stated goal is to cover 80 percent of the Internet equity. To be included, a company must derive at least 50 percent of its revenue from the Internet. A company must also have a three-month average of $100 million market cap and a three-month average stock price of at least $10 per share.

Several mutual funds track the Dow Jones Composite Internet. One is the Internet Index Fund (ticker symbol: M$-BEHC; internetindexfund.net).

Margin Call

The Internet stock market is not represented yet by a single major index, such as the Dow Jones Industrial Average or the NAS-DAQ Composite. Until it is, index funds must pick the index that seems the most likely to endure.

Goldman Sachs E-Commerce Index

This index produced by Goldman Sachs (ticker symbol: GS; gs.com) follows not only the e-commerce companies such as Amazon.com, but also companies that supply support and services to e-commerce companies and customers.

The index contained 64 companies as of March 2000 and is used by E*Trade E-commerce Index fund (ticker symbol: ETECX; etrade.com).

Internet 100

The Internet 100 Index is operated by *USA Today* newspaper's Web site (usatoday.com). The index tracks 100 Internet stocks and is split into several sections:

➤ **e-infrastructure**—Data, voice, and video carriers, and Web hosts and hardware suppliers

➤ **e-services/solutions**—Consultants, software/applications, and back-office services

➤ **e-advertising/marketing/media**—Internet advertising agencies and publishing companies

➤ **e-retail**—Consumer products and services

➤ **e-finance**—Banks, brokers, and credit companies

➤ **e-new media**—Advertising/subscription-supported communities

➤ **e-access providers**—Toll-supported access providers

ISDEX

ISDEX is an index of 50 Internet stocks operated by Internet.com (Internet.com). The index covers a broad range of Internet companies from e-tailers to hardware suppliers to information suppliers.

The mutual fund Guinness-Flight Internet.com Index (ticker symbol: GFINX; gffunds. com) covers this particular measure.

One of the concerns about investing in Internet index funds is picking the right index. Most of the Internet indexes are not widely reported, and there is no clear consensus leader.

Speak Up

Focused funds concentrate their investments in specific narrow sectors of the market. The idea is to take advantage of rapid growth in the sector. The downside is that when the sector tanks, so does the fund.

Risk Upon Risk

If index funds seek to follow the market as represented by a particular index, *focused funds* seek the opposite.

As the name implies, focused funds specialize in a particular market sector rather then covering a broad spectrum of stocks. Internet focused funds tie their fortunes to one part of the Internet economy, such as foreign Internet growth, Internet infrastructure, or business-to-business (B2B).

These funds offer the opportunity for large gains, but they also carry the heavy exposure that if the sector tanks, there is no fallback position. On the other hand, as the market for Internet stocks matures, there will probably be more volatility in some sectors than others.

One of these funds, Firsthand e-commerce (ticker symbol: TEFQX), concentrates on companies that provide infrastructure, software, or consulting services to e-commerce companies. This fund is so new that there are no meaningful financials to report, other than it has grown to $765 million net assets in just a few months.

A number of other focused Internet funds are scheduled to enter the market in 2000. While these funds may show spectacular results, that remains to be seen. Focused funds tend to defeat one of the strong reasons for investing in mutual funds by abandoning diversification. They are like betting on every horse in the race and hoping that the winner will pay enough to cover the losses on the rest of the field, plus a profit.

Some of the Best

Past performance is no guarantee of future results. Truer words were never spoken when referring to Internet mutual funds. Yesterday's winner is tomorrow's turkey.

The volatile nature of Internet stocks combined with many inexperienced managers can make for some interesting numbers. Here are some of the top funds from 1999:

Ticker	Fund	1999 Return
MFITX	Monument Internet A	273%
WWWFX	Internet Fund	216%
MNNAX	Munder NetNet A	175%
MNNBX	Munder NetNet B	173%

It's hard to argue with those numbers, but a lot has changed in the past year. Many of the Internet mutual funds are just too young to form any real opinions.

Like many numbers surrounding Internet stocks, you need to put them into perspective. These funds did great, if you got in at the beginning of the year and cashed out at the end. Most of us are not smart enough or lucky enough to figure that out in advance—but then again, nobody else is, either.

These funds did well because the underlying Internet stocks had a dramatic year with few corrections. There was a correction in January 2000, however, and another much larger correction in April 2000.

Even if we do not use the April numbers, these leading funds look a little different under a new light. Let's look at the first three months of 2000 and, more importantly, a trailing 12-month figure. The one-year trailing number looks at the previous 12 months as of the end of March 2000. *Trailing* numbers are almost always more significant than calendar year-end numbers, unless it is close to the calendar year end. Trailing numbers give you a moving picture of what is going on with the fund that is more reflective of current conditions.

Margin Call

Using past performance to pick mutual funds is never a good idea, but when it comes to Internet mutual funds, it is impossible. Investors buy the future, and that is doubly true of Internet funds.

Fund	3 Months 1999 Return	Trailing of 2000	12 months
Monument Internet A	273%	0.2%	37%
Internet Fund	216%	8%	31%
Munder NetNet A	175%	13%	62%
Munder NetNet B	173%	13%	61%

This is not atypical of Internet mutual funds. Munder funds seem to be doing better than the other two for the time period, but their *trailing twelve-month* returns are just a third of their calendar 1999 returns.

Of course, there is nothing wrong with 60-plus percent returns. However, these lower totals are reflective of a couple changes in the Internet mutual fund market. As funds grow larger, it is harder for them to move as quickly, and sustaining a triple-digit growth rate is a lot harder for a $3.5 billion-plus fund, which is where the Munder funds are, than the Monument fund, at $167 million.

Speak Up

Examining the **trailing twelve-months** is a way of looking at a fund's performance for the past 12 months from the current date. This "sliding" indicator is a better reflection of performance than tying numbers to a fiscal year end.

By the time you read this, those figures may have changed in the intervening period. The big correction in April 2000 surely hurt the funds in a dramatic fashion. Month-end figures weren't available, but the best this small group could do was to just barely break even for the Munder funds, while the rest were in negative numbers.

Although it is clear that mutual funds in general offer some protection against market fluctuations, that same protection is not as evident with Internet mutual funds. This is in part because the whole sector is so new and volatile that it may be asking too much to expect predictable results even from mutual funds. As managers of Internet mutual funds gain experience and the whole Internet stock sector matures, mutual funds may become a more popular choice than individual stocks for the average investor who may not have the time or inclination to research individual stocks.

Who Should Own Internet Mutual Funds

Are you a good candidate to own Internet mutual funds? That depends, of course, on several factors.

Internet mutual fund managers may not be any better than you at picking winners and losers. Because they invest in a large number of stocks, you could argue that they don't have to use the same amount of care as an individual investor buying one or a handful of stocks.

Another consideration is that the Internet stock market is still moving in tandem, which means that any bad news is likely to move the whole market. As the market matures, this will become less of a problem, but for the immediate future, things will be rocky.

Investors under the age of 35 who have a solid retirement plan in place may want to consider Internet mutual funds as part of an aggressive growth strategy. Investors getting close to retirement should consider Internet mutual funds with money they can afford to lose.

As a long-term investment, Internet mutual funds may make more sense than individual stocks. Fund managers can refresh the portfolio with newer stocks and discard those companies that aren't keeping up. Active investors can do the same thing, but most of us can't afford to own the same size basket of stocks that a mutual fund does.

Investors can also look for funds that invest a significant part of the assets in more established technology stocks. Although these stocks are subject to some volatility also, they tend to be treated more kindly by the market because most companies are making money.

A big negative is the expense associated with Internet mutual funds. Because some of the funds have had huge increases, it is easy to overlook a high expense ratio. As the market matures, investors will be more concerned about expenses. An expense ratio of 3 percent may not seem like a big deal when the fund returns 150 percent annually. However, as the market settles down, a 3 percent expense ratio on a fund returning 30 percent may not be acceptable.

Another way to hedge your investments is to pick funds with managers experienced in running a high-tech fund. You can find this information in the fund's prospectus or online with a service such as Morningstar.com.

An experienced fund manager and a low expense ratio are probably the two most important predictors of a fund's potential for success. They don't guarantee success, but they go a long way toward making it happen.

Help File

Although the Internet stock market is maturing, it has a long way to go. In the broader stock market, it is not uncommon for one sector to be down and another to be up. Internet stocks are still considered as a group by the market, so when one part does poorly, that affects the whole sector.

Double Click

Don't let huge increases in Internet funds hide sloppy management. When the market gets tight, poor management will make matters worse.

Like many Internet stocks, it may be hard at this point to see which of the funds are likely to be successful. Mutual funds have some real advantages of being able to reinvent themselves if things aren't working out with the current structure. It will be instructive to see how the funds rebound after a major correction. This is where an experienced manager may pay big dividends.

The Least You Need to Know

➤ Internet mutual funds may provide a cushion for a rocky ride as the Internet market matures.

➤ Experienced professional managers are worth looking for when considering an investment in Internet mutual funds.

➤ Focused funds have the potential for huge gains, but also for huge loses.

➤ Internet index mutual funds seek to follow the market in Internet stocks by investing in representative companies.

Chapter 19

Day Trading for Fun and Profit

In This Chapter

➤ Why day trading is not for the faint of heart

➤ How to get started

➤ Using fundamental and technical analysis

➤ Alternatives to day trading

If you are old enough to remember when the Dow Jones Industrial Average was under 3,000 and the stock market was not something most people worried about, you may be old enough to remember ads in magazines for the Charles Atlas body building system.

The ads showed a skinny guy (the original 90-pound weakling) at the beach with his girlfriend. Some bullies come by and kick sand on them. The skinny guy is determined not to let that happen again, so he gets the Charles Atlas body-building system. In no time, he goes from the 90-pound weakling to a 180-pound hunk. The bullies don't bother him anymore.

I was about 11 years old and skinny as a post when this ad was running. I thought the Charles Atlas system was the answer to my prayers, until I mentioned it to my father. He gently suggested that it was unlikely that an 11 year-old boy would bulk up to 180 pounds of muscle. He gave me my first lesson in "wishing don't make it so."

Like that ad, day trading has all the allure of an exciting lifestyle and fast money. Still, wishing don't make it so.

The Day Trader's Dilemma

Day trading has captured the imagination of a large number of people, many who weren't investors before they became interested. It has all the excitement of casino gambling, including the chance to make a lot of money in a hurry.

Despite the fact that by one study 80 percent of day traders lose money, people from all walks of life continue to quit their jobs for the often-lonely life of a day trader.

What is it about day trading that draws people to it like moths to a candle? Certainly, the prospect of quick and plentiful money is a big draw. However, there are other factors, including the attraction of being the "Lone Ranger"—you against the market, that many find compelling.

The day trader's dilemma is how to keep from becoming addicted to the trading, regardless of the money. For some, this is an addiction not unlike gambling.

What They Really Do

Before we get too far down the road, it might be helpful to outline exactly what day traders do and how they do it.

Basically, day traders try to identify stocks about to move in one direction or the other, and then capitalize on that movement by taking a position and quickly exiting that position when a certain profit or loss is registered.

Day traders may hold this position for anywhere from a few minutes to a few hours. As the name implies, many day traders never keep a position open overnight. In other words, when the market opens, they have no position and when it closes, they have no position; in between those two events, they may have done 50 to 100 trades.

A day trader's goal is to capture small price changes and make many small profitable trades. One quarter of a point may be enough to exit a position with a profit. This doesn't sound like much, but if you are trading 1,000 shares, a quarter point translates into $250 before commissions. Do that 100 times a day, and you are into big money pretty quickly. Of course, not every trade is profitable.

Different Brokers

Day traders use brokers that specialize in working with this type of account. These brokers differ from regular retail brokers in at least three significant ways:

➤ They offer a very different commission structure that makes volume trading practical.

➤ They offer a physical space in their offices for day traders to work. This allows the trader access to sophisticated trading software and quote systems.

➤ They offer a different margin requirement. The margins vary from broker to broker and depend partly on the trader's track record. The margin can range from 5–1 to 20–1. High margin allow traders to control much larger positions.

Commissions

The commissions charged by day trading brokerages vary from a flat fee per trade to a percentage of the profits. In addition, there may be charges for extras that some traders want.

Most day traders feel that a flat fee is the best route because you know your costs going into each trade. Most brokerages charge in the range of 1 to 2 cents per share. For example, if you traded 1,000 shares, the commission would be $10 at a brokerage that charges 1 cent per share, or $20 at 2 cents per share commission. Some firms may have a minimum commission to cover small trades.

Although that doesn't sound like much, remember that active traders often make 50 to 100 trades per day. At 1,000 shares (not an uncommon lot), you could be looking at $500 to $2,000 a day in commissions alone.

Like retail brokers, day trading shops offer the best deals to their best customers. The firms that charge a percentage of your profit are real bargains when you are losing money, but when you start making money, the picture changes.

Double Click

Hidden charges are the kind of unpleasant surprises most of us don't need. Read the broker's agreement carefully to be sure you aren't going to be charged for services that are important to you, such as itemized statements, bank transfers, and so on.

A great predictor of success in almost any form of investing is low expenses. Day trading is no different. Just be sure that you don't sacrifice the tools you need to save a few bucks here and there.

Some day trading brokers charge fees on top of commissions for everything from per-trade charges to access to certain levels of information, and so on. Remember, when the profit in a trade is an eighth or a quarter of a point, per-trade fees start to add up.

The Space

Many day trading brokers offer space in their offices for traders to use their sophisticated workstations and software. This is a must for day traders just getting started.

Although many books and Web sites cover the topic of day trading, there is no substitute for the trading tips (techniques, not stocks) that you can pick up at the firm.

Among the best references is the Web site for day traders on About.com (daytrading. about.com).

Many of these workstations have two or more monitors that display a number of different information sources, including real-time pricing and a variety of other news and data. Workstations used by brokers are connected to powerful networks and are nothing like your home computer. The workstations also have sophisticated software that helps traders manage the information and, more importantly, their positions.

Most of the trading systems are not goof-proof, though. They don't prompt you for confirmations of trades or positions. Hit the button, and the trade is gone.

The screens are divided into a number of different windows, so there is usually a lot going on. Pricing information may be in one or more colors, while volume information may be in another area of the screen. Although the screens look confusing, time and practice will make them easier to follow.

Doing It at Home

The most popular image of a day trader is someone still in pajamas hunched over a computer in a bedroom. A significant number of traders do their trading in this manner, although I can't verify whether they are in their pajamas.

There are two ways you can do day trading out of your home: You can use the Internet to connect with a broker, or some brokers will allow you to dial into the system from your home either over the Internet or through a direct connection.

Help File

Brokers and others see true real-time quotes in the market at the same time. Often "real-time" quotes offered for free on the Internet are still delayed because they are not connected directly to the market. In day trading, any delay, no matter how short, can mean the difference between a profit and a loss.

The Internet has given home traders access to many of the same systems and information as traders working out of a broker's office. It has also given rise to brokers who offer "bare bones" services. While these deep discount brokers may seem attractive, it is important to not skimp on the tools you need. A position of 1,000 shares that swings down a half-point that you miss because of delays can cost you $500 in that one trade alone.

If you are not using a broker's system that provides all the information and trading software you need, you will need to contract for these services. True real-time quotes and pricing information like that available in the broker's office will cost several hundred dollars per month alone.

In addition, your Internet connection should be something other than a regular dial-up modem. Cable, DSL, or ISDN are some of the alphabet soup services that are available in many communities, especially the larger ones. All offer advantages and disadvantages, but they will all be significantly faster than the fastest dial-up modem.

Your home computer is also no place to pinch pennies. A 3-year-old computer with a 15-inch monitor just won't get the job done. If you are doing day trading as your livelihood, give yourself a fair chance to succeed with the proper equipment and services.

Beware of Taxes

Day traders may make hundreds of trades a week. Some will be profitable and others will be losers. It is imperative that day traders keep very accurate trading records for tax purposes.

Normally, profits from selling securities you have owned less than one year are treated as ordinary income and taxed accordingly. This can impose a heavy burden on day traders who may have to pay self-employment taxes.

Some traders may qualify for special treatment by the Internal Revenue Service. Check with a qualified tax expert for specific advice.

The System

A romantic notion exists that day traders somehow have a "feel" for the market and make their trades based on "gut feelings." These types of day traders probably are out there, but most of them don't last very long.

In fact, experienced day traders may have a feel for the market, but it comes after a lot of experience and hard lessons. Serious day traders use information, logic, and strategy to guide their moves.

There are two basic types of analysis, whether you are talking about day trading or regular investing: fundamental analysis and technical analysis.

Day traders use a variety of tools to make their trading decisions. Most use a combination of fundamental analysis and technical analysis to look for patterns and variances in a stock's price. These tools, especially technical analysis, are very sophisticated. Traders who work out of a broker's office have access to professional-level information and technology to help them decide when to get in and when to get out of a stock.

Double Click

Day traders use a variety of tools. In addition to doing technical and fundamental analysis, they watch financial news on the Internet and visit stock boards and chat rooms, although always with a suspicious eye.

What follows is a brief overview of both systems. Numerous resources are available to help you learn more about both systems if you are interested. One, *Macmillan Teach Yourself Investing in 24 Hours*, was written by that brilliant writer, me (shameless plug).

Know the Fundamentals

Fundamental analysis asks these questions, among others: What is this company? What does it do? How much does it do it? Who buys its products? How much money does it make or lose?

This form of analysis tells the trader about the relative strength of a company in its market. This type of analysis is much more important to long-term investors because it gives them a picture of the company and some hints about its future prospects.

However, fundamental analysis doesn't address short-term swings in the stock's price. Investors are more interested in what the stock will be worth next year or in five years, while day traders are more interested in what it will be worth in five minutes. Day traders need information that will give them some clues about whether the stock is going to move today and how much and in which direction. Day traders don't care about the long-term prospects of the company because they are interested in the stock right now.

Fundamental analysis is helpful to day traders who follow specific stocks. It is helpful to know if the stock is particularly susceptible to interest rate changes, weather conditions, or other economic or natural conditions. For example, if you and the market anticipated that the *Federal Reserve Board* was going to raise interest rates, you might look for companies sensitive to interest rates to see if the anticipated rate hike is reflected by the stock's price already. If it did not appear that the market had already discounted the firm's stock, that stock might make a good short candidate.

Speak Up

The Federal Reserve Board (the Fed) controls the nation's money supply and interest rates. Its primary tool for working with the economy is interest rates. By raising interest rates, the Fed makes it harder to borrow money, which has the effect of cooling off the economy. When the Fed lowers interest rates, it is usually to stimulate the economy. The Fed's biggest fear is inflation.

Then the Technical Stuff

Technical analysis, on the other hand, is concerned only with trading volume and price data. These inputs give day traders the information that tells them when to buy and when to sell.

Most of this input is in the form of charts. Traders who work out of a broker's office have a real advantage with access to sophisticated charting equipment. The two words you hear most around technical analysts are *support* and *resistance*. These terms define the boundaries of price movement for the technical analyst. Day traders use a variety of charts to look for patterns within this framework.

Support

As the name sounds, this concept describes a "floor," if you will, under the price of the stock. A trader will look at a chart covering daily highs and lows of a stock over a couple of months.

What the trader is looking for is a price level that is approached several times on the low side, but that the stock never drops below. This is the support.

What this means is subject to interpretation, but in general it suggests that when a stock drops to this level, investors feel that it is undervalued and move in to buy. As the buying increases, the stock's price rises above the support again.

As you can see from this chart of Yahoo!, there appears to be a support level at $150—that is, until the April correction caused the price to crash through the support.

Double Click

Traders using technical analysis need to be on guard against external events that can trigger a breakthrough of either support or resistance.

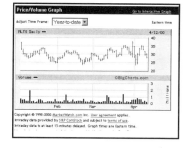

The support for a stock price of $150 is shown on this chart.

This is not a perfect example of a support chart, but I believe that it conveys a couple points:

➤ Before the April correction, a day trader may watch the stock fall to a certain point close to the support and jump in long, hoping that the stock will bounce off the support for a profit. Likewise, if the trader is short, he should consider covering the short as it approaches the support level.

201

➤ Charts are subject to a certain amount of interpretation. Technical analysis is not an exact science that gives you precise information on what a stock's price will do. Some traders will read more into a chart, and others will see less.

Margin Call

Sometimes a market moves so quickly that following charts becomes a task that requires you to never take your eyes off the screen.

This chart is a good example of why technical analysis by itself is not a foolproof system. I doubt that many people saw the April correction coming just from the charts. Many market observers believe that the ongoing struggle between Microsoft and the Justice Department over unfair trade practices triggered the correction.

Microsoft was found guilty of being a monopoly, and that ruling scared investors. Virtually all of these stocks suffered huge declines. Most people figured that there would be a correction sooner or later, and the Microsoft ruling was all the market needed to head south. In such a market, day traders might look for tech/Internet stocks that are somewhat out of step with their market, meaning they are not moving the same direction or with the same speed as their peers.

Resistance

Resistance is the opposite of support. If support is the floor, then resistance is the ceiling.

When you observe a pattern like that in the next figure of a stock's price rising up to but not going above a certain level, this is the resistance.

This stock is approaching 37 but does not go over.

This suggests that as the stock's price approaches the resistance level, investors begin to see the stock as overpriced and either don't buy or sell to take a profit. In either case, the stock's price retreats from the ceiling.

Although the peaks don't have to touch the resistance level, the closer they come and the more there are, the better. Day traders might use the occasion to short the stock as it approaches the resistance level or to put a stop in place before the stock gets too close to lock in a profit before the price retreats.

Different Looks

Dozens of different chart types exist, along with many interpretations of each. It is not within the scope of this book to look at all of them. However, these are important tools in the day trader's belt. If you want to pursue this type of business, you will need to learn much, much more about them.

What It Takes

It takes money to be a day trader—a lot of money. Most experienced traders say that you need a minimum of $25,000 capital to get started, and $50,000 would be better. Some day trading brokerages have a $25,000 minimum requirement to open an account.

The more capital you have, the bigger trades you can make, although most professionals say that you should start with 100-share trades until you have some experience.

Don't borrow your trading capital. The pressure to cover trading expenses and a sizable debt are too much for a trader just getting started. Also be prepared to lose your whole stake. This happens more frequently than not. In addition, you should also plan on not pulling any money out of your account for at least a year. This will give you the experience you need and, if you are making money, let your capital base grow.

Day trading and a full-time job don't mix either—day trading *is* a full-time job. You must plan to live off your savings or a part-time job that doesn't interfere with your trading until you are making enough to pull income out without eroding your minimum capital base.

Money management is incredibly important and requires a disciplined approach to day trading that many would-be traders lack.

Playing Games

Day trading simulations offered by some brokers and online sources is a good way to get a feel for the process. Trying your hand will help you get familiar with the terminology and technology of day trading without risking any money.

However, this is no substitute for actual trading. Playing a game and trading with real money (your money) are not the same. Anyone who has played poker for match sticks and for real money will tell you that.

Margin Call

Don't convince yourself that you are a "natural" just because you do well in games and simulations. Playing with your own money puts the exercise on a whole different emotional plane.

Still, simulations can get you acquainted with software, hardware, and other systems that day traders use. It will be worth your while to learn as much as you can about the mechanics of trading before you actually begin trading for real.

Emotions

Two emotions that will kill a day trader's chances for success: fear and greed.

Fear will paralyze you and cloud your decision-making. If you are afraid to trade or risk your money, look elsewhere for your investing strategy. Fear or low risk tolerance is not compatible with day trading.

Greed is just as incompatible. Although many people think this is the driving force behind day traders, it is not the reason most seasoned traders choose this line of work. They are more excited about the competition and the challenge of making good trades. Sure, they want to make money, but if greed is the only motivator, they won't last long. Greed, like fear, clouds your thinking.

A successful day trader is happy with a good trade and doesn't feel the need to make huge profits on every trade. The discipline to settle for small but consistent profits is the mark of an experienced trader.

The Rest of the Story

There is much more to day trading, money management, information management, and so on. If you don't think that day trading is for you, but you still want to be an active trader, consider any of these alternative strategies.

A couple alternatives are not full-time jobs, which you may find more appealing than giving up your regular job for an extremely risky career.

Double Click

Many online brokers will let you trade via telephone, pager, computer, or personal data assistant. These are nice extras if you need them, but they're costly if you don't.

These alternatives do not require a special brokerage account, although you probably will want a margin account instead of a regular cash account. No particularly expensive equipment or services are needed, and you can do these alternatives while still holding down a full-time job: price trading and swing trading.

Both of these forms of trading are similar to regular investing, but they differ in that positions are not held for the long term and may be terminated quickly the same day or several months later.

Price Trading

Price traders look for a stock that is moving in a particular direction that may indicate that the market has changed its mind about the issue. They are not concerned with making 100 trades a day; instead, they are looking for more than a quarter-point change.

Price traders, also known as position traders, look for stocks moving in a new direction and ride that as long as they can. For example, they might zero in on a stock that has been down for several sessions for no apparent reason other than that the whole market or market sector was down. This stock may be ready to rally as the market perceives it to be a bargain relative to the market or sector. Price traders may stay a couple of hours, days, or months in a position as long as the trend is in their favor.

These folks use more fundamental analysis to identify potential candidates, while relying on technical analysis to suggest entry and exit points.

Swing Trading

Swing traders may fall somewhere between price traders and day traders. They tend to hold positions longer than day traders but shorter than price traders.

These traders look for a flaw in the market's pricing of a stock and take advantage of movement in the opposite direction. Sometimes these flaws represent, for example, a downward trend in a stock's price for several days in a row.

Swing traders look for stocks that seem to be drifting in one direction, but that feel as if they should be headed the other direction. Some flaws in pricing can be corrected quickly, in which case the swing trader may exit the same day, or it could take longer.

Day Trading Internet Stocks

Day trading Internet stocks is a very dynamic situation, to say the least. Internet stocks tend to be very volatile even in intraday trading.

These can be excellent candidates for day trading, but you must approach them with caution. Many of the Internet stocks do not have a long history to observe, and their prices sometimes don't act in a rational manner.

The figure that follows shows Yahoo! after market close on April 13, 2000. You can see from the chart and the accompanying high, low, and close for the day that Yahoo! had an almost 14-point swing on this day, despite closing down just a fraction.

Notice the resistance at about 149 and the support at 134. One day's worth of price numbers is not enough to establish these two parameters, but the chart does illustrate what it might look like.

On this same day, eBay experienced a nearly 20-point difference between its daily high and low, while Amazon.com had a spread of 11 points. These spreads are a little exaggerated because of the April correction, but even in normal markets, the swings are wild.

Yahoo! took a wide swing during one day of trading.

What Do You Recommend?

I'm glad you asked. I wouldn't recommend that anyone take up day trading as a full-time job, and that's really the only way to do it. This is a demanding and challenging job with more risk than reward, in my opinion. If you want to take an active role in your investing, you can do so without risking the house every time you turn on your computer.

On the other hand, your tolerance for risk may be greater than mine. If you decide that day trading is something you want to pursue, learn everything you can before you quit your regular job. The more knowledge you have before you start, the better chance for success you have. Good luck.

The Least You Need to Know

➤ Day trading is very risky and is not something to be entered into lightly.

➤ Day trading requires a large amount of capital to start and a significant amount of savings to live on while you perfect your system.

➤ Day traders use both fundamental and technical analysis, but they rely more heavily on technical data.

Chapter 20

What Are Your Options?

In This Chapter

➤ How to use options on Internet stocks

➤ Where to get information about options

➤ The risks and rewards of options trading

➤ How employee stock options offer big payoffs

"There's more than one way to skin a cat," my grandfather used to say.

I never quite figured out why you would want to skin a cat or why knowing more than one way to do it was important. My grandfather was a wise man, but he died without sharing the value of this particular piece of wisdom.

I have come to accept that he was probably saying that there is more than one solution to a problem. In a round-about sort of way, that is the focus of this chapter on options.

The popular definition of the word *option* is "an alternative or another choice to be made." In the financial world, an option is a specific investment product that can be bought and sold.

When we talk about options on Internet stocks, both definitions are appropriate. Options give you another way to invest in Internet stocks, in addition to trading the shares themselves.

Options on Internet Stocks

When most people hear the term *stock options* in the same sentence as *Internet stocks*, their first thought is the perk that many dot.com executives receive instead of big salaries.

We will talk about stock options that employees receive as part of their compensation later in this chapter, in the section "Employee Stock Options." However, our primary concern will be options on Internet stocks. There aren't a large number of Internet stocks with traded options, but the number is growing all the time.

Although options are considered a risky investment, they can be used in a thoughtful investment strategy to profit from the tremendous interest in Internet stocks. A quick review of options might be helpful before we go much further in our discussion of options on Internet stocks.

Options in a Nutshell

Options give the owner the right, but not the obligation, to buy or sell the underlying security at a specified price by a certain date. They are created and sold on exchanges, not by the company. Option owners have no rights, such as voting or dividends, in the stocks of the underlying company. Options are derivatives—that is, they derive their value from the underlying security. Options can be exercised at any time during the life of the option. This gives the option investor the maximum flexibility within the established life of the option.

You need to understand a few unique terms for the rest of the chapter to make sense:

➤ **Call**—A call is an option that gives you the right to buy a stock at a certain price by a certain date.

➤ **Put**—A put is an option that gives you the right to sell a stock at a certain price by a certain date.

➤ **Strike price**—The strike price is the certain price mentioned in the two previous definitions. The strike price is also called the exercise price.

➤ **Expiration date**—The expiration date is the certain date in the previous definitions. It is the date when the options expire and is always the third Friday of the month. If the option is not traded or exercised before the expiration date, it simply goes away.

➤ **Premium**—The premium is what you pay for the option, plus commissions. If you buy a call option with a $2 premium, your cost is $200 (options are sold in round lots of 100 shares), plus commissions.

➤ **Writing**—Writing an option is the same as selling the option. If you write a call option, you receive the premium, minus a commission.

These are the basic terms that we will build on in this chapter.

Call options anticipate that the underlying stock's price will rise. You buy calls to participate in the increase or to lock in a lower price if you want to own the stock outright.

Put options anticipate that the underlying stock's price will fall. You buy puts to profit from the decrease in price. Although this involves the same strategy as shorting a stock, it is different in that the buyer is not obligated to do anything if the price of the stock rises above the strike price.

Margin Call

Shorting a stock involves selling shares that you do not own in anticipation that the price of the stock will fall and that you can replace the stock by buying on the open market at a lower price and then pocket the difference. If the price of the stock rises, you will be forced to buy the stock at a higher price than you sold it for and will suffer a loss.

When you short a stock and the stock rises, you probably will be required to buy the stock off the open market at a higher price to replace the shorted stock.

Pricing

Several factors figure into how option premiums are determined. The most obvious factor is the difference between the strike price of the option and the market price of the stock.

Strike Price

The strike price is fixed and cannot change, but the market price changes frequently. A call option with a strike price that is less than the market price is said to be "in the money." This means that you could exercise the option and buy the stock for less than the market price. You are in the money.

On the other hand, if the market price is lower than the strike price, the option is "out of the money." You would not exercise an option to buy a stock for more than it could be bought on the open market. To complete the picture, if the strike price and the market price are the same, you are "at the money."

A premium for a call that is out of the money will increase as the strike price approaches the market price. Obviously, if the strike price is less than the market price, the premium will be higher still. For example, take a look at this table:

Strike Price	Market Price	Premium
$50	$48	$0.50
$50	$50	$1.00
$50	$52	$3.00

These are completely made-up numbers, but they illustrate how the premium is affected by the difference between the market price and the strike price for call options.

The extent to which an option is in the money is called the *intrinsic value* of an option. The intrinsic value is one component of the option pricing formula.

Speak Up

The **intrinsic value** of an option refers to the difference between the strike price and the market price. For call options, if the strike price is lower than the market price, the difference is the intrinsic value. Likewise, if a put option's strike price is higher than the market price, the difference is intrinsic value.

Call options and put options move in opposite directions, so a put will have intrinsic value (or be in the money) when the strike price is higher than the market price.

Time Factor

Options are sold with a set expiration date eight months out. When the expiration date arrives, the option expires.

The time remaining before an option expires effects the price of the option. The more time remaining in the option, the higher the premium because there is a greater chance that the option will be profitable. Conversely, the closer to the expiration date an out-of-the-money option comes, the cheaper the premium becomes because there is less time to become profitable.

Because of this, options are said to have time value. This time value becomes part of the premium equation. Look at this in the money example:

Strike Price	Market Price	Expiration	Premium
50	52	October	$2.25
50	52	November	$3.75
50	52	December	$5.25

Again, these are made-up numbers, but you can see that the further out you go, the higher the premium is for in-the-money options. It should also be clear that the same would be true of out-of-the-money options. This is because more time means that the possibility a profitable option will become more profitable, so an unprofitable option will become profitable.

Volatility

Another factor to consider is the volatility of the underlying stock—and with most Internet stocks, we know that this is going to be high. The wide swings in price can take an option in and out of the money several times a day. Some investors incorrectly assume that volatility means that a stock will always tend upward in price during wide price swings. Volatility has no bias upward or downward on prices in and of itself.

I will discuss this in more detail a little later in the chapter (see the section, "Options Information," in this chapter) and will cover some tools to help you understand options.

Special Cases

There is a special class of options known as LEAPS, which stands for Long-term Equity Anticipation Securities. LEAPS have all the same characteristics as regular options, with the exception of the time period.

LEAPS can have a life of up to two years and eight months, as opposed to normal options, which expire in eight months. LEAPs were created to fit the particular needs of investors with long-term horizons.

Because LEAPS have a longer life than regular options, it is possible to participate in the stock's growth or decline over a longer period. This gives investors more opportunities to profit from changing market conditions.

Buyer or Seller

Like other securities, options can be bought or sold, putting you on either side of the trade. Each side of the trade, long or short, has different requirements and alternatives.

It is important to note that buyers of options, either calls or puts, are not under any obligation to do anything. They can trade the option, exercise the option, or simply let it expire worthless.

Double Click

Companies do not issue options, and they have no responsibility to the options investor. Options must have a buyer and a seller on each side of the trade to be completed. Out-of-the-money options nearing the expiration date will be hard to sell.

It is even more important to note that sellers, also known as writers, of options may be called upon to fulfill the conditions of the option. If you write a call option on XYZ stock and the option is exercised, you are obligated to sell to the option owner 100 shares of XYZ stock at the strike price, regardless of the current market price for the stock.

Likewise, if you write a put option and the option is exercised, you are obligated to buy the stock at the strike price, regardless of the current market price. People who write call or put options as an opening transaction are shorting the options the same way stock can be shorted.

Many options are exercised, but people wanting to profit from options generally trade the option or let it expire if it's worthless. You trade in the options market by entering an offsetting order. For example, if you buy a call option on XYZ stock for a premium of $500 and the price of the underlying stock rises, you can profit from the increase in premium by selling an XYZ call at the new premium. Your profit is the difference between the premium paid and the premium received.

First trade:

> Buy 1 XYZ call option for premium of $500
>
> Price of underlying stock rises

Second trade:

> Sell 1 XYZ call option for premium of $1,000
>
> Profit = Second trade – first trade
>
> $1,000 – $500 = $500 profit

One of the advantages of buying options is that they can be converted into actual shares of the underlying stock, if that is your strategy.

Buyers

People buy options for a variety of reasons, but as with most investments, they hope to make money on the trade or protect a position in the market.

Sometimes investors find options confusing because you can buy a "short" position in a stock by investing in a put option. It is important that you are clear on the differences between buying and selling options.

As I said earlier, buyers are under no obligation to do anything with their options. They can trade in the money option, exercise the option, or let the option expire worthless. Buyers pay a premium that is not refundable, but this premium is a fraction of the cost of the underlying security. This leverage makes options an attractive way to participate in the market without tying up a large amount of capital.

For example, many Internet stocks sell for more than $100 per share, even after a major correction. An investor would have to come up with $10,000 or more to buy 100 shares of the stock. An option on the same stock, however, could cost a fraction of that, depending on whether it was in the money. At a premium of $5 per share, the option buyer can participate in the stock's anticipated increases for a little over $500, counting commissions.

Here's how the numbers might look, assuming that you had $10,000 to invest:

Buying the stock:

Price per share	$100
Round lot purchase	$10,000

Buying an option:

Premium per share	$5
Strike price	$100
Round lot (20) purchase	$10,000

If the price of the stock goes up $10 per share, you could sell the shares for $11,000 and pocket a $1,000 profit (ignoring commissions).

Your options could rise to $6 per share. You could sell your options for a $2,000 profit, or exercise your options and buy the stock for $100 per share.

Like most things, though, it is not quite this simple. Twenty options will cost a lot more in commissions than one stock purchase of 100 shares.

Help File

The premium paid by option buyers and received by option sellers is not a down payment and is not refundable under any circumstances.

Reasons to Buy

There are some reasons to use options as a way to invest in Internet stocks:

➤ To benefit from the rise or fall in a stock's price without purchasing the shares outright

➤ To protect an existing stock position from a decline in market value

➤ To prepare to buy a stock below its market value

We have already seen how options let you participate in the rise or fall of a stock's price.

Many investors use options to protect an existing stock position. For example, if you bought XYZ stock at $100 per share and it had grown to $120 per share, you might want to protect that profit by buying a put at $120 per share. If the price of the stock drops, then your loss in the stock will be offset somewhat by the appreciation of the put option. You will still have the commissions to pay, but this is a way to protect your portfolio with options.

It is also possible to use options as a way to buy a stock below the market price. If you feel that a stock is going to experience a significant rise, but you didn't know when this was going to happen, you could buy a call at or near the market price, but with an expiration date months away. If the stock does rise during the option period, you can exercise the options and own the stock at a price lower than the market price.

Sellers

Options are not issued in the same way a corporation issues stock. Options are originated by the exchange they trade on, but the exchange acts as a facilitator of the process rather than as an owner.

Options must be bought and sold by investors. We have looked at buyers, so now let's examine the other side of the investment.

Option sellers are known as *writers*. Writers sell either calls or puts. Writers are obligated to fulfill the terms of the option if it is exercised. If you write a call option on 100 shares of XYZ with a strike price of $50 and the option is exercised, you are required to sell 100 shares of XYZ to the option owner at $50, regardless of the stock's market price. Likewise, writers of put options are required to sell the stock at the strike price, regardless of the market price of the stock.

Why would anyone choose to write options? In a word, premiums. Writers of options collect the premiums from the buyer (minus commissions and fees, of course).

Speak Up

An options **writer** is someone who sells options. Unlike the buyer, the writer is obligated to fulfill the terms of the option if it is exercised; options can be exercised at any point in the life of the option.

There are two ways to write options: covered and naked. This does not refer to your choice of attire while trading from your home. When you write covered call options, you own the stock. For example, if you own 100 shares of XYZ stock, you might want to increase your income against the stock. You could write a call option on the stock. You collect the premium, which increases your return from the stock.

The danger is that the option may be exercised, and you would lose the stock. It is unlikely that you would write an option with a strike price below your cost in the stock, however, so your risk is that you may not participate in stock's appreciation.

If the option is not exercised, you can repeat the process and collect another premium. Most covered call writers will buy an offsetting position to keep the stock in their portfolio if the price of the underlying stock makes the possibility of the option being exercised real. Once the option is exercised, the writer must fulfill the obligation and cannot buy an offsetting position.

Help File

Options can be exercised at any point in their life before or on the expiration date. When the owner of an option decides to exercise her option, a complicated system of randomly assigning the exercise to the writer is begun. This system means that writers do not know in advance whether the option they sold will be exercised until they are notified that it has been. Once exercised, an option's terms must be fulfilled.

Naked

The most dangerous way to trade options is to write a naked call. With a naked call, you are obligated to sell the stock at a specific price. This is called a naked call because you do not own the underlying stock. You collect the premium and if the option is not exercised, everything is okay.

However, you are in a dangerous position if the option is exercised. This means that you must go out a buy the stock on the open market, regardless of price. In a fast-moving market, highly volatile Internet stocks can move very fast, and you could find yourself having to buy a stock on the open market and selling it for much less than what you paid.

If you write a put option, you are agreeing to buy a stock at a certain price, regardless of the market price. Writing a put option is not as dangerous as writing a naked call because you know that your cost will be the strike price, minus whatever premium you collect. You might end up with a stock that you paid a lot more than the market price for.

Options Information

This overview of options was meant to get you thinking about the possibilities of using options to invest in Internet stocks. If you are interested in pursuing options as an investment strategy, though, you need to do a lot more homework.

The first thing you may want to consider is visiting the Web site of the Chicago Board Options Exchange (cboe.com). The CBOE offers a number of educational opportunities to better understand options and how you might use them. One of the best tools at this site is The Options Toolbox, which is a free download. The toolbox contains interactive educational material and an options calculator.

If you are going to invest in options, you need to understand and use an options calculator. Options calculators take the elements of an options premium we discussed and add two more elements: dividends and interest rates. Once these values are entered into the calculator, you are given some information about the theoretical price of the call or put option. The following figure shows the screen of the CBOE options calculator.

The CBOE options calculator gives you an idea of the theoretical price.

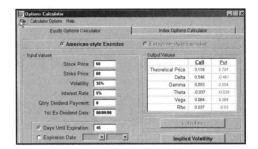

As you can see, the calculator gives you a tremendous amount of information to make informed decisions on options investments. I strongly suggest that you download this calculator and any accompanying educational material. It will give you a good idea of what goes into calculating options prices.

Overload

Options are a very acceptable way to invest in Internet stocks, but right now you may be thinking that this is way too complicated. Don't be discouraged. Options are not hard to understand, but they do have a language all their own that takes some getting used to. The more time you spend reading about options, the sooner this language will start to make sense.

Options are not any harder to understand than basic investing techniques; you just need to get comfortable with the language. That will come when you do your homework.

In addition to the CBOE Web site, you may want to check out some of the more detailed books on options: *Options As a Strategic Investment*, and *McMillan on Options*, both by Lawrence G. McMillan; and *Getting Started in Options*, by Michael C. Thomsett.

Using Options on Internet Stocks

Several options strategies work well with Internet stocks. As I mentioned, volatility is the great unknown factor in computing an option's true value.

Volatility and price fluctuation are the same thing, in this case. Volatility does not mean a stock will go up or down it means how much a stock will go up and down in a trading period.

As noted earlier, many Internet stocks have wide price swings in intraday trading. Because volatility is such an important part of the option price equation, Internet stocks can be very attractive and risky option purchases at the same time.

Here are some specific strategies you can use for Internet stocks, once you are more familiar with options.

Short-Term Speculating

Internet stocks lend themselves to short-term speculating because many are not yet mature enough to be considered for long-term investing.

Long-term investing is the most proven system of accumulating wealth in the stock market, but Internet stocks make it hard to know which ones are keepers and which ones will fade from view. In addition, even after major corrections, many are still too expensive from a valuation perspective to be considered for long-term investing.

Short-term speculating, on the other hand, is not particularly concerned with whether the company will be around in two years. Speculators are interested in taking a quick profit and moving on to the next deal.

Caution! Short-term speculating is not investing. This is no place for the beginner and is not the way to invest for your retirement or some other important financial goal. Having said all that, let's look at how you can use options to speculate in Internet stocks. One of the most favorable aspects of options is that they can be bought (or sold) for a fraction of the underlying stocks cost.

That's the good news. The bad news is they can be made worthless, and you can lose your entire investment. You might consider this day trading on a budget. One of the ways you can use options is to capitalize on intraday highs of a particularly volatile stock.

Double Click

You can find out whether an Internet stock you are interested in has options available by looking up the stock on the MSN MoneyCentral Web site. Once you have the stock up, you can look in the left column and see if "Options" is one of the headings. If it is, clicking on it will take you to the option quote.

For example, you can buy a call option on an Internet stock with a strike price that is at or close to the stock's previous intraday low. If the stock has wide swings during the trading day, you might take a profit within a few days after establishing a position. Set a profit target, and close out the position when you hit that goal. Settle for many reasonable profits, and keep your losses small—you may have the equivalent of a day trading strategy. This is a strategy that will require you to set limits on all your positions and to keep a close eye on the market.

Of course, if you had followed this strategy in the early part of April 2000, you probably would have seen all your call options expire worthless because of the decline in Internet stock prices.

Long-Term Speculation

If the short-term speculation is not your cup of tea, consider a longer-term strategy. One of the benefits of options is that you can control a position for a fairly long period of time without incurring any additional trading cost and while still keeping your initial investment low.

You may feel that a company is just about to explode, but you have no idea when that is going to occur. With options, you can control a position at a fraction of the cost of owning the stock outright. If you were wrong about the stock, you haven't tied up or lost a big chunk of your investment dollars.

Eight months, the length of a lot of options, is an eternity in Internet time. Taking a position with a call option in a stock gives you a long time to let the stock prove itself one way or the other.

Investors can profit if the underlying stock does take off by closing out a call option and pocketing the profits. On the other hand, you may decide that the stock is going to be a long-term hold; with the call option, you can buy the stock at the exercise price, which may be a lot lower than the market price.

Although they will probably cost more, LEAPS, the options with a life of almost three years, may be terrific vehicles for Internet stocks. That amount of time will certainly be enough to tell whether the company is going to be a winner.

Playing the Downside

People often forget that options let you participate in the downside of a stock. Puts give you the right to sell a stock at a certain price and may make a lot more sense than shorting the stock.

Volatility works both ways on an Internet stock's price. As quickly and as often as it goes up, the price can and will go down. Purchasing puts on Internet stocks can work for the same reason as buying calls does.

Ultimately, we want to find stocks that we can hold for a long period of time because that has been the best way to accumulate wealth in the past. However, there is no reason we can't profit on the weak and poorly conceived dot.coms that clutter the market. Goofy ideas that are poorly executed are prime candidates for buying puts, especially when options become available shortly after the company's IPO.

Employee Stock Options

Employee stock options have been the Holy Grail of the Internet community ever since the early employees of Microsoft and America Online, among others, became millionaires with their stock options.

Employee stock options were used for many years to attract top executives to companies. In recent years, many Internet startup companies have used them to attract and retain employees of all levels.

Basically, the plan is that young companies use stock options to give employees a sense of ownership in the enterprise and structure them so that it is advantageous for the employee to stay with the company for a minimum number of years. Without some incentive, it would be hard for companies to retain talented people who could offer their services to the highest bidder, which would probably be some more established company offering a huge pay raise.

The plans are almost as different as the companies offering them, but most have some similarities. An employee often must put in a minimum amount of time before being eligible, although this is often not the case for senior executives who get the options on the front end.

Then follows a vesting period before the employee can take full advantage of the options. Some plans offer an incentive up front but make the real benefits available down the road—say, three to five years later. This means that if the employee leaves before that time passes, he walks away from a large sum of money. This is the way companies hope to retain key employees for a period of time.

Double Click

There is nothing wrong with betting that a stock is overpriced and that you believe it will fall in the future. You are participating in market efficiency because there always must be a buyer and a seller to make the market work.

Margin Call

Employee stock options are only as good as the companies behind the stock. Be very careful about putting too much of your portfolio in a single stock, even if it is the company you work for.

How Good Are They?

After a major correction in April 2000, many dot.com employees were asking themselves that same question. Options, employee or otherwise, are only as good as the underlying stock. The feeding frenzy for Internet stocks in the late 1990s distorted the fact that many of the startups would not be around after five years.

Before deciding whether employee stock options are worth a lower salary and a commitment to the company, consider whether you think this company has a real future. Many of the dot.com millionaires in March 2000 were broke in April 2000. One company I am familiar lost 66 percent of its market value in a few weeks.

The senior officials of this company who were taking token salaries in lieu of stock options were probably wondering what hit them. If most of your net worth will be tied up in the stock of the company you work for, you are setting yourself up for a dangerous fall if something happens.

Diversify

One of the real dangers of tying up all your assets up in the company you work for is exactly what happened in April 2000. Diversification is the only way to protect yourself from market corrections that can wipe out big chunks of wealth. (Microsoft's Bill Gates reportedly lost $11.5 billion in the April 2000 correction.)

Whether you work for a dot.com or some Old Economy company, don't let stock in your employer occupy any more space in your portfolio than you would if you didn't work there. If things go from bad to worse you might lose your paycheck and any value in your company stock at the same time.

The Least You Need to Know

➤ Options can be another way to invest in Internet stocks.

➤ Stock options offer many advantages to the investor. They allow investors to participate in Internet stocks without paying the high prices these stocks carry.

➤ Do your homework before taking the plunge into options.

➤ Employee stock options can be a great way to participate in the growth of your employer, just be careful that you don't overload your portfolio with one stock.

Part 5

Blue Chips and Micro Chips

This part addresses the convergence or collision of blue chips and micro chips. Many of the more traditional companies are staking out their turf in cyberspace.

Some of these companies will make the transition and will be very successful. Others just won't get it and will find that they are slipping farther and farther behind.

In this part, we explore how some of those companies are making the switch and what investors can look for in evaluating investment opportunities.

If a pure Internet play frightens you, investing in more traditional companies that are using the Internet in innovative ways is the way to participate in the new economy without most of the stomachaches.

Chapter 21

New Tricks for Old Dogs

In This Chapter

➤ Bricks and clicks—can this marriage be saved?

➤ How mainstream corporate America woos the Internet

➤ Which companies stand to gain the most

➤ How to evaluate a traditional company's Internet strategy

I am reasonably sure that one of my prehistoric ancestors thought fire was a passing fad, and another that the wheel was the devil's handiwork.

Missed opportunities seem to have dogged my family for ages. A more recent relative had two pieces of Texas property in mind. He finally picked one that became a cotton farm of no consequence. The one he didn't pick has a name: Dallas.

Corporate America is slowly waking up to the fact that, like fire, the Internet is not a passing fad. Some of Wall Street's finest have wholeheartedly embraced the Web, while others have given it only token attention.

If a pure Internet investment is still too rich for your blood, consider some of the companies that are using the Internet to do business in ways that seemed impossible only a few years ago.

Mixed Marriages

Not too many years ago, corporate America's finest were predicting that this Internet thing was entertainment at best and a waste of time at worst.

About this same time, Internet cheerleaders were issuing visions of empty and decaying shopping centers because everyone was shopping online.

Sooner or later, the future becomes the present, and it usually is not what we thought it would be. There can be no doubt that the Internet has had a major impact on the world. Many things we thought we knew are now out of step.

You don't have to go too far back in history to see similar ways new technology has impacted our world. The telephone, the television, computers, and networks all changed the way we did business and conducted our lives.

Double Click

Toll-free calling is nothing more than a billing service that telephone carriers can offer. People used to think a 1–800-number meant running a special type of phone line to the office. Now, even residences can have toll-free numbers.

It seems to me that the introduction of toll-free telephone service created many of the same kind of opportunities that the Internet has allowed. For example, I know of a financial services company that did 90 percent of its business by mail and the rest by phone and walk-ins before offering toll-free access to its customers. Within a few years, the way the company did business changed: It did 90 percent of its business by telephone, and this company had more than a million clients. I have lost touch with the company, but I know that it is now offering services over the Internet.

Nothing But Net

Pure Internet companies have shown us totally new ways to relate to customers and to deliver products. Unfortunately, many also have shown us how to run through a bunch of cash and not have much to show for it.

Many investors find the pools of red ink and no prospects for much else too uncertain and thus have remained on the sidelines. It is clear that many Internet firms are moving toward profitability, but no clear timetable has been established.

I still believe that there are good investments in Internet stocks, and certainly some good speculative opportunities, but you have to be very careful where you step. Major market corrections have proved that Internet stocks are subject to wild swings and erratic performance.

Some winners will emerge in the near future out of the pure Internet crowd. In the meantime, many investors are looking for opportunities in existing businesses that are learning to use the Internet in innovative ways.

Clicks and Bricks

With all the hype about dot.coms, some of the better investment opportunities have gone largely unnoticed. They aren't going to give you 150 percent stock appreciation, but they will be around in 18 months—something many dot.coms won't achieve.

How companies have tried to integrate the Internet into their business models has run from laughable to inspired. Those companies with the most success are using the Internet as a way to reach customers and to deliver products and services.

The companies that don't get it have dumped Internet integration into their marketing departments or information services (computer) departments. This compartmentalization usually results in a half-hearted Web site and fails to take full advantage of the Internet's promise.

There has been and continues to be suspicion of the Internet as a marketing and sales tool. Managers of existing sales operations have feared that online sales will kill store sales, or at least pirate them away.

So how have the bricks and clicks worked out their differences? Let's find out.

Nothing New

Take a step back and look at the retailing scene. When you do, you'll realize that online selling is nothing new at all.

Companies such as Lands' End (ticker symbol: LE; landsend.com) have been doing online sales for years. The difference is that before the Internet hit, online meant telephone sales. The advent of toll-free calling (for the customer), credit cards to make purchases, and computers to track and process the sales created a whole new industry. There was a time when the media was all-abuzz about this crazy new way of retailing. Was it safe to give out your credit card number over the phone? How did you know whether you would receive your order, and would it be correct? Wouldn't the customer get a lot of busy signals around the holidays?

Sound familiar? All these concerns were swept aside, and hundreds of direct marketing companies sprang up. Existing retailers fought back with their own toll-free numbers and online ordering.

Virtual companies with no physical presence are nothing new, either. Back in the late 1980s, I ran a small (very small) virtual company. I had a vendor that took all the orders over a toll-free number and sent the orders to another vendor that processed them and then shipped the product. All I did was the marketing.

E-Tailing

The Internet sector that has generated much of the hype about online businesses is the e-tailing group. Led by Amazon.com, everybody and their brother have jumped into the Internet with both feet.

Unfortunately, many of these folks are finding the waters very shallow. The only thing keeping them afloat is the cash they received from their IPOs, which is disappearing at an alarming rate.

What happened to the promise of online retail sales? One of the reasons this sector has attracted so much money is that it seems like a can't miss business plan. Find a product, build a Web site, and rake in the money. However, each one of these components proved wrong.

Internet companies that wanted to operate like the small company I mentioned earlier had to license products or find wholesale connections. In either case, profit margins often become very thin.

In the early days, building a Web site meant hiring a couple of 20-year-olds and keeping them supplied with pizza. What e-tailers found out very quickly was that to be competitive, their Web sites had to be top notch. Instead of a few million, the price tag jumped into the tens of millions and those 20 somethings now make six-figure salaries.

The real shock for many Internet retailers was that customers didn't just flock to their Web site on their own. Marketing expenses skyrocketed.

Huge startup expenses and thin margins are not the formula for success in any economy. Even Amazon.com, with its huge customer base and tremendous advantage of being the first out, has not made a profit, although many believe that it will.

One of the things Amazon.com has done is to leverage its huge customer base by adding a wide assortment of other products and services. It remains to be seen whether this strategy will help the company turn the corner to profitability.

Help File

The promise of online retailing has not been fulfilled, yet it has come surprisingly close. Amazon.com is barely five years old and has no physical presence, yet it has achieved almost half of the sales of Barnes and Noble with more than 1,000 stores under a variety of names.

From Bricks to Clicks

Most large traditional retailers have joined the Internet world to one degree or another. It is too early to tell how much impact their Internet presence will have on the overall business model.

Two very notable entrants are K-Mart (ticker symbol: KM; bluelight.com) and Wal-Mart (ticker symbol: WMT; walmart.com). Both have jumped into the online world in a major way.

Wal-Mart has chosen to spin off its online store as a separate company. Some analysts believe that this will let the existing Wal-Mart management stay focused on the traditional retail business while giving the online store the freedom to make its own way.

The Bluelight.com folks seem to have an understanding of what makes the Internet work. They have forged partnerships with Yahoo! and offer free Internet access on its home page.

Wal-Mart's initial e-commerce effort was less than spectacular, and the company has also spun off Wal-Mart.com. The company has teamed up with America Online for a co-branded Internet service.

The strategy of spinning off the Internet business is not new and makes a lot of sense. Attracting the top Internet talent that it will take to make the e-commerce sites work will be a lot easier if the Web companies are not tied to the parents' salary schedules. A separate company can offer stock options and some of the other goodies that Internet workers have come to expect.

As an investor's note, it is unlikely that the Internet will have a material effect on these two retailing giants any time in the near future. However, the model of separating the retailer from the online store is one that other companies have tried in the past.

How You Do It

While there is a lot of fuss over e-tailing and bricks and clicks, some of the best Internet stories are being written by some unlikely characters.

One of the most unlikely characters to be a leading e-commerce trail blazer is W.W. Grainger (ticker symbol: GWW; grainger.com), a 72-year-old company that is a familiar name to purchasing managers of thousands of hard good products. Company's catalog contains 80,000 different products for the maintenance, repair, and operations (MRO) market and weighs in at more than 7 pounds. Its customers are all around the world, and the company maintains more than 530 physical stores and distribution centers.

Several years ago, the company began looking for a better way to do business and began an extensive Internet project. The project has led to four different Web sites that allow customers and suppliers from all over the world access to the full company product line, which exceeds 600,000 items. An extensive search function lets customers look for hard-to-find items. The company has positioned one of the Web sites to serve as a central platform for its own and other MRO products.

Grainger is leveraging its solid reputation and extensive industry contacts by using the Internet to reach customers in a way it never could before. If the strategy is successful, the company will see a broadened customer base and lower costs, although the initial money required for getting these Web sites up and running is extensive.

Double Click

Investors often overlook markets such as the MRO because they can't compete with triple-digit returns, yet these are basic bread-and-butter kinds of businesses that will be around for a long time.

As an investor's note, the Internet will not replace the company's stores, sales force, or even its catalogue in the near future. It will, however, drive more business to the company from existing customers and bring in new customers who will appreciate the automated services the company offers.

Look for companies that are taking advantage of the Internet's strengths and are integrating them into the current business model.

A Business Model

It is not surprising that some of the most successful companies to make the transition to the Internet economy are among those that have made the Web possible.

There are few better examples than Cisco Systems (ticker symbol: CSCO; cisco.com). The company makes networking systems—and after all, the Internet is a very big network.

Cisco sells to corporate customers and third-party vendors that build large networks. The company dominates its particular niche and has built an impressive company that ranks among the top five largest companies in the United States.

An astounding 80-plus percent of Cisco's business comes from the Internet, where customers can configure systems online with necessary hand holding kept to a minimum. Its Web site is very functional, with an almost Yahoo!-like feel to it. Scrolling down the product list is like reading a foreign language unless you are networking specialist.

As an investor's note, Cisco is one of the more expensive stocks on the market, but many investors feel that it's worth the money. Cisco is moving into new markets for telecommunications business, and it will be interesting to see whether the company can convert that business to an online model also.

A Partnership

One of the more interesting alliances that would not be possible without the Internet is that of General Motors (ticker symbol: GM; generalmotors.com), Ford (ticker symbol: F; ford.com), and DaimlerChrysler (ticker symbol: DCX; daimlerchrysler.com). The automakers have announced a plan to build an Internet-based portal that would link suppliers, partners, and dealers. The portal would be open to all automakers around the world and their suppliers. This *virtual marketplace* will be the largest of its kind.

This type of collaboration makes the tremendous costs of these virtual marketplaces more affordable. The portal will be a standalone business owned by the three automakers. It is expected that the enterprise will be given the go-ahead by government watchdogs because it will be a separate company open to any other automakers.

This type of cooperation would not be possible without the Internet, and as long as it doesn't become anticompetitive, it ultimately will benefit consumers and stockholders.

As an investor's note, the key item here is the notion of collaboration that benefits all the participants. This is a hallmark of the New Economy, and companies that employ partnerships and alliances stand a better chance of success than those that insist on standing alone.

Late Bloomer

Compaq Computer (ticker symbol: CPQ; compaq.com) was one of the early personal computer makers that knocked IBM off its perch as the market leader. Unfortunately, Compaq didn't keep going and eventually got run over by Dell and others.

Speak Up

Virtual marketplaces are Web sites where buyers and sellers can exchange information and work together more closely. The automakers' marketplace will allow vendors access to users and will create a competitive environment for pricing similar products.

The big problem was that Compaq was still selling through retail dealers and discount mail-order houses. Dell, which perfected the direct consumer sales model, and others were able to underprice Compaq. Much more tech-savvy consumers are buying computers, which are now commodities for the most part. These consumers realize that there is not much value in a brand if its prices are way out of line with the market. Most Windows-based computers are virtually identical once you take the cover off.

Compaq has seen the light, so company officials say, and is moving to substantially increase its direct-to-consumers and direct-to-business sales. Its Web site, which was a mess as late as 1999, has been cleaned up, and the company is finally getting in line with being online.

Investors would be wise to check out a company's Internet site before buying stock. If you had looked at Compaq's Web site in early 1999, you would have crossed that company off your evaluation list.

As an investor's note, it's hard to play catch-up in Internet time, but it is not impossible. Compaq is a good example of a company with a good product line that missed the boat the first time out. The Internet economy is not very forgiving, though, and most companies won't get a second chance—almost none will get a third chance.

Looking Beyond the Hype

The market has proven that its tolerance for fly-by-night dot.com wonders is not endless. These companies have been punished rather severely and will be punished again before it is all over.

This same lack of patience will extend to existing businesses that play fast and loose with the market. Investors want to see some real benefits to an Internet presence for existing businesses. Market corrections that clobbered the pure Internet plays are a wakeup call to all businesses that throwing money at dot.com ideas without any sense of where the company is going won't be tolerated.

The market has punished companies such as Compaq not because they have bad products, but because they have fallen behind their competitors in understanding and using the Internet's direct sales advantage. Dell has proven that a model of selling directly to the consumer model can and does work if it's done correctly. Dell has also proven that it can use the business-to-business model and retain most of the cost benefits of an Internet-based direct sales model.

In commodity businesses such as computers, the difference between "winners" and "what's their names" is cost control, marketing, and customer service. For most consumers, whether the computer they buy is a Dell, Compaq, or IBM is more a function of price and marketing than it is performance. Look for companies that translate lower costs achieved through Internet-based direct sales into market share.

The Least You Need to Know

➤ Bricks and clicks may have a distinct advantage over pure Internet plays if they know how to use the Internet's strengths.

➤ Mainstream corporate America is waking up to the fact that the Internet may not replace its business model, but will certainly shake it up.

➤ Companies that use the Internet to lower costs and expand market share stand the best chance for success.

Chapter 22

Mixed Marriages

> ## In This Chapter
>
> ➤ What happens when Internet and traditional companies merge
>
> ➤ How to look beyond the numbers
>
> ➤ What to look for in a successful merger
>
> ➤ What happens to the competitors after a merger

At some point in our lives, most of us realize that the world doesn't revolve around us. Some of us discover this much later in life than others, and I suspect that some people never figure this out. This change in world view causes us to look outward rather than inward. This may be happening to some of the leading Internet companies now realizing that there are benefits to partnering with Old Economy companies that can bring something to the marriage.

Unfortunately, the Internet to date has spent too much time contemplating its own navel and not enough time considering that when people give you money, they expect a return at some point in time. That may be changing, thanks to the merger between America Online and Time Warner. There will be other mergers and partnerships, and investors can learn a lot about what to look for by examining the AOL/Time Warner phenomenon.

Earth Shaking

On January 10, 2000, the world as we knew it changed. Everything we thought we knew about the world was turned upside down, and a brave new world emerged.

The press release announcing the merger of America Online and Time Warner (ticker symbol: TWX; timewarner.com) stopped just short of this declaration, but just barely. The marriage of the largest Internet company with the largest media company was all any of the pundits could talk about for days. All hype aside, this deal may be remembered in history as the beginning of a new era for the Internet and traditional media. Or, it may be remembered as another lost opportunity. Only time (pardon the pun) will tell.

Whatever you think about the merger (if you think about it at all), it is the best example of what happens when Old Economy media and New Economy distribution join forces.

It will be a while before the market knows for sure how wise or foolish this merger was. In the meantime, investors can use the merger as a laboratory to examine mergers of Old Economy companies with New Economy companies. What are the benefits? What are the pitfalls? What happens to the financial picture? How do you evaluate the surviving company? All these questions will be dealt with as we walk through the America Online/Time Warner merger. This will help us look at future similar mergers with a practiced eye.

Double Click

Mergers usually involve an exchange of stock in the old companies for stock in the new company. This is called a cashless merger. Other mergers may actually be buyouts in which one company buys the stock of another, usually at a premium to convince stockholders to sell their shares.

Big Deal

The joining of these two companies created a company worth $350 billion, with $40 billion in sales. The new company will be known as AOL Time Warner and will trade under the AOL ticker symbol.

Shareholders of the existing companies will receive shares in the new company, with AOL stockholders getting a share-for-share exchange. Time Warner shareholders will get 1.5 shares of the new company for their stock.

Even though Time Warner has five times the revenues and many times more assets than America Online, the new company will be known as AOL after the media shortens it. Steve Case, the America Online grand marshal, will head the new company, and AOL stockholders will control 55 percent of the new stock. The reality of this deal is that America Online swallowed Time Warner, a company five times its size.

That is not new; it happens all the time in corporate mergers. What is significant is that the surviving company will be known by the Internet half of the deal. Time Warner probably doesn't have the "person on the street" recognition that AOL does. However, when you start talking about the parts of Time Warner, such as CNN, *Time* magazine, Warner Bros. Studios, and so on, the company is at the top of anyone's recognition list.

What AOL Gets

America Online is the largest Internet service provider in the United States, with more than 20 million accounts and 50 percent of the market. That position is not likely to be lost anytime soon, but as more companies offer free Internet access (see the section "From Bricks to Clicks" on bluelight.com in the previous chapter), the pressure will build to reduce or eliminate fees.

America Online gains a ton of proprietary content ranging from news to music and movies. This content, along with its current offerings, may create a product so valuable that people will continue to pay even if free access is available elsewhere.

However, the asset that America Online covets the most is Time Warner's huge cable television system, the second largest in the country. That network can potentially connect 20 million households. This cable system can deliver America Online content through a *broadband* pipe that will work to dissolve the differences between televisions and computers. The cable system can also deliver local telephone service.

The marriage between America Online and Time Warner sets the stage for a whole new way of thinking about the Internet, television, and even telephones. Internet companies are starved for broadband delivery systems. Broadband service can be 100 times faster than regular dial-up connections, and you don't have to connect to the Internet every time you want to use it—you are always connected.

Speak Up

Broadband refers to the amount and speed of data that can be pushed through an Internet connection. If you think of your dial-up connection as a garden hose, then broadband is a fire hose. Broadband delivery is always "on," so you don't have to wait for a connection to the Internet.

If you have ever tried to watch video or download music files over a dial-up connection, you know how unsatisfactory it is. With broadband service like cable, you can see video just like on cable television and can hear music clearly and in real time. Imagine delivering Internet content at speeds that make it as exciting and as fast-paced as television, but with interactive capabilities. Advertisers will jump on broadband systems with both feet because of the rich media possibilities.

What Time Warner Gets

Time Warner is the premiere media company in the world, with content ranging from television stations to music, to movies, to publishing. The company also has a huge cable system capable of providing Internet access as well as television and telephone service. What Time Warner didn't have was a presence on the Internet of any significance. America Online dumps 20 million customers into its lap, along with new ways to make money from its existing content.

Time Warner is not alone among media giants that have failed to capitalize on their content over the Internet. Disney (ticker symbol: DIS; disney.com), Viacom (ticker symbol: VIA; viacom.com), and others have failed to convert their content to a dominant Internet presence. Many Internet veterans feel that the problem is that traditional media companies have not understood the difference between what they do and what the Internet does.

The Internet is built on the concept of interactivity, while traditional media is built on the concept of passive viewing (or reading). Any number of magazines have flopped on the Internet by simply putting their publishing products on the Web.

Even though Time Warner is a much bigger company than America Online, AOL is the 800-pound gorilla on the Web. It is the premiere Web property and, for the moment, is in a league by itself.

The New Company

AOL Time Warner will be the 1,600-pound gorilla on the Internet when the deal is finished toward the end of 2000. When you add Time Warner's content to the already content-rich America Online and marry the second largest cable system with the largest Internet customer base, the result may be the model for the future of media.

Television, news, music, and movies delivered to some customers at cable speeds will be hard to beat. Even if the rest of the market moves toward free Internet access, AOL Time Warner may be so content-rich that users will continue to pay for their services. Although some technical problems still need to be overcome, those will fall quickly as cable becomes the broadband delivery of choice.

Double Click

We will talk in more detail about broadband delivery in Chapter 24, "The Big Push," but understand now that it is the future of the Internet.

Imagine the ability to have several of these activities piped into your house at once. Your daughter is doing her homework on the Internet, your son is listening and watching a music video, your spouse is watching a classic movie, and you are updating your portfolio while watching the cable financial news station, CNNfn, in a window on your computer screen. Admittedly, this is not the way most families might want to spend quality time, but you always have the off button if it gets too much.

The point is that for one monthly fee, all this and a whole lot more is yours via AOL Time Warner. How will your local Internet service provider compete with that?

Potential Problems

This deal may sound like it was made in heaven, but potential problems could reach out and make this the biggest mess since New Coke. America Online and Time Warner executives will share management duties. Both are well-managed companies, so there is no doubt that the talent is there. The big question is whether they can work together to manage a company that *must* work together or lose all the advantages listed previously.

Management types are fond of talking about "corporate cultures" and how they mesh or repel. Time Warner has no real experience running businesses that are immediately accountable and accessible to its customers. America Online knows that if it screws something up, it will hear about it instantly and in large numbers. Can Time Warner executives deal with a customer base that has immediate access? America Online's management also has no experience running a company five times its size and in a totally different industry. Most of Time Warner is profitable, but that could change if the America Online managers fail to see the need for keeping its cable system running smoothly with regular maintenance, for example.

Margin Call

Pulling together two unrelated companies is a real management challenge. First, management must convince itself to forget about the former companies and to think about the best interest of the new company. Second, management must convince the rest of the employees. Neither is an easy task.

In addition, America Online has a "feel" about it that could be in danger if too much change is instituted. Admittedly, the Internet is about change and constantly giving your customers a fresh look. However, many who use the Web—and especially those who use America Online—are not really interested in the technical side of the Internet. They are there for ease of use and content. If AOL Time Warner upsets this balance, the 1,600-pound gorilla may become a chimp.

Investors should be aware of potential pitfalls in any merger between Old Economy and New Economy companies. This deal is too young to know whether it will work. The press release announcing the merger sounds like the combination is the greatest thing since sliced bread. On the other hand, critics have wondered if this hybrid will inherit the best or the worst characteristics of its parents.

Financial Concerns

Obviously, investors want to know how any merger will work financially. Will the resulting company be stronger or weaker than the sum of its parts?

Time Warner has been a profitable company for a long time, but *goodwill* charges from previous acquisitions have kept net income in the red zone until recently.

America Online has only recently become profitable, which is a significant feat by itself. The new company will have a huge goodwill bill of almost $150 billion to swallow, which should keep earnings depressed for years to come.

America Online shareholders will end up owning a company that bears almost no resemblance to the one they had owned. Time Warner brings a huge chunk of debt, something America Online has not had to deal with, to any real extent.

Speak Up

Goodwill is the difference between the book value of a company and the price paid for it by an acquiring company. Goodwill puts a value on the nonquantifiable assets such as customer relations. It must be depreciated over a period of years, which means every year the company incurs a noncash expense that reduces its net income.

America Online shareholders have also been used to some pretty spectacular growth numbers. Those days are over. The larger any company becomes, the harder it is to sustain the same percentage increases. Growing a company with a top line of $40 billion is a different story from growing a company with a $6 billion top line. The law of large numbers suggests that 10 percent of $40 billion is a lot harder to achieve than 10 percent of $6 billion.

Mergers of this type also bring out the tremendous cost savings that the two companies together will achieve. Somehow the lofty numbers suggested at the time of merger seldom materialize, at least not as swiftly as promised. Time Warner and America Online have said that the merger could result in more than $1 billion a year in savings. That's doubtful. However, over time it is possible that with a firm hand on expenses, some savings will drop to the bottom line. Still, cost savings don't create themselves. They must be actively pursued and conquered. Do not be surprised at layoffs within a year or two of the finalization of the merger.

Time Warner throws off more than $1.5 billion in free cash flow, while America Online pumps out more than $1 billion that can be used in a variety of ways. It may be very tempting to dump it into the Internet side of the business but that may or may not be the best use of the cash.

Investors need to understand that most of the time, the resulting company is very different from the two parents. This is going to be especially true for America Online shareholders. Is this the kind of company that you want to own? Does the resulting company still fill your financial goals?

Time Warner has paid dividends for years. What will be the policy of the new company? If current income is important to your financial needs, this is a question that you need answers to before you can make a buy or hold decision.

My guess—and it is a guess, at this point—is that AOL Time Warner will not be as wonderful or as horrible as some have said. If management can pull it off, however, AOL Time Warner will be a stock that you will want for a long-term investment.

Trouble in Paradise

How will you know if the merger is not working or is in trouble? Fortunately, this deal will be under a media microscope from the beginning. It is doubtful that much can go wrong without the whole world knowing about it very quickly.

If you are following less popular mergers, though, what trouble signs should you look for? Frequent turnover in the executive suite is often a clue that things are amiss. I am talking about senior-level staff leaving, especially in bunches. This can be a sign that corporate cultures are not meshing.

It is not unusual to see some turnover after a merger. Managers end up with duties that they didn't anticipate or working with people whom they don't understand. Sometimes projects will be announced with great fanfare, only to disappear from the news screen later. This can be a sign of conflicting priorities and goals within the merged executive staff. Disappointing financial results become routine when the new organization can't focus on core businesses and values.

The Bottom Line

Back to our earlier example, we don't know and won't know for some time what the bottom line on the AOL and Time Warner merger will be. It does, however, push us in some definite directions.

If America Online's primary motivation was getting access to Time Warner's cable system, as seems obvious, this is the first tangible and substantial vote for the broadband future that most Internet professionals and users dream about.

This move may be the push that other broadband and potential broadband partners need to accelerate the rollout of a variety of broadband services.

Double Click

Sometimes the market is waiting for a market leader to take the first step in a new direction. This first step is often seen as validating the new direction. The AOL and Time Warner merger has validated cable Internet access.

The Baby Bells and local telephone companies have been slowly rolling out their own broadband product, digital subscriber lines (DSL). DSL comes in several flavors, but basically it operates over existing telephone lines, which gives it a slight edge over cable. Cable may go *by* a house, but not *into* the house, while telephone lines are already in place. DSL offers many of the same benefits as cable, but it is not currently delivering movies and television stations the way cable does. It has some physical limitations, but it is competitively priced in many markets with cable Internet service.

The people who lay awake at night thinking about such things envision a day when homes will have a broadband connection to the Internet through a home network that will allow a variety of devices and users to access the Web. They talk about the post-PC era, when we won't need computing power to access the Internet. All the processing, software, and data will reside on the Internet, and we will simply access it from a variety of devices.

That is impractical with dial-up connections, but with universal broadband access, it does make sense. Imagine accessing the software you need to do a job along with your proprietary data mixed with information from the Internet. Access would be available from a variety of devices. If you travel, you could access your data via the Internet as easily as if you were in your office.

Mergers of content-and-delivery companies such as America Online and Time Warner put us a step closer to that reality. Once the tide begins running in a certain direction, it will be hard to stop. Where does that leave the other Internet players?

What Will the Competition Do?

How competitors react to a merger can create some real investing opportunities if you keep your eyes open. Pop quiz: Which Internet company is the next likely merger candidate?

Buzz. Time's up. Everyone who said Yahoo! go to the front of the class.

Yahoo! is the other premiere Internet company, and although it is not a content generator, it has a dominating presence on the Internet. Yahoo! has cut several deals with offline companies, most recently K-Mart's online alter ego: bluelight.com.

Yahoo! is still not in the content-generating business, but it is making inroads into the access market. Company officials have said that they are happy to be an aggregator, that is a collector of content as opposed to a producer of content, but the America Online, Time Warner merger has to be causing them to reconsider.

Many believe that media companies such as Disney will be pushing for a partner of Yahoo!'s caliber as a defensive measure. Other nonmedia candidates include AT&T and Microsoft, among others.

What Should Investors Do?

When you consider the higher financial standards being applied to Internet companies along with the mergers and partnerships being formed, you have to conclude that the Internet is preparing for a consolidation.

If that is the case, smaller and weaker companies will be running for cover or will be run over. Several major Internet companies are approaching profits, and although its net income may be negative for a while, AOL Time Warner is likely to be the kind of company the stock market can understand.

The days of investing in anything dot.com are rapidly coming to end. If you can invest in market-dominating companies, why would you invest in clotheshanger.com?

Make no mistake, I believe that there are still big winners to be found in Internet stocks. The Internet is not about to become dominated by two or three giant media companies. There will be plenty of room for smart, well-thought-out companies to pay handsome returns for investors willing to take some risks. What you can quit worrying about are the oddball ideas that have nothing but a dot.com to sell.

The Least You Need to Know

➤ Mergers that marry content, delivery, and customers should be very attractive in the future.

➤ Internet companies that isolate themselves face extinction in the coming consolidation.

➤ Successful mergers are characterized by a common-sense fit of products and services.

Chapter 23

What Price Glory?

In This Chapter

➤ Measuring the impact of an Internet strategy

➤ Where to look for signs of success

➤ An investment model that follows the money

The promise of technology has always been lower expenses and higher productivity. I suspect that the first typewriter salesman used these same benefits in his presentation.

Computers, the old room-size ones, were supposed to reduce payroll by eliminating jobs that the machines could do better and faster. In many cases, that happened, but at the same time the computer required more people to attend to it, so any payroll impact was lost.

Personal computers took computing power out of the techie's hands and distributed it throughout the organization. It took many years, but by the mid-1990s, the productivity increases that were hoped for really began to happen. Some would say that those productivity increases are what sustained the longest economic boom in history.

The Internet has promised many benefits, but for many organizations, it has delivered only cost overruns and frustrated management. How do you place a value on a company's entry into the world of cyber commerce?

Internet Strategy

It is important to get out on the table now the fact that no single Internet strategy will work for every company.

One of the problems investors face is the unrealistic expectation that the market places on Internet stocks. This is the same problem facing companies considering an Internet strategy.

Folks who live and breathe the Internet, but who don't get up from their computers very often to look at the real world, sell Internet strategies to senior management. Successful companies that throw out a working business model for an Internet strategy based on unrealistic assumptions are asking for trouble.

Some companies will find that they can migrate large parts of their sales functions to the Internet, while others will use the Internet as a way to stay in touch with customers or vendors. The same model doesn't work for everyone.

It will be helpful to go over the types of products and services that do well on the Internet and those that don't.

Understanding Commodities

A *commodity* in this usage refers to a product or service that is so well known to the customer that little or no help is required to complete the sale. Customers know what they want and shop for price, service, and so on.

Many consumers consider computers commodities. I currently own three computers. Counting computers that I have owned and ones supplied by employers, I have probably used 15 different systems. I am not an expert, but I do know what I need to get the job done. I bought my last two computers over the Internet. I can't imagine ever needing to go into a computer store again.

Speak Up

Commodities are common, everyday items, at least to most of the customers that purchase them. The term suggests that there is no significant difference in the same item made by different manufacturers.

Niche Markets

Cisco Systems builds and sells networking hardware for large corporate and government networks. The company has a large number of products and discrete components.

Most Cisco customers understand what the equipment does and how it fits together, so Cisco sells more than 80 percent of its merchandise on the Internet. The customers know what they need and how it all fits together. If they have questions, they can find technical help at the Cisco Web site.

Internet companies that can target a specific market have an advantage over firms with less focused customer bases. Cisco would have a hard time selling $15 billion worth of products if it had to explain to every customer what a router was and why it is important to a network.

You don't sell $15 billion worth of product a year without an effective sales function. Like power computer users, corporate networking executives don't need a lot of hand-holding to make purchase decisions. The Internet works for Cisco because its market is well versed in its products and functions.

Portals

Companies that use the Internet to reach suppliers and vendors are often successful in achieving their goals. In these cases, the goal is not to sell products, but to buy products.

This highlights another Internet strategy: lowering costs and tightening communication with the suppliers. Many manufacturers are using a system called "just-in-time delivery" to control costs. Just-in-time delivery of components ensures that the manufacturer doesn't fill warehouses with material waiting to be processed. This keeps inventory costs down and profits up.

For the just-in-time system to work, the manufacturer and supplier must be in constant communication. Problems with delivery can shut down a production line. Not only can the Internet facilitate this communication, but it also can help purchasing managers locate new or alternate suppliers.

World Vision

IBM ran a series of television ads touting its e-commerce products that made this point very well. In one commercial, a group of Japanese businessmen are sitting around a table. The man in charge is saying, via subtitles, that the cost of valves is too high. The poor subordinate who gave the price protests that there is only one supplier.

A younger man with a laptop computer says that he has a bid over the Internet at half the price. When asked who the vendor is, the young man replies, "Mitch Co."

The camera cuts to an American wearing a work shirt with the name Mitch stitched over the shirt pocket. He is looking at his computer and saying something in Japanese that probably translates to "how about that" or such. The music and his accent let you know that Mitch Co. is in Texas.

My work at About.com—through *Investing for Beginners* (beginnersinvest.about.com)—confirms the international reach of the Internet. The day I wrote this chapter, I had e-mails from people in Uganda and India wanting information about investing. Not a week goes by that I don't have some foreign inquiries.

Measuring the Impact

How do investors figure out whether an Internet strategy is going to work and what impact it will have on the company's financial picture?

Unfortunately, you can't always know. How a plan is executed can mean the difference between success and failure. Here are some broad signs to look for when evaluating a company's Internet strategy.

Margin Call

One of the most costly mistakes companies make in executing an Internet strategy is not planning how their target market will know about the site. Without a well-funded plan, companies might as well put up a billboard in the middle of nowhere and hope that a customer drives by.

Well-Defined Goals

What does the company hope to accomplish? When you read in company literature or in a press release that the company is going to double sales because of the Internet, be skeptical.

It may happen, but it almost certainly won't happen overnight. Plenty of Internet tales tell of sales going through the roof, but you never hear about the ones that flop.

How are customers, new as well as existing, going to find the Web site? More than a million sites exist on the Internet. How will this one stand out from the rest? If significant marketing resources aren't devoted to promoting the site, nothing much will happen.

The Internet is old enough that we should be past the naïve hopes and expectations of a few years ago. Unfortunately, too many executives still don't get it.

Realistic Costs

There is a good rule of thumb about the Internet: It costs more than you think—a lot more. Gone are the days when your neighbor's 15-year-old can slap together a Web site and off you go.

A company's Web site says a lot about the company. Throw up a cheesy site, and that's the impression the company will have. Top-quality Web sites cost money. The more function is built into the site, the more it is going to cost. If a company sells products off its Web site, the site also must be tied into accounting, distribution, inventory, and sales systems.

A top-quality e-commerce site will probably cost $25 million to $50 million. Small companies can get by on much less, but the size of company you will invest in can't afford to nickel-and-dime an e-commerce site.

Realistic Time Frame

It takes time to coordinate all the departments that need to be involved in a major Internet initiative. Leave a department out of the loop, and disaster strikes. Another IBM advertisement illustrates this point.

In this ad, a rather glum-looking man introduces himself to a support group by saying, "I'm Bob, and I'm stupid." The leader of the group admonishes him that there are no stupid people in this support group.

Bob tells the group that his company was going to spend millions on a Super Bowl ad. That ad was supposed to drive millions of people to the Web site. Someone asks what happened, and Bob says, "The Web site crashed, I forgot to tell the Web guys." The leader of the support group looks at Bob and says, "That *was* stupid, Bob."

A company that claims its Web site will be up in three months is probably nine months off, or its site will be so bad that it will drive business away.

In addition to getting the company all working in the same direction, the company needs a strategy to tie the target audience into the Web site. It is a little easier to convince vendors and suppliers to convert to a Web-based system (after all, they want to keep the business) than it is to convince customers. Customers need to see an immediate benefit to them, or they will be reluctant to change. Customers aren't stupid, and if a company assumes that they are, it is in for a rude awakening.

Help File

The bar for acceptable Web sites is constantly being raised. Yahoo! proves that you don't have to build the most graphically sophisticated site to have a winner, but the site does need to be easy to use and full of the content your customers want.

In the mid-1980s, I attended a week-long meeting at Columbia University with other folks in the financial services business to talk about where we were headed as an industry. One of the hot topics was debit cards. Several of the major retailers represented at the seminar were talking about issuing private-label debit cards through local banks. When customers used them to buy an item, the money would automatically be taken out of their account and deposited into the store's account.

Obviously, banks were charging for this service, and the retailers wanted to pass that fee on to the customer. However, it was pointed out that everyone but the customer benefited from this type of transaction, yet the customers were being asked to pay for it.

Follow the Money

Pure Internet plays are difficult for many investors to justify when valuations are through the roof. Even after the big correction in April 2000, many of the leading Internet companies were still in the stratosphere.

Investors hooked on huge Internet growth numbers may find things too tame in the rest of the market. However, money invested in a going business with an operating history that is older than the chicken salad in the back of your refrigerator may seem more secure. It may not be any more secure, but it will feel like it. The question investors need to address is whether a company will fall behind because it lacks an Internet strategy or because it has a poor Internet strategy.

Double Click

Cisco Systems was not an Internet company from the start. The company has transformed its sales operation into an Internet-based function that is extremely efficient. However, its main business is still making networking hardware.

Ample cases in fairly recent business history show companies that have missed a turn that everyone else made. Beginning in the 1950s and through the 1970s, many college graduates wanted to work for IBM, either as engineers or corporate officers.

IBM had a reputation for training the best managers of any company in the United States, and although IBM didn't lose many managers, other companies snapped up former IBM managers. During most of this time, IBM dominated the mainframe computer market. IBM dominated it so thoroughly that it was forced to change some of its sales and service practices because they were ruled anticompetitive.

Then came the turn. Personal computers led by Apple were all the rage. IBM jumped in with both feet but assumed that its reputation would carry it in this market. IBM left the door open, and in came Compaq Computers, followed by a host of others. When computers were sold out of computer stores, IBM did fine. However, the market became more price-sensitive. Mail-order businesses began undercutting retailers significantly, and it wasn't long before most of the computer stores and franchises disappeared.

The mail-order houses and superstores that sold several brands replaced them. Margins in both businesses were thinning. More competitors joined the market, which was growing quite rapidly. IBM, which probably could have dominated the personal computer market, as it once dominated the mainframe market, became just another manufacturer losing market share.

Fast-forward to the 1990s. A young man in Austin, Texas, named Michael Dell began selling his computers directly to consumers, bypassing retailers, wholesalers, and discounters. Dell established an Internet strategy that turned his company into the leading e-commerce site on the Internet. Dell was able to sell computers cheaply, but more importantly, it customized products to each customer's needs, if the customer wanted that customization.

IBM missed this opportunity, along with Compaq and most of the other computer manufacturers. IBM and Compaq now are shifting their sales strategy to the direct method pioneered by Dell.

Too little, too late? It's hard to say just yet, but rest assured it is unlikely that IBM will ever ascend to its lofty heights again. This doesn't mean that the company is a bad investment, and it does mean that IBM will have a hard time matching growth numbers with the Internet crowd. After all, I am not suggesting that you should or should not invest in IBM. That is a decision you must make on your own. I simply use this company as an ongoing example of how established companies can use the Internet to reinvent themselves.

You know that a company is serious about reforms when it takes actions that will hurt sales and growth in the short run. Wall Street is not forgiving of steps backward even if in the long run it will be to the company's benefit.

Double Click

When a company warns that a strategy is going to hurt sales or earnings in the short term, you can be fairly sure that the company is serious about the effort.

The conversion to direct sales had a negative effect on IBM's numbers in the first quarter of 2000 and will probably continue to cause problems for some time to come. As the company pulled out of retail relationships, their products were less available, and sales suffered.

When we talked about Internet strategies earlier in this chapter, I mentioned the problem of convincing customers to do their shopping on a Web site instead of in a favorite store. Even for a company with the size and reputation of IBM, that transition is not an easy one.

IBM finds itself in an interesting position. One business the company has been pushing heavily is its e-commerce expertise. The two television ads I referenced earlier in this chapter were both for the e-commerce solutions that IBM sells. The company's well-deserved reputation for service will work to its advantage in this market, and IBM will offer opportunities to sell network servers, a growing market for all computer manufacturers.

However, IBM's credibility as a provider of e-commerce hardware, software, and consulting services could suffer a severe blow if its own e-commerce site fails to sell its own computers.

I am writing part of this book on an IBM ThinkPad laptop computer. I bought this computer online, but not from IBM. At the time I was looking (late 1999), an online discounter had the computer on sale for $300 less than what it listed for on IBM's site. It is not unusual to see this price difference when a company relies on retailers to sell its products. The company doesn't want to undercut the retailers. It will be interesting to see how IBM updates its Web site to transition from a corporate site to an e-commerce site.

What Can You Learn?

Of what value is all this talk about IBM? Although IBM is not new to the Internet, it will be instructive to watch the transition from the IBM your dad knew to the IBM of Internet time.

I will be watching the company's Web site and how it evolves in the process. Don't assume that just because it is IBM, things will work or even will go smoothly. Fortunately, IBM is well followed by stock analysts, and ongoing reports will tell how the transition to direct sales is going.

Watching IBM struggle through this process will help you better understand the problems and opportunities that companies face as they convert from Old Economy to New Economy.

Second Best

Companies can pay a tough price for letting the market get too far ahead of them. IBM is a case in point, but this is not the only one.

Most of the full-service and discount stock brokerages looked on in amusement as E*Trade and other online brokers took the Internet by storm. One by one, however, those brokerages have fallen into the Internet camp.

One of the criteria you can use in evaluating how an Internet strategy will impact an existing company is to ask some of the same questions that you would ask when evaluating an Internet company. Does the Internet strategy give the company a distinct advantage over its competitors? Will the Internet strategy move it from the number 2 or number 3 company in its market segment to number 1?

Is the Internet strategy defensive or offensive? You will probably get more bang for your investment buck if you bet on an offensive strategy. A defensive strategy will likely just keep the company from falling further behind.

Does the Internet strategy play to the Internet's strengths of personalization and interaction? Here's a tip: If an e-commerce site directs you to call a customer representative to take your order, you are at a second-rate site.

Margin Call

If an Internet strategy does not give a company some kind of advantage, you should ask yourself why you want to buy that company's stock.

Understanding Opportunity

Investing in established companies that are moving to an Internet presence is a lot less nerve-wracking than chasing pure Internet stocks. You have an ongoing company with a history and some comfort in that.

Not every company that tries to move all or part of its operation from Old World economy to New World economy is going to succeed. This doesn't necessarily mean that the company is doomed to failure, but for companies that face strong competition from Internet, significant erosion in market share is a possibility.

Look for companies that can use the Internet to take a big step forward. Look for companies that use the strengths of the Internet. Look for companies that are willing to commit the necessary resources to making an Internet strategy work. Find these companies, and you will find some good investment opportunities.

The Least You Need to Know

➤ Some items and services work better on the Internet than others.

➤ An Internet strategy that is well thought out, with reasonable goals and time frames, is more likely to succeed.

➤ Some strategies are defensive and will likely take the company nowhere, while offensive strategies give the company a chance to move forward.

Part 6
Is That a Good Idea?

The next big opportunities for Internet investors lie in the changing nature of how we connect to the Web and what we do once we are connected.

There are several keys to this future. The first one is the notion of widely available and affordable high-speed access to the Internet. This connection is always on, so it is ready to use instantly.

Another key is the notion of Internet everywhere. This means that the Web is not confined to wired connections, but is available almost anywhere you can go with a single account.

In this part, we also look at how the Internet will change our lives in even more ways than it has already. You will be connected to a variety of networks all the time, and they will work together to provide you with the information you need.

Chapter 24

The Big Push

In This Chapter

➤ Why broadband delivery to the home and office is a golden opportunity

➤ How cable, wireless, and phone lines all offer possibilities

➤ What candidates are emerging as potential leaders

➤ Why the companies that set the standards will be worth billions

During the mid-1980s, I discovered that you could dial in to some databases to collect information. I hooked up with one on the West Coast that offered access to published articles from a large number of publications.

If you wanted to find what had been published on a certain topic, you could do a search, and the system would give you extracts of the story. You could then buy any of the stories you were interested in and download them.

It seems to me that I paid about $20 a month for the service, plus a per-minute charge of around a dollar. The stories I downloaded also came with a price tag. My modem operated at about a third of the speed of modems today, so this was not a cheap process.

However, it did get me hooked on online services. The more I used them, the faster I wanted the system to work. Internet users are in much the same situation. There is a real need for speed, and delivering speed to the home and office is a gold mine waiting to be worked.

This chapter will give you a glimpse into one part of the infrastructure that supports the Internet economy. The importance of high-speed delivery systems to the Internet cannot be overstated.

In this chapter and the following chapters, we are going to look at major developments in the Internet economy that represent opportunities for investment. Understanding these developments will sharpen your eye for investments in Internet stocks.

Speed Defined

The term used to describe high-speed Internet access in general is broadband, and it was mentioned earlier in Chapter 22, "Mixed Marriages." The term refers to the concept of bandwidth, which has to do with a lot of stuff I don't understand.

The analogy I used earlier in the book of a garden hose being similar to dial-up connections and a fire hose being broadband says it pretty clearly. They both deliver water, but the fire hose obviously delivers a whole lot more a whole lot quicker than the garden hose.

Computers can deliver information at a tremendous speed, thousands of times faster than the typical dial-up connection. This garden-hose connection is a bottleneck slowing down the Web.

If you really want a technical explanation of broadband, ask someone with a pocket protector full of pens. For this book, broadband is a generic term used to describe high-speed Internet access. It can take several forms and competing technologies boast superior service.

Speed Builds

I am not the typical Internet user. Between my online work, books, and other writing and editing projects, I am online three to five hours a day.

I work out of my home, and that makes me one of a growing group of folks choosing to either go it on their own or telecommute to a regular job. My Internet access is absolutely vital to my livelihood. The dial-up connection I use is adequate but inconvenient. Every time I need to be online, I have to dial in, and that means the phone is tied up. I live in a small town, however, so this is the only affordable service available at this point.

It would be nice to have more speed, but what I really want is to have the Internet always connected so that I don't have to dial in for a connection and so that other family members can access the Internet at the same time. All this is possible with one of the high-speed Internet access systems.

Several years ago, I worked for a company that had high-speed Internet access connected to the office network. If an employee wanted to look up something on the Internet, all that person had to do was launch a Web browser, and he was connected.

Easy access makes the Internet more accessible and increases usage. Of course, if employees are visiting porno sites or online gambling casinos, this might not be a good thing.

Speed Sells

Consumers aren't the only ones lusting for more speed. Web site builders and advertisers both want more universal speed. A common problem both groups face is structuring content for a variety of access speeds.

Most systems connected to the Internet are using a dial-up Internet service provider (ISP) and modems with speed of 33,000 to 56,000 bits per second (bps). Many of these systems also have a 15-inch monitor to view the Web.

Help File

It might be helpful to understand how pages are viewed on the Internet. Your browser and computer determine how a page looks. The two main browsers, Internet Explorer and Netscape, do not always display a page the same way. Web site designers write code that is delivered to your computer and interpreted by your browser. If your monitor is small, or if you do not have the correct font installed, the page will look different on your system. Most Web pages are designed these days to fit any size monitor, but the standard size is still considered to be 15 inches because this is the most common size in use.

Web designers and advertisers must work within these limitations so that content can be delivered with a minimum amount of waiting on the consumer's part. They also want the entire width of the site to fit on whatever size monitor the consumer is using.

Add to this the fact that the two major browsers (Netscape and Internet Explorer) don't always treat pages the same way, and you can see that Web designers have their hands full.

For example, a page of text, such as a story on CNN.com, probably doesn't need to change for a broadband connection. If you visit this news site often, you probably are familiar with the audio and video clips available for many of the stories.

Margin Call

Audio and especially video files are huge and require a long time to download at regular speeds. Broadband will make it possible to see video with the kind of clarity you have on your television.

A broadband connection would let CNN.com deliver that audio or video without any hesitation. The video clips on regular dial-up connections have to load, and even then they would be jerky and grainy. With broadband, the images will appear much like scenes from your television, clear and steady.

Designers of e-commerce sites would have an additional tool for broadband users. A company spokesperson or icon could appear on pages to introduce new products or demonstrate how they work. The user would see the presentation as "live" television.

At the higher ends of broadband, the distinction between your television and your Internet connection begins to blur. The major difference, for now, will be your Internet connection's interactive capability.

Advertising

As anxious as Web designers and content producers are for universal broadband access, advertisers are practically foaming at the mouth.

Advertisers are already plugged in to the interactive capabilities of the Internet. Many of the ads you see on Web sites have some interactive features. The advertiser wants you to click on the ad, which will send you to another page with more ad details.

You only need to turn on the television to see what advertisers have in mind for the Internet. Most ads, regardless of where they appear, want you to do something—call a number, visit a showroom, buy the product, or whatever.

The Options

There are at least four competing technologies for broadband delivery. It is unlikely in the near future that one technology will dominate the market and become the de facto standard.

Each of the technologies has strong points and weak points. Consumers in many localities often have only one technology to choose from, but that will be changing. Let's look at the four technologies. The list that follows ranks the technology by its market penetration, although this list will change rapidly as more companies offer the services.

➤ **Cable**—Up to 3 Mbps (megabits per second)

➤ **DSL**—Up to 1.5 Mbps

➤ **Satellite**—Up to 400 Kbps (kilobits per second)

➤ **Wireless cable**—Up to 1.5 Mbps

Cable

Internet access via cable is the most widely distributed technology at the time this book is being written. Cable Internet access operates over the same cable that brings television into your house. It requires a cable modem that is usually included as part of the monthly fee or that can be bought separately. Cable Internet access can run from $20 to $40 per month in addition to what you pay for cable television.

So far, this is the fastest service available, although advertised speeds and actual speeds vary a great deal. One of the current problems facing cable is that the service slows down when too many people are using the service at the same time.

Cable television reaches most of the U.S. population, whether the residents sign up for it or not, so most of the infrastructure is in place. However, if your cable service comes from a small local or regional vendor, it may be a while, if ever, before you have Internet access. There were about 1.8 million cable Internet subscribers at the end of 1999.

The technology needed at the cable office and the technical support that users require may be more than small systems can handle. Cable modems require a technician to install the system, and finding and training those people will not be easy in small markets.

The cable Internet connection is always on, which means that as soon as you launch your Web browser or e-mail program, you are connected. There is no dial-up or passwords to deal with and forget. This "always on" feature presents some drawbacks, however. The connections have a permanent electronic address on the Internet, which means that it is theoretically possible for a hacker to enter your system without your permission. Software called a firewall can protect your system.

Another problem involves people who travel and want access to their Internet accounts. Unlike with dial-up connections, road warriors can't easily access cable Internet accounts.

Margin Call

Without going into a lot of technical terms (which I wouldn't understand), it is important to understand that an "always on" Internet connection is a fixed target with a permanent address on the Internet. When you use a dial-up connection, you are assigned a different address every time you connect.

DSL

DSL, which stands for digital subscriber line, is the most likely challenger to cable for broadband Internet access. A handful of different DSL services actually exists, and each service has its own different twist.

Some are faster than others, but they all have most of the same qualities and drawbacks. DSL service is based on existing telephone wires, which makes it potentially easier to roll out than cable service.

The basic service allows you to access the Internet at speeds of 256 Kbps and up. You will need a DSL modem, but your regular telephone line will do. Without the need for a technician to set up DSL, users can install many of these systems themselves.

With DSL, you get the same convenience and concerns as cable's "always on" technology, and you can use your telephone and surf the Web at the same time. In some markets, you can buy as much bandwidth (speed) as you need, with tiered pricing for faster speeds.

Because of the distance implications from the phone company's central office, DSL is better suited to more densely populated urban areas. Local telephone companies are the usual source of DSL service, although some third-party vendors lease the service from the phone companies and then resell it. Other companies are stringing their own lines. DSL requires you to be within a certain distance of the phone company's switching office, however, so the farther away you are, the slower the service.

The phone companies have been slow to offer DSL service to residential customers, preferring the more lucrative commercial accounts. However, many believe that the merger of America Online and Time Warner will light a fire under the telecoms to broaden the service or let cable walk away with big chunks of the market.

Satellite

The two main players in the broadband game are cable and DSL, but some minor players are making waves as well. One of the nosiest—at least, in terms of how "visionaries" see the Internet growing—is satellite service.

Help File

Any broadband service that requires laying new wires will be at a distinct disadvantage over cable and DSL. Wireless alternatives avoid this type of capital outlay.

The current state-of-the-art connection is based on a combination of satellite and dial-up connections. Basically, you are connected to the Internet via a regular dial-up account, but this is used only for uploading or sending requests to the Internet. When a Web site is found, it is sent to you via satellite at much faster speeds than a dial-up connection could provide. Most Internet users would find this system workable because your tiny requests for information take the slowest route, while the return takes the fastest route.

The real promise of satellite is two-way communication between the computer and the satellite. Several companies are flirting with this technology, and it is worth keeping an eye on.

Wireless Cable

Wireless cable delivers the same speed of service as cable, but it operates more like a cellular phone system. The provider builds a transmission tower on a hill or tall building. Every house and office within line of sight of the tower has access to the high-speed service. An antenna is installed at the user's home facing the tower.

Although there are several players in this market, wireless cable has not caught on with the public.

The Players

There are only two real options for investors at this point: cable and DSL. Although DSL badly trails cable, it has the potential to catch up in a hurry.

Two major players dominate the cable market: Excite@Home (ticker symbol: ATHM; home.net) and Time Warner's Road Runner cable service. Excite@Home has about 61 percent of the 1.8 million cable subscribers. AT&T owns parts of both systems, which makes it a significant player as well.

The equipment manufacturers include the well-known names Motorola (ticker symbol: MOT; Motorola.com), 3Com (ticker symbol: COMS; 3com.com), and Cisco Systems. None of these strikes me as leaping ahead of the pack unless one comes out with a way to stabilize bandwidth with multiple users.

The DSL market is dominated by the telcoms such as SBC (ticker symbol: SBC; sbc.com); U.S. West (ticker symbol: USW or URL:), being bought by Quest (ticker symbol: Q; uswest.com); Bell Atlantic (ticker symbol: BEL; bell-atl.com); and BellSouth (ticker symbol: BLS; bellsouth.com). SBC is the clear leader, with U.S. West next. The two Bells are far back of these leaders.

Some of the smaller players in the DSL market are worth looking at as well. They include Covad (ticker symbol: COVD; covad.com), Northpoint (ticker symbol: NPNT; northpointcom.com), and RhythmsNet (ticker symbol: RTHM; rhythms.net). Some of these firms lease the service and resell it to customers, while others, such as Convad, are stringing their own fiber-optic lines.

On the equipment side, we find Cisco Systems again, along with Lucent (ticker symbol: LU; lucent.com), 3Com, and Nortel (ticker symbol: NT; Nortel.com). Some of the smaller vendors worth a look include Nokia (ticker symbol: NOK; nokia.com), Paradyne (ticker symbol: PDYN; paradyne.com), Netopia (ticker symbol: NTPA; netopia.com), Copper Mountain (ticker symbol: CMTN; coppermountian.com), Efficient Networks (ticker symbol: EFNT; efficient.com), and Westell (ticker symbol: WSTL; westell.com).

Place Your Bets

It is hard to guess where the market for broadband is going in terms of delivery systems. Forrester Research estimates that broadband services will be an almost $8.8-billion industry by 2003. The 1999 totals were only $740 million, so there is a lot of money to be made.

Right now, the nod has to go to cable Internet services. Many observers believe that the merger of America Online and Time Warner establishes cable as the de facto standard. Cable certainly has the edge, and with AOL behind the technology, you can be sure that it will get a good push. However, I think that it is way too early to count DSL out. SBC is a powerhouse, and once it gets things rolling, this company will be a tough competitor.

Double Click

Expect to see some consolidation in the cable television industry as providers jockey to lock up market share for cable Internet service.

Unfortunately, the big companies are probably going to dominate this market segment because of the tremendous up-front costs. This means that this market will not likely explode unless some of the smaller companies take off.

Investors interested in this market should keep an eye on the Internet stock Web sites I have mentioned throughout this book for news, especially about the smaller companies.

Some Issues

Some potential regulatory and legal problems arise as cable and DSL service becomes more widespread. Independent Internet ISPs are very concerned that they will be cut out of the market.

These ISPs have asked—and, in some cases, demanded—that the cable and DSL providers grant them access to the delivery system. It is unclear at this point where all the legal and regulatory issues are heading, but the demand for these services will ensure that they are delivered in some form.

The Standard

Normally, investors look for the market leader that will set the standard for every other company to follow. In the case of broadband Internet access, there are likely to be several leaders in each of the competing technologies, at least for the short term.

Eventually, it seems likely that the standards will revolve around how the consumer views the Internet rather than what technology was used to deliver the content. Personal digital assistants (PDA) and subnotebook computers require a different delivery than a system with a 21-inch monitor. If the Internet industry can agree on a standard for delivery, you can expect a boom in Internet devices.

Broadband delivery to Internet devices will be just as important as broadband delivery to your desktop. The company or companies that develop this standard will reap tremendous rewards. Earlier in the book, I cited Qualcomm as an example of what can happen to a company when its technology becomes the standard.

Yet standards are two-edged swords. On one hand, they can stifle competition and create monopolies. This is the sword hanging over Microsoft. On the other hand, standards allow a wide variety of software to be developed that can be guaranteed to run on anyone's machine (unless you own an Apple).

For all the nasty things you can say about Microsoft and its Windows operating system (and you can say plenty), the company has provided a standard for software and hardware companies to work from. If we still had the choice of 8 or 10 operating systems, the computing public would not have near the choices of software that we have today.

A Future Vision

The current buzz among folks who think about the future a lot circulates around the concept of "Internet everywhere." This concept suggests that we would be connected to the Internet permanently, accessing it when and where we wanted.

Picture this invisible blanket covering the Earth. The blanket consists of the Internet and its ability to follow you, no matter where you go. You will be able to interact with the Internet through a variety of devices, including gadgets we haven't even thought of and many that are commonplace today but that will have added functionality in the future.

This "Internet everywhere" has replaced the telephone, television, and personal computers with a variety of devices that draw their functionality from the Internet rather than from internal resources, like processors. To some people this sounds like Utopia, while to others it sounds like hell. Many technological issues need to be addressed, but not as many as you might think. Equally important are social issues and concerns about privacy.

The remaining four chapters of this book talk about a future in which the Internet plays a more prominent role in our daily lives. It may seem like pie in the sky, but so did the notion of television, computers, and many other technologies that we now take for granted.

The Least You Need to Know

➤ Broadband delivery is a market on the verge of explosion.

➤ There is no clear technological leader now for broadband delivery, although there are contenders such as satellite that may surprise everyone.

➤ Cable and DSL will be the most popular technologies in the near future.

Chapter 25

Interactive Multimedia Toilet Cleaner Commercials

In This Chapter

➤ Why the ads won't go away

➤ What would happen if you only saw ads about items that interested you

➤ Privacy issues that could be an obstacle

➤ Targeting the market

The interactive nature of the Internet makes it potentially the most exciting and lucrative advertising vehicle ever invented. For the first time, customers can interact immediately with the advertiser.

New technology makes it possible to specifically tailor advertising to individual customers. This wide open market is ripe for investing in Internet advertising agencies and the many other companies involved in bringing marketing to the Internet.

Investing at this root level in the Internet economy may produce long-term gains. Read on and find out what you should be looking for.

In the Beginning

The Internet was born as a forum for exchanging ideas and information in a noncommercial environment. The early proponents wanted to keep it that way, and while they looked down their elitist noses at the great masses of the unwashed, they couldn't keep it to themselves.

The development of the World Wide Web gave the rest of us a chance to use the Internet—and the rest, as they say, is history.

I can remember reading about the Internet during the last century and thinking, "This sounds great, but how is anyone going to make any money with it?" So much for my foresight. Although the Internet has developed in many ways like the direct marketing industry, it has grown on its own time schedule, which is much faster than anything else that has caught the public's eye. When something catches the public's eye like the Internet has, it won't be long before businesses are finding ways to make money from it.

The Early Years

It was very common to hear all sorts of analogies about the Internet in the early days. Analogies help us understand things that we really don't understand by comparing them to things that we do understand.

Among the early analogies were these:

➤ It's like publishing a magazine—you fill up the space in between the ads with stories that will attract readers who will see the ads.

➤ It's like television—you fill up the space in between ads with entertainment that will attract viewers who will see the ads.

➤ It's like direct marketing—you find a niche market and then fill up the space in between ads with stuff to sell to the niche market.

Obviously, all these analogies had a common thread, and that was using the Internet to attract viewers who would see ads. Advertisers would pay for the exposure. The other obvious thing about these analogies is that they were all wrong. While there are elements of truth to each one, none describes the Internet with a great deal of accuracy.

One of the problems with analogies is that if you carry them too far, they often fall apart. Unfortunately, too many businesses accepted them at face value and jumped into the Internet without really understanding what they were doing.

The Here and Now

The painful correction that began in April 2000 had the effect of a cold shower for many of the overheated Internet investors running on the notion that a "buy any-thing dot.com" strategy couldn't lose.

It had the same effect on a number of companies that were preparing an initial public offering (IPO) before the correction. Many pulled back, realizing that investors are starting to demand a reasonable business plan that considers profits a worthy goal in a reasonable amount of time.

In this chapter, we focus primarily on Internet companies that use advertising sales as their primary or sole means of generating revenue. It might be helpful to have a quick primer on Internet advertising so that you can better understand how it works.

An Advertising Primer

If you are familiar with the way traditional advertising is sold, you will find Internet advertising easy to grasp. Here are the basics.

Internet advertising is sold primarily on the basis of cost per thousand (CPM) impressions. An impression (a term held over from print media) is a page view, or every time a visitor views the page, whether he sees the ad or not.

Right away you can see that position is important and can affect the cost of the ad. Ads at the top of the page, which is what you see first, cost more than ads farther down on the page. These may not even be visible unless the visitor scrolls down the page.

The more viewers a site can deliver to an advertiser, the more that site can charge for the ads. Popular sites charge from $30 to $80 CPM for their ads. The big issue is counting the page views or impressions.

For a variety of reasons too boring to reiterate, impressions, page views, and other activities captured by tracking software don't catch all the looks at a particular page. This information is supplemented with additional data gathered by surveys and statistics.

There is a continual dialogue between advertisers and Web sites to get at a fair way to count visitors. One of the ways sites can capture visitors' data is to use *cookies*. Cookies identify users by some magic that allows the site to place on the computer a code that identifies the computer.

Every time that computer requests a page from the site, the site checks to see whether a familiar cookie is present. This also is the way sites "remember" who you are when you register with them.

Help File

The Internet advertising industry is still going through some growing pains. Traditional media has worked out most of the issues between advertisers and publications or electronic media. The industry is working to come to an agreed-upon formula for calculating advertising revenue.

Margin Call

Cookies are small files exchanged with Web browser that contain information helpful to Web sites. If you don't want to accept cookies, you can change the settings on your browser, although some sites won't let you in if cookies are turned off. Both Internet Explorer and Netscape Navigator allow you to change the settings.

Activity on a site is captured in a log on the server where the site is located. This log captures a tremendous amount of data (and some of it very personal) that specialized software can analyze. Advertisers and Web sites have experimented with a variety of payment methods, including paying only for times that a visitor clicks on the ad and is sent to the advertiser's site.

Test, Test, Test

Not surprisingly, several online advertising agencies help companies design, place, and test their Internet ads. These companies track ad performance and modify campaigns as they go to reflect better information about which ads work and which don't. One of the tools these companies use is a profile of visitors. Profiles are built using information from the cookies about what pages were visited, what action was taken, and so on.

Although this may sound sinister, there is nothing new about profiling in the advertising community—it has been going on for years. The purpose of profiling is to put ads in front of you that you may actually use.

The A.C. Neilsen Company has been doing the same for years with television viewers, although participation in their surveys and studies is voluntary.

Direct marketers have used profiles for years. In its simplest form, a marketer may buy the subscription list from a certain magazine and mail ads for products that it thinks readers of this magazine would buy. For example, a company that makes outdoor menswear might buy the subscription list of a hunting magazine, thinking that hunters are more likely to buy outdoor wear than readers of a chess magazine.

Double Click

Developing profiles of existing and potential customers is an important part of marketing. Successful profiling reduces advertising costs by eliminating ads directed at people unlikely to buy the product or service.

Most profiling efforts are much more sophisticated, though. Marketing researchers might interview buyers of certain products and then compare the results. They may find that people who have bought product X may also be inclined to buy product Y.

For example, people who invest in conservative mutual funds may also be interested in other conservative investments. However, you may also find that they (as a group) would also be interested in an umbrella insurance policy for their home, which affords more protection that a plain homeowner's policy.

Market researchers, both traditional and on the Internet, know a whole lot more about you than you think. Most of the information they gather comes either from public records (motor vehicle records, the Census, and so on) or from information that you voluntarily submit every time you fill out a registration form for a product or answer a questionnaire.

Most of this information is not about you personally, but about your demographic signature. For example, if you are married with children and live in your own home, you belong to a broad group that is going to be marketed to by advertisers with products that this group is known to buy.

So What?

Good question. What does all of this have to do with investing in Internet stocks? Actually, it is quite important because many companies are betting most of their future on advertising revenues.

The whole issue of profiling, while basically nothing new, takes on a new dimension when is becomes very personal in a way that frightens some people. Several online advertising agencies, including DoubleClick (ticker symbol: DCLK; doubleclick. net) most recently, have taken a lot of heat about the privacy issues profiling raises.

The difference in online profiling is that it can track you as an individual, as opposed to a group. (Actually, it tracks your computer's browser. If you use a different computer, Web sites will not recognize you.)

If advertisers can't be specific about the market they want to buy, this may erode confidence in the Internet as an advertising medium. Advertisers know the least about the Internet's effectiveness just by virtue of how new it is.

Internet advertising hit $4.62 billion in 1999, according to one report. That's not chump change, but it's a drop in the bucket compared to more traditional venues such as television and magazines. When you split $4.62 billion among the many Web sites, there is not a lot to go around. However, these numbers are expected to grow substantially in the coming years. The operative word here is *expected*. A general economic downturn could force advertisers to curtail all but the proven vehicles. This could spell disaster for sites that rely on advertising dollars for all or most of their revenue.

Help File

Internet advertising is expected to double every year. Like most statistics and projections about the Internet, this one is probably overstated in the long run, but it could be fairly accurate in the short run.

One group of Internet observers believes that an advertising-only strategy is not sustainable for the long run. Web sites that are based on advertising revenue are content or services providers. Their mission is to drive as much traffic to the site as possible. The more traffic, the more advertising revenue is generated for the site.

What the sites have to do to generate traffic and develop content can be very expensive. Many of the sites resort to traditional advertising themselves in order to generate advertising dollars. Is this getting confusing? Some of the large Internet sites can command huge advertising CPMs because of the traffic they generate. Most sites, however, are finding that advertising revenue alone is not going to get them where they want to be financially.

The strategy has been to develop traffic by forming alliances and partnerships with other sites through referral programs and other devices. Even the powerhouse Yahoo! which commands the highest page view of any site, has diversified its income streams away from pure advertising. In the past 12 months, Yahoo! rang up sales of $713 million; however, about one-third of that total came from nonadvertising sources, primarily facilitating and referral fees.

Here to Stay

Even though I have raised questions about the efficacy of an advertising-based revenue strategy, I do not believe that this strategy is going away any time soon. These strategies do provide major revenue streams, and those should get bigger.

Advertising is an ingrained part of our culture. We may not like it, but we expect it and tolerate it. In some cases, we learn as much from advertisements as we do from other information sources. We expect free content for the most part and understand that it is advertising that is paying the bills.

How It Is Changing

In the goofy world of the Internet, companies are trying all sorts of gimmicks to get people to look at ads.

One company is paying people to surf the Web. To sign up, you must fill out a detailed questionnaire about yourself and put up with ads on your screen. If you turn off the ad, which you can do, you don't get paid.

For about $12 a month, you can paint a bull's eye on your back for every advertiser that thinks it can sell you something to shoot at. Free e-mail, free Internet access, and free DSL service are just some of the gimmicks being offered to get ads in front of people. Some observers think that the notion of free services for ad exposure is potentially an explosive option.

Growing Opportunity

The Internet has pretty well saturated the top part of our economy in terms of income and education. Maintaining its growth as the market has less disposable income is going to be a problem.

This is becoming a *real* problem. The federal government is even getting into the act, as are a number of private nonprofit groups. All are exploring ways to extend the benefits of the Internet to lower-income families.

This *digital divide,* as it is being called, threatens to keep lower-income families locked in jobs and careers with fewer opportunities than people with access to better education.

Although prices have come down and continue to drop, many families can't afford even a bare-bones computer and $20 a month for Internet access.

Advertising-sponsored computers and Internet access may be an answer for these folks. However, let's not nominate advertisers for sainthood just yet. If they can't see tangible results from these efforts, they will drop the ads.

The New Ads

Most of us probably would agree that we are all bombarded with too many advertisements. The problem is that most advertisements are broadcasts—that is, they are delivered indiscriminately by almost every medium.

Speak Up

The **digital divide** is a separation of the population into those who have access to technology and those who don't. It threatens to further divide our country at a time when we should be pulling together.

Two new developments in the online advertising world have implications for investors. The first is how online advertising agencies are working hard to make Internet adverting more effective. These companies are worth watching as potential investments, and it is also worth noting how online companies are using this technology to shore up advertising-based revenues.

The second development is how online advertising is changing as broadband Internet access becomes more common. I talked about this some in the last chapter, but it is worth putting into a specific advertising context. Marry these two technologies, and online advertising sales could skyrocket.

A Gold Mine

Earlier in this chapter, I talked about profiling as a way to target ads at consumers that may actually be interested in the product. Although these techniques are fairly sophisticated in the offline world, they cannot be implemented as quickly as in the online world.

We all agreed earlier (I saw you nod your head) that we were exposed to too many ads. But what if the only ads you were exposed to were for products and services that interested you?

I will confess that I have "techno lust." I am interested in computers and electronic gadgets. When the catalogs come from discount computer operations, I read them cover to cover. If most of the ads that I saw online were for these items, I would probably look at many of them. If every site I visited on the Web featured ads for products and services that interested me, I would be more likely to buy than if I was confronted with ads for just anything.

And what if you were visiting the same site that I was at the same time, but you saw only ads for products and services that interested *you?* That would be, as they say, way cool or something like that.

Brave New World

The ability to *serve* ads to individuals on the Web will become a widespread reality in the not-too-distant future. Software using cookies will track you through the Web, building information on what you like and don't like based on the pages you visit and the ads you click on.

Combine this with information that I may voluntarily offer, and advertisers would have the information they need to target specific ads at me. When I visit a site that is participating in the program, I am tagged with a cookie that follows me around the Web.

If I visit another site that is also participating in the program, the cookie will tell the ad server what kind of ads I am presented. I am oversimplifying the process that is actually very complicated, but the pay-off is significant.

Advertisers don't like to pay for people who will never be customers, but they are willing to pay handsomely for prime candidates. A key metric for advertisers is keeping the cost of acquiring a customer to a minimum. A system very much like I have just described would go a long way to helping advertisers precisely target customers.

Help File

Despite appearances to the contrary, thoughtful and effective advertisers are not interested in spraying their message over the whole population. Targeted marketing is much more effective and cost efficient.

Double Click

Serving ads refers to the ability of the site's network to deliver ads to a specific page when it is requested.

I talked earlier in this chapter about privacy issues, and this certainly raises some. Although this system is not much more intrusive than your state government selling your driver's license information (most do), it still raises some legitimate questions. Ultimately, it may have to be a completely voluntary system to avoid the toughest privacy issues. In any event, some form of this idea will make real inroads in the on-line advertising business.

One of the companies to watch is AvenueA (ticker symbol: AVEA; avenuea.com), which is among the leaders in rolling out this kind of system.

Multimedia Mania

In the last chapter, I talked about the wider availability of broadband Internet access and how this was changing the face and function of the Web. I made the point that advertisers were among the most anxious groups awaiting wider acceptance.

The reasons are obvious. Advertisers, especially those with television roots, have creative departments accustomed to producing rich multimedia-type advertising. The Web is currently limited to what it can display by some physical constraints and the extra time it takes for media-rich ads to download.

Many consumers may not be aware that their computer display is actually a fairly low-resolution device. One of the problems that certain e-tailers and advertisers have had to deal with is this low resolution, which is often not flattering to products and may not be the same color on two different systems.

Most monitors will reproduce a palette of "Web-safe" colors, but these are spot colors or single colors. When you combine the spectrum of colors to produce a full-color image on the Web, you never know quite what it will look like on a user's monitor.

I am not sure if broadband will help this problem, but it will give a boost to what may be the sleeper system—Web TV. This concept, which hasn't taken off like the proponents hoped, uses a set-top box to connect your television with the Internet. Most systems feature a wireless keyboard. Web TV has some major drawbacks, however, one of which is that it does not display some sites like they were designed. The system also has limited capabilities in terms of what you can do. Web TV's main problem may be that it is just ahead of its time.

Broadband potentially has a lot to offer Web TV. For one thing, it can deliver content that is more compatible with the television set's features.

For advertisers, broadband to Web TV or regular computers has the promise of serving up more than bouncing squirrels or other stupid graphics that clutter up my screen now.

Double Click

Remember that the current leading form of broadband delivery is the same cable that is already connected to your television. You can see why this combination has possibilities.

When combined with the system of delivering ads the consumer wants to see, you have some exciting possibilities. For example, I am interested in wireless networks for home office use. I believe that I would click on an ad for a wireless system that featured a spokesperson describing the product, talking about system requirements, and answering frequently asked questions. Another click, and a technician is showing me how to install the system and software.

Rather than show still photographs, you could see a trailer advertising the latest *Star Wars* movie or a short video on that resort on Pango Pango that you've been thinking about as a vacation destination.

What Investors Need to Know

There are two reasons why you need to keep an eye on the Internet advertising industry. First, a number of sites rely heavily on advertising for most of their revenue. If the online advertising dollars continue to double every year (doubtful in the long term), some Internet companies may actually start making money.

Some of the companies worth watching as potential investments are those mentioned in this chapter and others that will be riding the online advertising wave.

Second, if the economy suffers a protracted general downturn, some of the advertising-revenue-based companies may be in serious trouble.

Internet advertising and all the marketing and support functions that surround it offer fertile ground for investment. As with all Internet investments, stay on top of developments and watch for leaders to emerge.

The Least You Need to Know

➤ Internet advertising is here to stay, although it will continue to evolve.

➤ Privacy issues are real threats to online advertising campaigns.

➤ Broadband Internet access will help advertisers produce more compelling ads.

Chapter 26

The Check Is in the Network

> ### In This Chapter
>
> ➤ Why there is no reason to ever go to the bank again
>
> ➤ It's not a checkless society yet, but we are closer
>
> ➤ Security issues that will have to be overcome
>
> ➤ Personal financial services on the grow

My, how times have changed! Not too many years ago, banks spent a lot of money on advertising their friendly and helpful staffs. Smiling faces of tellers graced billboards, newspaper ads, and television. Yes, you are family when you are part of our bank. Open a new account and get a toaster.

Two years ago, when we moved to a new town and state, our experience with the bank was quite different. The woman who set up our checking account recommended one particular account because it had the lowest fees.

She said that we should get the check (debit) card and use it instead of checks to keep fees down. She also warned us that we should never, unless it was absolutely necessary, use a live teller. It seems that there is a fee to use a live teller. My, how times have changed!

Internet Indispensable

There are probably still folks out there who think that the Internet is about playing games and looking at girly pictures. If you have read this far in the book and are still not sure why you should bother with considering investing in Internet stocks, this chapter may change your mind.

Market and technological forces are moving many traditional businesses in directions that we never imagined only a few years ago. Online stock brokerages have gone from an idea few believed would work to a major force in the investment community. Personal financial services won't be far behind.

The more our personal life gets intertwined in the Internet, the more indispensable the Web becomes. The following is a short overview of where we have been and a longer look at where we are going, with an emphasis on investment opportunities along the way.

Who Needs Banks?

Okay, we still need banks, but many of the services that banks have traditionally offered no longer require your physical presence at the bank.

Help File

Deregulation forced banks to compete with a variety of industries that they had never faced before, including investment firms, insurance companies, and so on.

This trend began with deregulation of the financial services industry in the 1980s and continues with migration to the Internet. During the mid-1980s, I had the opportunity to work on chartering a new bank. That process gave me a quick look inside the banking industry and how it makes money.

The old model was this: A bank paid 3 percent interest on deposits and charged 6 percent interest on loans. If a bank made well-secured loans to established businesses and avoided anything controversial, it would succeed. Of course, it is a lot more complicated than that.

Banks have a fairly complicated business model, and even back then, it was obvious that "personal" service needed to be a profit center or needed to be kept to a minimum.

Many banks began to charge for previously free services and enacted fees for fairly common services. If you bounced a check, they hit you with a $25 to $50 fee. If you let your balance fall below the minimum for your account, the fees mounted. If you wrote more checks than your account allowed for free, you paid for every additional check. This is still in effect and is probably nothing new to you.

Customers have been able to get account information over an automated telephone system for many years. Some banks began experimenting with online banking in the late 1980s and the early 1990s. This was obviously before the Internet, but even then banks and customers could see the advantages of accessing account via a personal computer.

You dialed in to the bank's network and could look at account balances and transfer money between accounts. A few banks even tried some bill-paying services. This type of access never really caught on with the banks or most of their customers, though. Going online was still a very new and mysterious thing then, and personal computers at home were still somewhat unusual.

The product that really got people thinking about putting their personal finances on a computer was Quicken, made by Intuit (ticker symbol: INTU; intuit.com). Like word processing and spreadsheets, Quicken was one of those programs that suddenly gave utility to personal computers. Cleverly designed to look like a checkbook, Quicken was a way to capture all your financial transactions. Early versions touted their ability to help you balance your checkbook.

It wasn't long before people began to see all sorts of benefits, including organizing expenses for taxes, tracking investments, writing checks, and paying bills online. The early bill-paying feature involved a third party that actually took the money out of your account and wrote a check for you. Quicken is extremely popular and has grown into a full personal finance-management package.

I credit Quicken with giving people the confidence to do their personal finances on a computer and, by extension, to become familiar with online financial transactions.

Internet Banking History

Internet banking began with Security First Network Bank in 1995. Like a lot of Internet banks, it is connected with a brick-and-mortar bank. It is sort of ironic to read the corporate histories of some of these banks that are well over 100 years old.

Since then, a number of other banks, including most of the truly large banks, have opened Internet branches or affiliates. There are some advantages to using an Internet bank that is part of a "real" bank, and there are some disadvantages. We'll explore those in a minute.

Not many pure Internet banks are banks that were started up as Internet banks rather than as a branch of an existing bank. This makes current investment opportunities somewhat limited, but I predict that personal financial services will become an explosive growth industry in coming years.

The key factor for investors is that these banks must pass the same regulatory oversight as all banks. Deposits are federally insured, and the internet banks must meet the same equal housing

Margin Call

Just because it looks like a bank doesn't mean that it is one. Look for the Federal Deposit Insurance Corporation (FDIC) logo on the Web site. If it is there, then bank deposits are insured up to $100,000 against loss due to fraud or default by the bank. If the deposits are not insured by the FDIC, be careful.

regulations as brick-and-mortar banks. Security concerns still circulate, but the industry has worked hard to keep customers' accounts safe.

What It Looks Like

Internet banking offers a full range of banking services, although not all Internet banks (i-banks) offer the same level of product diversity. The following description of products and services is general in nature and may not apply to every i-bank.

Open an Account

Opening an account at an i-bank is an easy online process. Some i-banks may require you to send postal or fax a signed check card that will identify your signature. You can even fund your new account with a wire transfer from your old bank.

Like regular banks, i-banks offer a variety of accounts with different features. Also like regular banks, i-banks offer the best deals to folks who keep the highest balances.

Access

The main feature of i-banks is that they are open 24 hours a day, seven days a week, as long as you have a computer and Internet access. Can't sleep? Pay some bills.

As handheld Internet devices become more popular, look for i-banks to make access to your account through your cellular telephone or personal digital assistant (PDA) just as easy as with your computer.

Good Deals?

While you might think that without the hassle of maintaining a physical bank, i-banks could offer cheaper rates and better deals, you would be only partly right. You'll find some good deals on certain banking services, but not all. As with all financial products, shop around before you buy, and don't assume that i-banks are cheaper on all products.

Large accounts get better deals than small accounts. (Remember the "big dogs eat first" rule from Chapter 10, "Five Rules You Need to Know.") Read the small print for fees, or you may find some ugly surprises on your first statement.

Easy Bill Payment

No, they won't pay your bills for you. However, i-banks can make the process very simple. Many of us have reoccurring bills such as utility payments, mortgage payments, car loans, and so on.

These bills can be paid one of two ways. First, for bills that are the same amount each month, such as a house or rent payment or a car payment, you can configure your account to automatically pay the bills on a certain date. You might need to make a rent payment at the end of the month for the next month's rent, while the car payment can be made in the middle of the month.

Those bills that reoccur but at different amounts, such as utility bills, can be paid by manually entering the amount in a screen and specifying when you want the bill paid. Some i-banks will guarantee that the payment will reach its destination on time if you have set up the account correctly.

Bill Presentment

This is a fairly new service that some i-banks are just getting starting. With this feature, cooperating vendors submit a bill to the i-bank, and it is posted to your account. You look at the bill for accuracy and authorize payment with one click. Bills are kept in your file in case you have a question later on or you need the bill for tax purposes.

Some i-banks are compatible with Quicken and allow transferring information. Bill presentment will be a big item with business-to-business Internet companies. We'll look at the commercial application of this service in the next chapter.

Loans

Many of the i-banks offer a full range of loan products, including mortgages, home equity, and credit cards.

Those i-banks that are part of traditional banks have ready access to these services. Pure Internet i-banks usually form alliances with lenders to facilitate the services. Loans are available from i-banks, but you may need to visit a partner of the bank for complicated loans such as home mortgages.

Investments

Stock brokerage services are offered by many of the i-banks either through an in-house service or in partnership with a discount brokerage.

This is an area where you should pay close attention to commissions and fees. It is possible that you would be better off with a direct account, especially if you are an active trader.

Cash Is a Problem

Cash—taking it out or putting it in—is a problem for i-banks. If an i-bank is part of a regular bank, then customers have access to automatic teller machines (ATMs), assuming that they live close by.

However, because i-banks are generally national in reach, dealing with cash is a problem. Most ATMs charge a fee for transactions if you are not a bank customer, and most ATMs will not accept deposits. Some i-banks will give you a break on ATM fees, but not all. Think about your cash needs, both withdrawals and deposits. If they are significant, you may want to consider maintaining a local bank account for that purpose.

A few i-banks are working deals with ATM networks to give their customers access to the ATMs without fees. It is likely that more of these alliances will be formed in the future because this is a major drawback of Internet banking.

Special Services—Not

Another drawback of i-banks is their lack of special services such as traveler's checks, safe deposit boxes, financial counseling, and so on.

These are not necessarily services that you need everyday, but if they are important for some reason, maybe an i-bank isn't for you. Before you decide whether an i-bank is for you, make a list of bank services that you use frequently and those you access only infrequently. Be sure that the i-bank can handle the critical tasks with relative ease.

The Future

You may not be ready for an i-bank account today, but my guess is that within the next three to five years, you will seriously consider one. It might be helpful to think of what this would look like for you if you had broadband Internet access.

Many of the services and products available on the Internet today will be incredibly enhanced by an "always on" fast connection to the Internet. This level of service will change the whole process of accessing the Internet from a multistep effort to a flip of the switch. I have discussed this briefly in Chapter 24, "The Big Push," and will do so in detail in Chapter 28, "Online with Your Toaster."

Think about how you access the Internet at home. More than likely, the computer is in an office or a spare bedroom, or wherever there is space.

The telephone line must be free, and you have to boot up the computer and then wait. You have to access the ISP and hope that the line isn't busy, and then you wait. You have to log on to the i-bank and then begin the process of doing business. When high-speed, "always on" Internet access is the norm, however, many of us will have a home network that will allow access to the Internet from multiple locations or anywhere with a wireless network.

Double Click

High-speed "always on" Internet access will make using the Internet as easy as flipping on a switch. This ease of access will fundamentally change the way products and services are perceived on the Internet.

We will have portable devices that will allow us to access our i-bank account as easily as turning on the radio. Want to check a balance while cooking pasta? No need to stop what you're doing and leave the cooking for 10 minutes while you go through the slow process described previously. Simply turn on your Internet device in the kitchen, and in seconds you are looking at your account. The pasta is never over-cooked while you're waiting to log on.

Choices

Right now there aren't many pure Internet i-banks. One of the leading ones is Net-Bank (ticker symbol: NTBK; netbank.com). Unlike most of the other i-banks, NetBank started from scratch with no customers, yet it has experienced some phenomenal growth. In April 2000, the bank reported its eighth consecutive quarterly profit. How many other pure Internet companies can you name that have put eight straight profitable quarters together?

Pure Internet banks are not without their detractors, of course. Traditional bankers insist that consumers want a personal touch in doing business. Maybe some do. I personally wouldn't care if I never had to set foot in another bank.

Huge banks such as Wells Fargo (ticker symbol: WFC; wellsfargo.com) and Bank of America (ticker symbol: BAC; bankamerica.com) have large numbers of customers with Internet accounts. Some observers believe that their size and large number of physical locations gives them an advantage by providing physical access to the bank, as well as Internet access. This solves the "where do I get cash?" problem

Strategy

Investing in the few pure Internet banks may not be the best immediate strategy. However, as the market matures, pure Internet i-banks will prove their viability or will fold into a brick-and-mortar bank. I believe that pure i-banks are being overlooked because investors aren't thinking beyond how the service works today and considering how it might work in an "always on" high-speed Internet access environment.

The argument that a physical presence with real people is needed to complete complicated transactions such as home mortgages is not very compelling. Smaller banks have been partnering with independent home mortgage companies to do the paperwork for years. There is no reason that i-banks couldn't form such partnerships. Even brick-and-mortar banks use this arrangement to extend their service areas beyond the immediate vicinity of the bank.

Help File

Online banks have not made a compelling case as your only banking relationship. As the market matures and consumers become more comfortable with the idea, online banks should experience tremendous growth.

A compelling reason to use an i-bank is the convenience of never again having to change banks because of a move. Instead of you finding a new bank, your current bank follows you. Despite the talk of a less mobile society, I believe that we will continue to be a people on the move. A bank account that moves with you makes the process easier. Even if it is not a permanent move, but just a business or pleasure trip, your bank is always there.

Security Issues

Security concerns about online banking are technically not any different from the issues addressed by online brokers. However, there is more of a psychological barrier when it comes to people's checking accounts.

Although online banks are more secure than online brokerages, it will take a while for people to become comfortable with doing most of their business online. Banks have operated huge electronic networks for years, so there is plenty of expertise in security. Like all things new, online banking will take some time to be accepted.

Personal Financial Services

I have focused on online banking because that is the best defined at the moment, but there is a growing movement to encourage people to transfer personal financial services to the Internet as well.

Quicken, which I mentioned earlier, has a version of its popular software on the Internet. Your data is entered, processed, and stored on the Internet. Quicken is just one of several companies offering products on the Internet. This strategy meshes with the broadband concepts I raised in the last couple of chapters and will expand on in the next two chapters.

A personal financial services package such as Quicken that resides on the Web has some significant advantages, especially in a world where "Internet everywhere" is a reality. In this reality, computing power, software, and data reside on the Web, not in a computer.

In the next chapter, I will talk about the "post-PC" era, which Microsoft officials, among others, have acknowledged as the next era in computing. The advantages of having your personal financial services program reside on the Web start to make themselves clear when you realize that you would have access to this information anytime and anywhere. You would never have to buy software upgrades again because the software on the Web would be automatically updated.

Your personal financial services program would tie your bank accounts, investment accounts, insurance, and other vital financial data together in a manageable bundle. If you made a change in one area, every other area affected by the change would be automatically updated. What's more, your taxes would be calculated and updated every day. The program would warn you, if you want it to, about tax consequences surrounding certain actions. If you were required to file estimated taxes, it would be done automatically, with the proper forms sent to the taxing authorities and the money taken from whatever account you told the program to use for tax payments.

Also in this scenario, your investments would be updated as frequently as you wanted them to be, including real-time updates. The program would signal you through your cell phone that a stock you were interested in was at or near your purchase price. It also would warn you if a stock or other investment dropped below a certain point.

Many people find that they are so busy making money they have no time for managing their money. These Internet-based programs will take over much of the management function based on parameters you decide to use.

Your Strategy

This is an emerging area without any strong investment possibilities in the immediate future. Keep your eye on financial services, and you will see an explosion of new ideas and products in the coming years.

The next two chapters deal with expanded looks at some of the concepts introduced in this chapter. At the beginning of this book, I suggested that investing in Internet stocks was buying into the future. Part of a successful investment strategy is anticipating where the Internet is headed and watching the new market leaders emerge.

The Least You Need to Know

➤ Online banking is a reality and will grow at a tremendous rate.

➤ Not everyone is ready for online banking, but a large number of people are.

➤ Online banks offer most of the important products and services that brick-and-mortar banks do.

Chapter 27

Work Is Where the Internet Is

In This Chapter

➤ Is the personal computer becoming extinct?

➤ Why home office workers are ripe for Internet-based products and services

➤ Why you might rent your software

➤ Business-to-business opportunities

I can remember reading an article in *Popular Science* magazine in the late 1950s about this new thing called a laser. Scientists seemed pretty excited about it, but no one in the general public could see much use for it.

The magazine even offered a kit for sale so that you could make your own laser, but about all it would do is pop a balloon at a distance of a few feet. When engineers hooked up a large power supply to more sophisticated lasers, though, those lasers could cut through steel plating. Now, here was something the public could understand: a death ray.

Now lasers are used for everything from the most delicate eye surgery to printers for personal computers, to sophisticated measuring devices, to CD players, to, yes, even death rays. Lasers are so commonplace now that no one gives the technology much thought.

One day in the not-too-distant future, the Internet will be such a part of our lives that we will notice it only when something goes wrong. Forward-looking investors will spot opportunities before the herd catches on to what is happening.

Coming Full Circle

The world of computers is finally coming full circle, but in a way that none of the early pioneers could have imagined.

I think it is fair to say that computer technology has enabled the creation of more wealth than any other resource, natural or otherwise. I have no proof of this statement, but if you think about it, almost nothing in our economy or daily lives escapes being influenced or shaped by computers.

Even if you don't own a computer, you use one every time you make a phone call, start your late-model car, or, well, you get the idea. Computers are such a part of our lives that we don't see or think about most of them.

In the beginning, computers were tended by specialists who ran jobs submitted by various departments within an organization. Then came the great movement to distribute the power out of the hands of the ordained and on to the desks of the masses.

Double Click

People don't need a computer on their desks. What they need is access to software and data that is secure and highly portable.

The circle will be completed when we move processing back to centralized locations but retain full access to the power and data. We will be able to access this power with a wide variety of devices and from almost any location.

The End Is Near

You will be hard-pressed to pick up a business or technology publication these days without reading something about the "post-PC era." Depending on whose view of the future you subscribe to, personal computers as we know them will give way to "Internet devices."

Internet devices are machines that act primarily as a connecting point to the Internet. They may or may not have a processor, memory, or a hard drive. Your cellular phone will be one example, and your personal digital assistant (PDA) will be another.

In this situation, your software and data would reside on the Internet, and you could access them from virtually anywhere. The processing power would be on the server, not in your Internet device. Access to the Internet would be virtually universal, high-speed, and always on.

In the post-PC world, you wouldn't have to worry about lugging your laptop on business trips. You could have a wireless PDA about the size of a laptop that would weigh less than 1 pound and that would be as thin as a pad of paper. For the truly mobile, your Internet device would respond to voice commands.

Hotels would have flat-screen monitors and keyboards in every room. You'd turn this on and log in to your business. All the software and data you'd need would be at your fingertips.

Later in this chapter, I talk about application server providers (ASPs), which are the folks that make the software accessible on the Internet.

Investors Take Note

Where will the opportunities be in this post-PC world? Look for new devices to compete with Palm products. As you will remember from earlier discussions about Palm, the company makes a very popular PDA called the Palm Pilot. Certain models of the Palm Pilot have wireless Internet access capabilities. People use them to read e-mail and to keep track of appointments and customer contacts.

Several vendors, including Microsoft, are rolling out competing products aimed at the PDA market. Some of these products include wireless Internet connections. These devices are coming out faster than you can keep track of them. For example, Research in Motion (ticker symbol: RIMM; rim.net) makes a wireless e-mail device called Blackberry. The Blackberry is 3.5 inches by 2.5 inches by .75 inches. It has a full keyboard and an LCD screen. It operates on a single AA battery. It also has a built-in wireless modem that is always connected to the Internet, unless you turn it off or stray out of the coverage area.

Margin Call

A number of the new Internet devices require that you be connected to their ISP. This is a problem that will have to be worked out before the devices can be widely accepted. It is pretty clear that most consumers will not want the hassle of multiple accounts.

You are not going to type any long messages with this device, but you can use it for entering stock symbols to look up prices or to actually trade on-line with the appropriate software. Check out the Research in Motion Web site for the full details—I think you'll be shocked.

One of the steps that will make the Web a greater part of our lives is to have hardware available at reasonable prices so there will be multiple points of connection in the same house. Not many people want or can afford to have computers sitting around the house so that they have access to the Internet from several rooms. Internet appliances are one answer, and they are here now. Netpliance (ticker symbol: NPLI; netpliance.com) makes a device called the i-opener that consists of a flat panel display and a keyboard. The i-opener would fit easily on most kitchen cabinets. This is a small device that is connected directly to the proprietary ISP, which means no dialing out and so on. You can send and receive e-mail, visit Web sites, and view news. According to Netpliance, you just take the i-opener out of the box, plug it in, attach the phone line, and start using it. As I am writing this, the i-opener sells for $99, plus a monthly ISP fee.

A device like this may one day be found in every hotel room. It is inexpensive and easy to use, and you can have all the fun of the Internet without struggling with a computer.

If that is too complicated, CIDCO (ticker symbol: CDCO; cidco.com) makes a product called the mail station. The self-contained unit has a small screen and a full-size keyboard and works only for e-mail. The unit costs $99, and service is $9.95 per month. That's a great idea for people who want to keep in touch by e-mail but have no other interest in the Internet.

Europe is actually way ahead of us in wireless connections, which means that a lot of growth is possible in this area. Many of their connections are through cell phones. Growth in cell phones with Internet capabilities is soaring. The cell phones now have e-mail capabilities and can access special sites designed for their small screens.

One of the forerunners in this area is Nokia (ticker symbol: NOK; nokia.com). Its cell phones are leaders in Internet connectivity and are an example of where phones are headed in the future.

A new buzzword that you will encounter is m-commerce, for mobile commerce. This vision of the future sees a time when your cell phone or PDA will interact with other devices to let you make purchases. For example, you are at an airport waiting to catch a plane and want something to read. You go into the newsstand and find a couple of magazines. The clerk rings them up, and you punch in a code on your cell phone or PDA. The cash register acknowledges the charge to your credit card, and off you go.

Better yet, what if you could pay a cab fare the same way or buy tickets to the movie or get a soda out of a machine? The technology to do these transactions is already here. It is just a matter of rolling it out. These innovations won't happen overnight, but they will happen, in some form or the other. Infrastructure and security issues are just two of the major concerns that will have to be overcome.

I have not touched on nearly all the devices and applications forthcoming—that's another book. I simply would like to leave you with the idea that there will be plenty of good opportunities for a long time. Don't feel like you have to get in on the very next deal that comes along. Wait until you are ready and comfortable to make your investments.

Home Office Revolution

Increasingly, people are spending more of their work time in home offices. Some estimates I have seen indicate that more than 16 million people spend all or parts of their workweek in a home office.

Thanks to computers and telecommunication services, it is possible for workers or small business owners to operate out of their homes. The business world has become much more accepting of this concept, and a number of companies are finding that they can let employees telecommute with great success.

I work out of my home. I have agent in New York City, editors in Indianapolis, New York City, Arizona, and San Francisco that I do business with, yet I have never met any of them in person. I also publish a newspaper and other publications for a non-profit church group. They e-mail me material from Colorado, Kansas, Missouri, Kentucky, Illinois, and North Dakota, and I compile it. The thread that ties all this together is the Internet. While it would be possible to do this without the Internet, I suspect that many folks would find the logistics very cumbersome and it would take a lot longer.

What Do We Need?

The small office–home office (SOHO) needs many of the same products and services that large operations use, but in different quantities and levels of service.

SOHOs have the same human resource concerns as large companies. Providing benefits for employees—or yourself, if you are self-employed—is a growing Internet business. Companies that provide outsourcing for these services are in big demand by SOHOs.

Lots of companies out there are selling products and services over the Internet. The ones that succeed are the companies that provide solutions, not just gadgets.

We Need ASPs

ASP is not the snake that gave Cleopatra a bad time, but a way to serve up software and data on the Internet. ASP stands for application service provider and describes a company that rents access to software and data over the Internet.

At first, this sounds like a goofy idea. Why would you want to rent software or have your files on some strange server? The answer is cost and convenience. Here's how this works in very simple terms. Your small (or large, for that matter) business needs access to some heavy-duty software, such as database programs. You can't afford or don't want to hire the professionals needed to put together a sophisticated database and keep it running. Here's where the ASPs enter the picture. They configure the latest software to your company's needs and keep it updated and running. You enter the data and crunch the numbers.

Other folks have put their accounting online, where they can afford a more sophisticated package than if they had to buy the software. Human resources reporting systems are another area where ASPs are filling the bill.

Some of the packages are fairly specific for certain types of businesses or professions. For example, Elite.com (ticker symbol: ELTE; elite.com) offers a time and practice management software bundle for attorneys. The package is targeted at small offices and solo practitioners who pay a monthly fee to use the package. The sophisticated

287

software helps them compete with larger firms. Because the software resides on the Internet, lawyers can access it from anywhere there is an Internet connection.

Software packages that track time, do billing, and support case management are used by large firms and can be quite expensive. With an ASP, small offices can afford to have the same technology at a fraction of the cost. In addition, the software is updated as needed by the server (and you never need to purchase and install the latest upgrade).

Double Click

Even small companies need highly sophisticated software to compete with larger firms. ASPs provide an affordable alternative to an in-house computer department.

Other packages are targeted at doctors and other professionals. A company called Wireless MD (wireless-md.com) has created a system that uses a variety of wireless devices to connect doctors to hospitals and other information sources over the Internet. Doctors can view patient records, order prescriptions, and admit and discharge patients. The system works on a number of wireless platforms as well as wired computers. Like the system for attorneys described previously, this is an example of ASPs creating specific tools for specific industries.

Larger e-businesses might take advantage of a system from Bottomline Technologies (ticker symbol: EPAY; bottomline.com). The company offers a suite of programs designed to manage corporate billing, payment, and management functions. Its system manages payments and helps companies manage their cash flow. In April 2000, the company was picked by a division of United Parcel Service to provide electronic bill presentment and payment (EBPP) services to business-to-business customers. The system will focus on both the biller and the payer, with the goal of expediting the process from shipment to delivery to payment.

Some security issues concern people, especially attorneys, who almost certainly have sensitive data in their files. The ASPs are doing everything they can to convince all potential clients that their information is secured.

Another problem for small or home offices is that an ASP needs a broadband connection. The high-speed and always-on features make broadband a must to run ASPs. However, as broadband spreads, more SOHOs will have the speed they need to take advantage of the ASPs.

Business-to-Business (B2B)

Like the UPS system mentioned previously, a number of ASPs are targeting business-to-business (B2B) applications. These systems are designed to facilitate e-commerce.

Part of the push behind moving software off the desktop and on to the Internet is the trouble businesses are having recruiting qualified computer specialists. One of the big benefactors of the B2B growth is Ariba (ticker symbol: ARBA; ariba.com), an Internet company that sets up and runs exchanges. These exchanges provide a virtual marketplace for companies and vendors to buy and sell products and services.

Ariba has been at the forefront of this technology and is considered a leader in the market. However, as of this writing, Ariba's stock was hugely expensive, riding the excitement over B2B.

Some estimates put the dollar value of B2B at well over $1 trillion by 2003. Companies such as Ariba charge a small fee for every deal cut in the exchange. However, as I reported in Chapter 21, "New Tricks for Old Dogs," some large companies are taking on the exchange by themselves.

The Missing Pieces

This may all seem a little overwhelming and a little far-fetched at the same time. However, that doesn't change the fact that it is coming.

Motorola reportedly plans to ship 200 million digital phones in 2000. All of them will have a special browser to connect to the Internet. Many of the phones will go to overseas customers who are adapting to wireless technology at a faster pace than Americans.

Airtime charges have kept many consumers out of the wireless market, but that is changing. More competition is driving down prices, and some national carriers are offering flat rate plans. To make wireless even more accessible, cooperative agreements and the end to proprietary ISPs will make Internet everywhere a quicker reality.

Margin Call

Wireless service will not really take off until service providers figure out a way to hand off connections between competing systems. This kind of cooperation will make a bigger market for everyone.

More wireless transmission towers and/or satellite facilities will have to be built to accommodate the new wireless world. Bandwidth problems for wireless devices will need attention.

Networks Rule

Although we may still use the term "personal" to describe computers and other Internet devices, it doesn't truly reflect the shift from the standalone devices of the 1990s to the connected devices of the twenty-first century. The Internet will act as the umbrella network that we all are connected to in a variety of ways through a variety of devices.

You may find a couple terms helpful: LAN, PAN, and WAP (oh, boy—more acronyms). These three terms are becoming more important as we move from the single user mind-set to the notion of networks.

LAN stands for local area network and may be familiar to you. Larger offices are connected with a LAN, and we will talk more about these networks in the next chapter. PAN stands for personal area network and represents the notion that carrying a wireless Web device makes us a walking network that can interact with other networks. WAP stands for wireless application protocol, which is a standard way for wireless devices to interact with each other and networks such as the Internet.

Double Click

Wireless and wired connections of the future will be high-speed, always-connected networks that will interact with other networks.

Bluetooth, which I discussed in Chapter 3, "The Internet," is a technology that lets wireless and wired networks interact, sometimes automatically. In the near future, when you want a soft drink out of a vending machine, you will simply make your choice and get the drink. Your Bluetooth-equipped PDA will transmit your credit or debit information to the Bluetooth-equipped machine, which will then serve your soft drink.

Your cell phone will be always on and always connected to the Internet. It will let you know when you have e-mail or will scan your stock portfolio on a regular basis and alert you when certain events happen. If you want to read your e-mail on a more comfortable screen, the phone will forward it to your PDA or a nearby PC, if you wish.

The Least You Need to Know

➤ Internet devices will become more popular and cheaper.

➤ The need for personal computers will be reduced as more applications become Web-based.

➤ Wireless devices will provide always-on, always-connected service to the Internet.

Chapter 28

Online with Your Toaster

In This Chapter

➤ How the network will rule

➤ How your house will work with you

➤ Here come the Jetsons

➤ Good morning, Dave

When I was growing up, we had an electric wall clock in our kitchen. The clock would gain a couple of minutes every week, and my father jokingly explained it by saying that we had "fast electricity."

Many families still find that the kitchen is often the center of activity in the morning and evening as members come and go to work and school. These are times when information about the outside world would be helpful. Few families, however, keep a computer in the kitchen. If you want to know about the weather, you turn on the television or radio and hope that you catch the forecast.

Wouldn't it be convenient to have an Internet device about the size of a pad of legal paper with a touch-sensitive screen stuck to your refrigerator? Want to check the weather? Touch an icon. Want to check the family's schedule for the week? Touch an icon. Want to know when the school bus is five minutes away? Touch an icon and listen for the warning tone.

My dad would probably call this "fast electricity," too.

Networks Rule

The twenty-first century will be known as the era when networks ruled—well, at least for the first 5 or 10 years. After that, who knows?

We closed out the twentieth century with bigger and more powerful personal computers. They could do phenomenal computing jobs and encouraged us to get more power and faster processors. The ugly truth was that the main job PCs perform is word processing in one form or another, and you can't really tell the difference between a 300 MHz fired word processor and an 800 MHz driven word processor.

Of course, PCs do a lot more than word processing, and their ability to perform complicated tasks better and faster is truly amazing. I use fairly sophisticated desktop publishing software for some of my projects, and it does run faster with a more powerful processor and more memory.

An estimated 50 percent of the households in the United States have one or more personal computers. These computers are used for a variety of projects, including homework, e-mail, games, Web-surfing, and even some business applications.

Home networks are becoming very popular for the same reasons they are so necessary in businesses: sharing resources. People who came home from the office that was connected to a local area network (LAN) wondered why they had to buy a second printer for the kids or stop what they were doing so that the kids could print out their homework.

Fights over the Internet and whose turn it was to log on became sources of friction and trouble. The answer was to connect the home's computers in a LAN so that the kids could share the printer and Internet access.

This was fine as far as it went, but sharing a dial-up connection wasn't much fun, and the simple networks were confined to sharing printers, an Internet connection, and transferring files. I have a simple peer-to-peer wireless network between my laptop and my desktop computers. The network allows me to transfer files and share the printer and an Internet connection. The main convenience for me is that I can take my laptop downstairs to work and still have access to the printer in the office and an Internet connection. I don't have to be "plugged in" to any wired network, which gives me the freedom to work where I want.

Actually, the wireless system gets out of range if I go too far away from the desktop. These systems clearly have a way to go before they offer the true convenience they advertise.

What's Next?

Here's where investors can start looking for new products and technologies that will take home networks to the next step.

One of the big differences between most current home networks and your office network may be that at the office, some or all applications reside on the network server and are available for all to use.

For example, at the office, you may have a database program that allows everyone connected to the network to work on the database at the same time. The server prevents two users from working on the same record at the same time. This is no different in function than the application service providers we looked at in the last chapter.

However, that doesn't sound like something the home network could use—or does it?

The other thing the office network does is give everyone on the network access to the Internet through a high-speed connection. Now, this sounds more like something the home could use. As broadband service becomes more available to residences, the network will take on more importance.

Ignoring the technical issues for a moment, having a super-fast cable or DSL connection to the house opens the opportunity to connect more computers to share the speed. Right now, this is done with a piece of hardware called a router. Home network experts believe that the future of home networks is in connecting not only computers, but also Internet devices that offer a portal to the Web but no real internal processing power. In other words, these devices are not computers in the sense that we functionally understand them.

Called gateways, these devices would be the equivalent of the office network server. The gateway would provide a connecting point for all the computers, Internet devices, peripherals (such as printers), the home security system, environmental controls, some of the appliances, the entertainment system, and, from the outside, a high-speed Internet connection.

The gateway allows you into the network from the outside and keeps out those to whom you want to deny access. It coordinates the house and family members so that all are more efficient. Let's look at some of the components.

Computers

Connecting all the traditional computers makes sense. We have already discussed the advantages of sharing printers and Internet connections.

Because this is a true network with a server, another function might be to make available on all the

Speak Up

A **personal information manager,** also called a contact manager, is a software package that helps you organize and keep current all the people in your business or personal life. These might be customers, vendors, or just friends. The PIM records names, addresses, phone numbers, e-mail addresses, Web sites, and so on for easy retrieval. It also keeps your appointments and calendar.

computers (and other devices also) the family information manager (FIM). The FIM is much like the *personal information managers* (PIM) that you may be familiar with, such as ACT and Microsoft Outlook. The Palm line of PDAs and others are sophisticated PIMs.

Your FIM contains all the familiar functions, such as address books, contacts (plumber, electrician, and so on), and a family calendar. Everyone old enough has access to the FIM and notes important dates and deadlines on the calendar function. At some point in the future, the FIM will poll the school's database and download Junior's homework assignments. No more missed book reports.

Internet Devices

Like the home's computers, the Internet devices will be connected to the gateway. The refrigerator display I referred to in the beginning of this chapter would have a wireless connection to the gateway.

A touch screen, much like PDAs are today, would manipulate it. By touching an icon, you would see the family calendar. By touching another icon, you could display the weather. Another icon would let you read e-mail, while yet another would let you program the security system and environmental controls for when you are gone during the day.

The children may have Internet devices like the ones I discussed in the previous chapter. These devices would have a screen and a keyboard and would fit on a small desk with ease. The kids could do their homework over the Internet and turn it in to the school's Web site.

Home Security

Your home security system could be connected to the gateway, which would allow you to program it from any of the internal devices or from an external device connected to the Internet.

Some new homes are currently being wired for security systems while they are being built. It would be simple to wire a new home for a LAN. The system not only would watch out for burglars, but it also would alert you or the authorities to anything unusual, such as fire or smoke.

Environmental Systems

The benefits here are obvious. You would set the temperature to raise or lower as your needs dictate. Smart thermostats can do this now, but the new systems will be accessible over the Web.

Appliances

You thought I was kidding when you saw the title of this chapter, "Online with Your Toaster." Actually, I *was* kidding about the toaster. However, there is a significant interest by appliance makers in kitchen aids that are smart, interactive, and, in some cases, Internet-connected.

Some cutting-edge companies in the thick of the smart appliance push include General Electric (ticker symbol: GE; ge.com), Maytag (ticker symbol: MYG; maytagcorp.com), and Whirlpool (ticker symbol: WHR; whirlpoolcorp.com), among others. Their partners? Microsoft, Sun Microsystems (ticker symbol: SUNW; sun.com), and others.

In the near future, these smart appliances will display recipes, respond to voice commands, and be more interactive. The next step is to connect some of the major appliances to the home gateway so they can be accessed from the Internet.

Some of these appliances may have Internet devices built in, like the screen on the refrigerator we mentioned earlier. The current move seems to be toward making the appliances smarter. The real benefit will come when they become active helpers rather than passive tools. Refrigerators that keep track of what you are running low on and make shopping lists when asked would make planning menus simpler. Menus could be constructed from a database of what foods the family enjoys while considering nutritional needs.

Help File

Interactive and *connected* will be the terms to describe appliances of the future. This may seem like overkill, but it will free up your time for more important activities such as spending time with the people important to you.

If two dishes (one for the kids and one for the adults) need to be prepared, the refrigerator or stove could access the database on the gateway, prepare a weeklong menu, and print a shopping list of what you need to make the dishes.

A low-fat meal for the adults would not be a problem because the database could access a nutrition Web site for low-fat recipes while preparing a nutritionally balanced meal that the kids would eat. As the main cook in our family, I want one of these!

Entertainment Systems

Broadband Internet connections, such as cable, can stream live video or audio over the home networks. However, unless displays are radically upgraded, you are not likely to use your Internet devices to view the latest *Star Wars* movie.

Your television will be another story. It likely will be a high-definition digital display that may hang on your wall like a picture. What is displayed, whether it is from the cable television network or the Internet, will be indistinguishable from one another.

You won't have to settle for what the cable television channels offer, either. If you are not happy with their selections, you can flip over to AOL Time Warner and download a DVD version of *Casa Blanca* or any other movie that you want to see. The download would take less than two minutes. In fact, if you decide that you want a romantic evening with your partner, you might arrange the download from your office so that your "date movie" is cued up and ready whenever you are.

If you have more time than most, you can program your stereo system with a selection of music that you have downloaded from the Internet while you are riding the train home in the evening.

Hello, Jetsons

The Jetsons was a television cartoon show from the 1970s that chronicled the life of a family in the future. George Jetson complained about his two-hour workday. The kids had all sorts of automated gadgets to help them with their homework and, in general, enjoy life. Mrs. Jetson had a robot for a maid, and the dog had an IQ of 100 or so.

Futuristic looks at everyday life have been the staple of television, movies, comic books, and novels for years. The first part of the twenty-first century will take us many steps closer to those times.

All domestic (and many foreign) automobile makers are or soon will be shipping cars with onboard Internet connections and *global positioning systems*. Not only will this system tell you where you are, but it also will give you audio directions to where you need to go.

Margin Call

Global positioning systems (GPSs) are devices that use signals from three satellites to calculate your exact position. Some of the devices are accurate to within a few yards of your exact position. They are used in navigation at sea and in airplanes, and now as either handheld devices or units built into cars.

Cars with Internet connections have raised some jokes along with safety concerns. You thought drivers talking on cell phones were dangerous—wait until you get behind one surfing the Web. These systems may actually become obsolete within a few years if the "Internet everywhere" scenario becomes a reality. Your PDA or cell phone could serve the same functions and be with you wherever you go.

Another cartoon character that fits here was the police detective Dick Tracey. As we've mentioned, Tracey had a two-way television receiver on his wrist that kept him in contact with his officers. Tracey's communication device may not appeal to you, but "wearable" computers and Internet devices might. A connected pair of virtual glasses may create a "display" in front of you, appearing to float in the air. A small video camera built into special glasses would allow you to transmit what you are seeing to others on a videoconference hosted on the Internet.

"Good Morning, Dave"

It seems that some part of computer technology is always lagging behind other parts. During the 1980s, processing power of PCs increased dramatically, along with sharper displays and more memory.

Printers, however, didn't seem to make much headway. It wasn't until the latter part of that decade that laser printers for PCs became available. I believe I remember paying almost $4,000 for the first laser printer I owned—a LaserWriter by Apple. Thankfully, printers have improved dramatically, and the price has dropped. I recently bought a laser printer that has better quality and that prints at a higher speed than my first printer, and it cost less than $350.

The one thing about my computers today that is essentially the same as the first computer I had back in 1983 is the keyboard—or, more appropriately, the input device.

People who don't know how to type or who can't type for some reason are at a real disadvantage. Although many PDAs and other similar devices use icons for navigating, as the PC does, it is still inconvenient if you can't type at a reasonable speed. The answer, which has been around for a long time, is voice recognition. Various attempts have been made to get computers to respond to natural language with limited success.

> **Double Click**
>
> Several programs will read what is on the screen for the visually impaired, but true voice-recognition programs will understand conversational speaking.

Some computers in specific applications can be maneuvered by voice, but they respond to very limited and specific commands. The title of this section comes from the movie *2001: A Space Odyssey,* and the words are spoken by Hal, a computer. (That's a great movie, by the way.) What Hal can do is respond to conversational language rather than specific commands. This ability to respond is seen again and again in a variety of science fiction movies, television shows, and novels.

In the television series *Star Trek* (and all its subsequent spin-offs), the crew can ask the computer questions, and the computer responds. They always begin with the word "computer" to let it know that the words are directed its way.

Voice-recognition programs require some heavy-duty processing power, though, and until recently, the average PC just didn't have the horsepower to do the job. The programs also require an excellent sound card in your computer and a good microphone.

I have a version of the leading voice-recognition programs on my laptop. I have tried to dictate part of this book, but I found that the program made too many errors, and I spent more time correcting the errors than I saved from not typing.

Help File

The answer in the past to questions over topics such as voice recognition has been to keep raising the processing power of PCs. I am not sure that will be the answer of the future, though. ASPs running super computers might make more sense for really processor-intensive applications rather than making everyone own a desktop super computer.

One of the big problems is that if the software doesn't get the word right, it substitutes another word that sounds like the original. This means that when I run the spell-checker, it skips over these wrong words because they are spelled correctly. Most of the mistakes I make typing will be picked up by the spell-checker.

A Big Step

The problems of voice recognition are significant, but the payoff is, too. When we can free ourselves of keyboards and mouse devices, we will have taken a big step toward mastering the technology instead of accommodating the technology. That step is a big one from a philosophical perspective, but not very far down the technological road.

Double Click

The Internet device hanging on your wall in the future will double as artwork when you aren't using it. You can program it to download pictures of the world's greatest art, photos of your last vacation, or scenes from the great outdoors.

I don't know how the voice-recognition problems will be solved. Maybe with high-speed Internet connections, we can use ASPs with large computers to do it for us. I do know that the payoff will be significant. For example, imagine that you are a salesperson getting ready for your day's work. Despite video-conferencing, you find that your best sales are made in person. As you are getting dressed in the morning, you ask your Internet device hanging on the wall of your bedroom for your schedule. The device displays the schedule, but it also reads your appointments for the day. It ends the report by telling you that there are driving directions loaded into your PDA to each account.

As you are driving to the first call, you ask your PDA to tell you about the person you are going to meet. The PDA accesses your contacts database and gives you a quick summary of the person's name, family status, hobbies, and so on. The PDA also reminds you that this customer enjoys talking about sports, so it gives you the latest sports news in summary form.

Your PDA has been programmed to check the company accounting system, and it reports to you that this customer has a rather large invoice outstanding of more than 90 days. You'll have to gently encourage this customer to get current.

I could go on, but you get the idea. Everything I have suggested is possible within the next few years. With the exception of quality voice recognition, all the technology is here now.

Investment Opportunities

How anyone can say that we have missed the investment opportunities of a lifetime if we didn't get in early on the Internet is beyond me. This is a shortsighted comment without basis. We have only peaked at the tip of the iceberg. There is much more lying beneath than you or I can imagine.

Our challenge as investors will be to do our homework and to be patient. Don't feel like you have to jump at every deal that comes down the street. There will be another deal—and another and another.

The other challenge will be to curb our natural tendency toward greed. Greed destroys; it never creates. Investing is about a reasonable return for reasonable risk. Keep that in mind, and you will have 90 percent of the problem solved.

No Utopia

I don't want to paint the world as a Garden of Eden just because technology is making our lives easier. We still will have the problems of poverty, both financially and technologically.

Our challenge as a society and as members of the world community will be to extend the benefits of technology to as many people as possible and to use that technology to make life better for everyone, not just the technological haves.

Happy investing!

The Least You Need to Know

➤ Networks are the road to success.

➤ Being connected to a greater whole is more important than standing by yourself.

➤ Networks will manage your house and help you manage your life.

Investment Review

Here's a 10-minute review of basic investment strategy and guidelines with some cautions for Internet stock investors.

For a more complete survey of investing basics, pick up (and pay for, please) a copy of my book, *Macmillan Teach Yourself Investing in 24 Hours*, which is available where fine books are sold.

Buy Quality

Many investors make the mistake in thinking that an inexpensive stock (under $5 per share) is a good deal because they can buy a lot of it for not much money.

You are much better off buying 10 shares of a quality stock than 100 shares of junk. Speaking of junk, never buy penny stocks. Penny stocks generally sell for $2 a share or less and are not listed on any major exchange.

Tons of "get rich quick" schemes involving penny stocks circulate around the Internet. Most of them are swindles. Penny stocks are not regulated like the regular stock market. You will often find people touting them in chat rooms and on message boards.

The oldest scam in the book is called "pump and dump." Basically, a person takes a big position in one of the penny stocks and then gets all over the Internet talking about phony deals with Microsoft or new patents or some other revelation that is going to make the stock shoot up.

People start buying, and the price goes up. More people see the price going up, and they start buying. The price continues to go up until the con artist dumps all of his stock at a fat profit.

The stock tanks, and everyone loses.

Buy and Hold

The best method of building wealth is to buy and hold stocks or mutual funds for the long term. Plan on holding your investments for at least five years. Buying quality investments is always the least expensive strategy in the long run.

Obviously, if an investment isn't performing and there doesn't seem to be any reason to suspect that it is going to turn around, dump it.

Investing in Internet stocks may force you to re-evaluate holding for long periods. The internet market is so dynamic that changing fortunes are common. Don't feel like you need to be in a hurry to invest in Internet stocks. You will have plenty of good opportunities for years to come.

Speculating, which is buying and selling within a short period of time, is not a proven way to make money in the stock market. In fact, if you are not careful, it is a proven way to lose money.

I am not a big fan of speculating because it is a high-risk strategy. However, if you are willing to spend a lot of time watching the market and your stock, it can pay off. Just don't get greedy.

Keep Expenses Low

One of the killers of investing profits is high cost of trading. If you will be making a lot of trades, use a deep-discount broker. You can find a ranking of online brokers at Gomez.com.

Most information site and advisory services will let you sign up for a free trial before you commit to a subscription. This is a good idea because you can work with the Web site for a while to see how you like it.

If you are considering about day trading, sit down and think about it really hard. Some people make lots of money day trading, but most don't. One of the reasons that it is hard to make money is that the equipment and data services are very expensive.

Use Mutual Funds

Mutual funds are a great way to invest if you don't have the time or the inclination to do the homework necessary for individual stocks.

Some mutual funds focus on Internet stocks; I discuss in Chapter 18, "Mutual Admiration Society." More Internet funds will be joining the market in the coming years.

One of the key items to watch on any mutual fund is the expense ratio. That number reflects your total cost of owning the fund. Good funds should have expense ratios of 1.5 percent or less.

Finding an expense ratio that's this low may be difficult with an Internet fund, but keep this number as low as possible. Another alternative is to buy aggressive growth mutual funds. Many of these funds have up to 40 percent of their investments in tech and Internet stocks.

Watch the Risk

Your stomach may be the best investment gauge you have. If you get a sinking feeling in your stomach at the thought of a certain type of investment risk, don't do it.

No great return potential is worth losing sleep over. Plenty of lower-risk investments won't make you queasy and still will help you achieve your goals.

Diversify

You should always spread you investments out over a number of stocks or several mutual funds with different compositions and objectives.

This diversification will keep you from losing everything if the only market sector you invest in goes south. Mutual funds are a great way to achieve diversification.

Have Fun

Investing can and should be fun. If you enjoy what you are doing, odds are, you will do a better job.

If you can't stand the thought of spending time researching investments and keeping up with the news, stick your money in a top-rated mutual fund and forget about it, but keep putting money in on a regular basis.

Glossary of Investing and Internet Terms

This glossary contains definitions to all the investment and Internet terms in this book, plus a few more for good measure.

10-K An annual document that must be filed by companies. It contains complete financial information about the previous year along with other information investors need to know. It is like an annual report without pictures. *See also* annual report.

10-Q The quarterly equivalent of the 10-K and focusing on the previous quarter.

12b-1 distribution fees Fees charged to shareholders by the mutual fund company to provide for advertising and marketing as well as "distribution" costs.

401(k) plan A qualified defined contribution plan offered by employers. It allows employees to have a certain percentage of their salary deducted and invested in the plan. The deduction is pre-tax, so current income tax is reduced. The plan usually offers five to seven mutual funds to which the employee can apply his deduction. In some cases, the employer may match a portion of the employee's contribution. The deposits and earnings are tax-deferred until withdrawn in retirement.

403(b) plan Similar to the 401(k) plan, the 403(b) is offered to religious, educational, and other nonprofit groups. This plan is also known as a tax-deferred annuity plan because the investments must be annuities.

active investing Frequent trading and significant personal commitment to investments characterize active investing.

active investment strategy An investment strategy that places primary decision making with the investor. This strategy prefers actively managed mutual funds to index funds and often prefers individual stocks to mutual funds.

actively managed mutual fund Funds that meet their investment objectives by actively buying and selling securities. These funds may have high expense ratios and create tax liabilities, which are passed through to the investor.

administrative fees   Fees are charged by the mutual fund company to maintain and administer a fund.

after-hours trading   A fairly new way to trade stocks and securities after the major markets have closed. Some brokers are facilitating this activity.

annual report   A document that all publicly traded companies, including mutual funds, are required to produce. It presents the financial results for the past fiscal year, which are audited by an accredited accounting firm.

application service providers   Companies that house software on a Web site and "rent" it to customers.

asset allocation   The process of distributing your investment assets in a manner that is consistent with your investment goals. This allocation will change as your life circumstances change.

B2B   *See* business-to-business.

back-end load fund   A mutual fund that charges a sales fee when you sell your shares.

back testing   The process of using historical data to construct an investing plan that produces spectacular results and then suggesting that it will work in the future.

balance sheet   An account of a company's assets, liabilities, equity, and net worth at a certain point in time. Part of the annual report.

bear market   A market characterized by significant long-term declines in market value, as shown by falling market indicators.

beta   A measure of a stock's volatility. The higher the number over 1, the more volatile the stock is. The number one represents the market as a whole, so the beta measures how a stock reacts relative to the whole market.

blue chip stocks   The most prestigious and solid companies on the market. It is thought that the term comes from the fact that blue chips in poker are the most expensive ones.

bond mutual funds   Mutual funds that invest in bonds and may target long or short maturities and different issuers. Triple tax-exempt bond funds are sold in specific states, and residents may enjoy tax-free income from the bond fund.

bonds   Debt instruments that represent an obligation on the part of the issuer to repay the debt. Governments and private corporations may issue bonds.

book value   The stockholders' equity after all liabilities have been paid.

broadband   The amount and speed of data that can be pushed through an Internet connection. If you think of your dial-up connection as a garden hose, then broadband is a fire hose. Broadband delivery is always on, so you don't have to wait for a connection to the Internet.

bull market   A market characterized by significant long-term growth in stock market value, as shown by rising market indicators.

business-to-business   Business-to-Business or B2B describes Internet companies that sell to other businesses as opposed to individual consumers.

buy and hold investment strategy   An investment strategy that suggests that buying and holding quality investments for the long term is a successful strategy.

buy and sell   From an investment perspective, the approach of buying an instrument that gives you the right to sell, and selling an instrument that gives you the right to buy. *See also* call option and put option.

call option   An option that gives the owner the right, but not the obligation, to buy a stock at a certain price within a specified time frame.

capital gain   The profit from the sale of an asset. Capital gains are realized when you sell a stock or bond for a profit, and when a mutual fund does the same. Capital gains are passed on to mutual fund shareholders. Any asset sold for a profit and held less than one year is subject to ordinary income tax by the owner. This is known as a short-term capital gain. An asset held for more than one year and sold for a profit is a long-term capital gain and is taxed at 20 percent.

cash equivalents   Financial instruments that represent a deposit of cash. These include certificates of deposits, money market accounts, and savings accounts. They are characterized by their high liquidity.

certified financial planner   A professional designation that someone has extensive training in financial planning. Many certified financial planners charge a fee only for their services, while others may take a commission of the products that they recommend.

click and mortar   A term coined to identify traditional companies that have integrated, or tried to integrate, the Internet into their existing structure. For example, Compaq Computer's Web site directs customers to nearby retail stores for certain products.

closed-end mutual fund   A hybrid type of investment that offers shares for sale only once. After that, no new shares are sold. The remaining shares are traded like stocks and can be bought and sold on the open market.

commissions   Fees brokers charge to buy or sell securities for you.

commodities   Common, everyday items—at least, to most of the customers that purchase them. The term suggests that there is no significant difference in the same item made by different manufacturers.

common stock   The primary unit of ownership in a corporation. Holders of common stock are owners of the corporation with certain rights, including the right to vote on major issues concerning the corporation. Shareholders, as they are known, have liability limited to the value of stock they own.

compounding   The mathematical means by which interest is earned on the principal during one period, and then interest for the next period is earned on the resulting principal plus interest in the first period. Another way to say this is interest earning interest.

correction   A polite term for a full-scale retreat by a market sector or the whole market. It is usually caused by some external event, such as interest rate hikes, and usually lasts for only a short time.

critical mass   The volume of business necessary to generate profits. This varies from company to company depending on a number of variables, but it is an important goal for the company.

cross selling   A way to offer customers who have just bought some merchandise the opportunity to buy something else. An Old Economy example would be offering socks to a man who had just bought a pair of shoes.

day trader   Someone who engages in aggressive trading using an Internet connection to a broker or a terminal in the broker's office. Day traders may make dozens of trades each day with the hope of making numerous small profits.

day trading   A very aggressive form of trading that seeks to capitalize on small moves in a stock's price. The day trader looks to make small profits and then exit the position.

depression   A long-term (multiple years) decline in the national standard of living.

direct investment plans (DIPs)   A way to buy stock directly from a company without using a broker.

discount brokers   Brokers that facilitate the buying and selling of securities, but that don't make product recommendations. For the most part, they are order-takers. Discount brokers charge commissions that are considerably less than those of full service brokers. Online brokers are discount brokers.

diversification   The calculated spreading of your investments over a number of different asset classes. This cushions your portfolio if one part is down because different asset classes (stocks, bonds, cash, and so on) seldom move in the same direction. In mutual funds, you achieve diversification because the fund owns 50 stocks instead of a few.

dividend reinvestment plans (DRIPs)   Plans that allow owners of stocks and mutual funds to reinvest dividends into the investment program. You also can set up a DRIP and make periodic payments as a way of buying stock without going through a broker.

dividend yield   A figure calculated by dividing the current price per share into the annual dividend per share. The resulting percentage tells how cheap or expensive a dividend is relative to the stock price.

dividends   Portions of a company's profits that are paid to its owners, the stock-holders. Dividends usually are paid quarterly. Not all companies pay dividends; the board of directors makes that decision. Companies that don't pay dividends reinvest the profits in the company to finance additional growth. These are often referred to as growth stock. Companies that pay regular dividends sometimes are known as income stocks.

dogs of the Dow   A passive investment strategy built upon buying high-yielding stocks of the Dow Jones Industrial Average.

dollar cost averaging   An investing technique that makes regular deposits in an investment account regardless of market conditions.

Dow Jones Industrial Average   Also known as the Dow, this index is the best known and most widely quoted in the popular press. The Dow consists of 30 companies considered leaders in their industries. Together they account for a significant amount of the value in the market. Although not as reflective of the whole market as other indexes, the Dow is watched earnestly.

earnings-based evaluation   Evaluation of a stock based on the relationship between earnings and stock price, the price/earnings ratio (P/E), and the P/E and growth ratio (PEG).

e-commerce   The buying and selling of goods and services over the Internet.

e-economy   The New Economy that many believe is being created by Internet companies, based on interaction with and personalization for the customer.

economic indicators   A key measurement of the economy's health, such as unemployment, wages, prices, and related factors, that gauges the health of the economy.

economic risk   The danger that the economy could turn against your investment. An example would be investing in a real estate company during a period of high interest rates.

economics   Area dealing with the production, distribution, and consumption of goods and services, as well as the factors that affect the economy, such as taxes, inflation, and labor.

entry barriers   Obstacles that companies must overcome to participate in a certain line of business. For example, retail sites that sell other people's products have a very low entry barrier because anyone can sell the same or equivalent products.

equity   What remains after all liabilities have been paid.

equity-based evaluation   Relates the company's equity to the stock price. This method uses price-to-book ratios and return on equity to find this relationship.

execution   The actual consummation of a buy or sell order. A good execution is at the target price and in a timely manner.

expectation bubble   The value added to a market or stock by investors who expect growth to continue on a straight line upward. The investors are willing to pay a premium for this future benefit, even if the benefit is in their imagination.

expense ratio   The total of all fees charged to shareholders by the mutual fund.

Federal Reserve Board   Also know as the Fed, this entity controls the nation's interests rates by setting the key interest rates charged to banks. Alan Greenspan has headed the Board for many years. An old Wall Street saying has it that when he sneezes, the market gets a cold. A change in interest rates will have a dramatic effect on the markets if it was not anticipated. Raising and lowering interest rates is analogous to turning up or down the heat while cooking.

fill   An order to execute a buy or sell order for securities. A good fill is at the price sought in the shortest amount of time.

fiscal year   The bookkeeping year for a company. It may or may not correspond to a calendar year.

focused funds   Funds that concentrate their investments in specific narrow sectors of the market. The idea is to take advantage of rapid growth in the sector. The downside is that when the sector tanks, so does fund.

full-service brokers   Brokers that offer comprehensive services to persons wishing to invest, including recommendations on specific products and proprietary research.

fundamental analysis   A method for evaluating a stock on the basis of observing key ratios and understanding the underlying business.

futures   Contracts that obligate the owner to deliver a specific commodity or financial instrument by a certain date. Futures facilitate a more stable market for the producers and consumers of commodities. In addition to agricultural products such as cattle, orange juice, and lumber, futures are sold on a number of financial instruments.

Global Positioning Systems (GPS)   Devices that use signals from three satellites to calculate your exact position. Some of the devices are accurate to within a few yards of your exact position. They are used in navigation at sea and in airplanes, and now are handheld devices or are built into a car.

going public   The process of offering shares of stock of a privately owned company to the public.

goodwill   The difference between the book value of a company and the price paid for it by an acquiring company. Goodwill puts a value on the nonquantifiable assets such as customer relations. It must be depreciated over a period of years, which means that every year the company incurs a noncash expense that reduces its net income.

growth investment strategy   A strategy that identifies companies with significant growth potential and that is willing to ride out frequent market fluctuations.

growth mutual funds   Mutual funds that seek investments in stock of companies with potential of rapid and sustained growth.

growth stock   A stock that usually pays no dividends but puts profits back into the company to finance new growth. Investors buy growth stock for its potential price appreciation as the company grows.

income investment strategy   An income strategy identifies sources of immediate income, whether through income stocks or bonds.

income mutual funds   Mutual funds that invest in stocks and bonds that provide high levels of current income.

income statement   A financial document listing income and expenses of a company that reveals how much was made or lost. Part of the annual report.

income stock   Characterized by the current income that it produces in the form of dividends. Utilities often are classified as income stocks for the strong dividends they pay.

index   A way to measure financial activity. An index has an arbitrary beginning value. In investing, indexes are often tied to certain groups or sectors of stocks. As those stocks rise or fall, the index either rises or falls.

index mutual fund   A mutual fund that seeks to mimic some key market index, such as the S&P 500. Index funds are known for very low expense ratios because they do little buying or selling unless the underlying index changes.

inflation   Too much money chasing too few goods. The result is a sharp rise in prices without any extra value added, making money worth less. Inflation leads to rising interest rates and a cooling of the economy. If the economy slows down too quickly and too far, it may slip into a recession or even a depression.

infomercials   Late-night program-length (usually 30-minute) television ads that are often structured to look like news stories.

initial public offering (IPO)   The first time a company issues stock for sale to the public. The company is said to be going public when this happens. The offering is highly regulated and often is surrounded by a lot of media attention. Hot technology stocks often see immediate price increases of 300 percent or more.

Internet   A vast network of computers that allows anyone with access to connect to this network and tap into tremendous amounts of available information.

Internet access   The portal through which you access the Internet. Local or national companies called Internet service providers offer this access to the vast majority of users.

Internet service provider   A local or national company that gives you access to the Internet, usually through your existing telephone line. The going rate is about $20 per month.

311

intraday   Prices that occur within a single trading day for the same stock. Speculators and day traders follow them closely.

intrinsic value   The difference between the strike price and the market price of an option. For call options, if the strike price is lower than the market price, the difference is the intrinsic value. Likewise, if a put option's strike price is higher than the market price, the difference is intrinsic value.

investing   Using your money to make money, while minimizing risk. Investing is proactive.

investment clubs   Groups of people who get together to learn about investing and collectively make investments.

investment goals   Financial goals that you address with your investments.

large-cap stock   Stock for any company with a market capitalization of $8 billion or more.

limit order   An instruction to your broker to buy a stock when the price drops to the level you set.

limit order to sell   An instruction to your broker to sell a stock when the stock climbs to a predetermined level.

limited partnership   A legal entity that is formed for a specific purpose. In the case of venture capital firms, a limited partnership acts as the general partner, meaning that it has management responsibility, while the other partners contribute money to the deal.

liquidity   The characteristic of a financial instrument to be converted to cash. A mutual fund is considered highly liquid, while an apartment building would be highly illiquid.

loaded fund   A mutual fund that charges a sales fee or commission, which is paid to the broker who sold the shares. The load may be up front or deferred.

long and short   Somewhat the equivalent of "buy and sell," but with an investing twist. If you enter an order to "go long 100 shares of IBM," it means that you want to buy IBM. Likewise, to "short IBM" is to sell the stock. Long also describes your position in a stock. For example, your brokerage statement might show that you were "long 100 IBM," which means that you own 100 shares of IBM. Your account also could show that you were "short 100 IBM," which means that you sold 100 shares of IBM short. *See also* short selling.

lost opportunity costs   When you fail to act on an opportunity because your money was tied up, or when you pass up a chance for profits because fear or the lack of information holds you back.

management fee   Also called the investment advisory fee, this is the amount charged by the mutual fund company and used to pay the fund's manager, who is responsible for making sure that the fund meets its objectives.

margin   A way to finance your stock purchases. Your broker will lend you up to 50 percent of the purchase price. For example, if you had $5,000 to invest, you could buy $10,000 worth of stock. You pay interest on the loan and repay it when you sell the stock. If the price of the stock falls below 75 percent of the original price, your broker will require you to deposit more money in your account or to sell the stock and pay back the loan.

market capitalization   Also called market cap, this is a way of measuring the size of a company. It is calculated by multiplying the current stock price by the number of outstanding shares. A stock trading at $55 with 10,000,000 outstanding shares would have a market cap of $550 million.

market cycles   Periods of up markets and down markets that have been historically documented.

market indicators   A collective name for a number of indexes and other measurements of market activity.

market order   An order to buy or sell that is placed with your broker and that requests the best price at that moment. Market orders are filled the fastest.

market value risk   The danger that your investment will fall out of favor with the market or may simply be ignored.

market/viewer value (MVV)   A way to place a value on the number of viewers that visit a Web site. The number of viewer is an asset and MVV is a way to relate the stock's price to that asset.

mid-cap stock   A mid-cap stock would be any company with a market capitalization of $1 to $8 billion.

money market accounts   Special savings accounts usually offered by financial institutions that pay a higher interest rate than regular savings, but that require a higher minimum balance. They are not the same as money market mutual funds.

money market funds   Mutual funds that invest in very short-term cash instruments. These funds are often used within a family of mutual funds to park uninvested cash. These are not the same as money market accounts.

money market mutual funds   Mutual funds that invest in short-term money market instruments. You often can withdraw money on short notice without penalty. Some offer check-writing privileges.

Moody's Investors Services   A service that analyzes and rates investments, including bonds, along with Standard and Poors.

multiple   Another term for price/earnings (P/E) ratio.

mutual funds   Funds representing a pool of individuals who have pooled their money and hired a professional management company to invest the money. Each mutual fund has specific goals and objectives that drive its buy and sell decisions. Mutual funds may invest in stocks, bonds, or both.

NASDAQ   Also known as the over-the-counter market, the NASDAQ is the new kid on the block. Trades are executed over an electronics network of brokers. Many of the companies listed here are fairly young, and this is the home of many of today's high-tech stars.

National Association of Securities Dealers (NASD)   A self-regulatory body of securities brokers that is supervised by the Securities and Exchange Commission. The NASD licenses and examines brokers and handles consumer complaints.

net asset value (NAV)   The net asset value is the mutual fund equivalent of a share price. This is the price you pay when you buy into a mutual fund. Unlike stocks, mutual funds have no problems with fractional shares. The amount you deposit is divided by the NAV to arrive at your shares. The NAV is calculated by subtracting the liabilities from the holdings of a mutual fund, and then dividing by the outstanding shares.

New York Stock Exchange   The oldest and most prestigious of all stock exchanges. The NYSE is home to most of the blue chip companies.

no-load fund   A mutual fund that charges no sales fees or commissions either up front or deferred.

online brokers   Brokers that allow investors to buy and sell securities over the Internet without ever talking to a human. Online brokers offer the least expensive commissions.

options   Give the owner the right, but not the obligation, to purchase or sell a specific number of shares of a stock at a specific price. Options are bought and sold on the open market.

options writer   An investor who sells options. The writer, unlike the buyer, is obligated to fulfill the terms of the option if it is exercised. Options can be exercised at any point in the life of the option.

passive fund   A fund in which there are no investment decisions. An index fund would be a passive fund.

passive investment strategy   An investment strategy that seeks to put most of the work into a professional's hands or that adopts strategies that are more mechanical than analytical. Dogs of the Dow is a passive investment strategy.

penny stocks   Penny stocks are a special category of low-priced (usually $1 or less) stocks often issued by highly speculative companies. They are the focus of numerous stock scams and manipulations.

personal digital assistants (PDAs)   New devices that are being used to access the Internet. They have built-in modems and cellular phones to connect with an Internet service provider.

personal information manager (PIMs)   A software package that helps you organize and keep current all the people in your business or personal life. These might be customers or vendors or just friends. Also called a contact manager, a PIM records names, addresses, phone numbers, e-mail, Web sites, and so on for easy retrieval. It also keeps your appointments and calendar.

portal   A Web site that acts as a starting point for deeper levels of discovery. In addition, a portal often categorizes information and directs the user to specific locations. Portals also offer additional services such as e-mail. Alta Vista and Excite are portals.

portfolio   The collection of all your investing assets.

position   A description of your current holdings. If you owned 100 shares of IBM, your position would be "long 100 IBM."

precious metals mutual funds   Mutual funds that invest in stocks and bonds of mining and trading companies of precious metals (gold, silver, and so on).

preferred stock   As the name implies, preferred stock is a different class of stock with additional rights not granted to common stock owners. Among these rights is first call on dividends.

price trading   A trading program that looks for stocks that are about to change direction in price for some reason and attempts to get in before the change occurs.

price/earnings growth ratio (PEG)   A ratio that is used to look into the future relationship of earnings and growth. It is calculated by dividing forward earnings estimates into the price/earnings (P/E) ratio.

price/earnings (P/E) ratio   A way to show how a company's earnings relate to the stock price. The P/E is calculated by dividing the current price of the stock by the annual earnings per share. The higher the P/E, the more earnings growth investors are expecting.

price-to-book ratio   Dividing the current stock price by book value per share. This relationship shows the value of the equity as it relates to the stock price.

primary market   The first sale of the company's stock. This is often to institutional investors and brokerage houses. Money from this sale goes to the company.

profit-sharing plan   A plan that passes a portion of the company's profits to the employee's retirement account. These plans often are used in connection with 401(k) plans. The employer makes all the contributions but is not obligated to pay out a portion of the profits.

prospectus   A legal document that potential shareholders of mutual funds and initial public offerings of stocks must have before they can invest. The prospectus lists complete financial details of the fund as well as the associated risks.

put option   Gives the owner the right, but not the obligation, to sell a stock at a certain price within a specified time frame.

315

ratio   Simply a comparison of the relationship between financial items. For example, price/earnings ratio shows the relationship between a company's earnings and its stock price.

real estate investment trusts (REITs)   Investment vehicles that are similar to mutual funds in that they are traded as securities. Thus, they are more liquid than other forms of real estate investments.

real estate limited partnerships   An investment vehicle that pools investors' money and buys income-producing properties.

recession   A period marked by declining standards of living and rising prices. Officially, a recession is marked by a decline in the nation's gross national product for two consecutive quarters.

return   Another term for yield. Return is expressed most often as a percentage.

return on equity   A way to look at how earnings relate to stockholder equity. Annual earnings are divided by stockholder's equity.

risk   A measure of the possibility that an investment will not earn the anticipated return.

risk tolerance   A way to judge how much risk you are willing to take to achieve an investment goal. The higher your risk tolerance, the more risk you are willing to take.

round lot   The standard transaction unit in stocks (100 shares). Any order not divisible by 100 is considered an odd lot and may trigger a fee from your broker.

Russell 2000 Index   The Frank Russell Company, now a part of Northwestern Mutual, developed this index of 2,000 smaller companies. Numerous other indexes also measure other market segments.

sales-based evaluation   Evaluations that look at how sales and price relate. This measurement works well for companies with no earnings and uses the sales-price ratio.

sales-price ratio   Dividing the stock's market capitalization, plus any long-term debt, by sales for the preceding 12 months.

search engine   A specialized piece of software that searches the Internet for words, primarily in Web site descriptions, that match the request.

sector mutual funds   Mutual funds that invest in various sectors of the economy, such as technology or healthcare.

Securities and Exchange Commission (SEC)   The chief regulatory body over the stock markets and companies that are publicly traded.

Securities Investor Protection Corporation   A private government-sponsored agency that provides insurance to protect your assets at a brokerage firm if the brokerage fails. Coverage is up to $500,000 per account. The insurance does not protect against trading losses.

server   A piece of computer hardware that Internet companies use to respond to queries of its database. The computer serves up the requested files.

short selling   The process by which you sell a stock that you do not own in anticipation that the price is going to fall. Your broker borrows the stock from another client. You sell the stock and put the money in your account. If you are correct, you buy back the stock at the lower price and pocket the profit. The original owner then gets the stock back. This is all perfectly legal.

small-cap stock   Stock in any company with a market capitalization of $1 billion or less.

socially responsible mutual funds   Mutual funds that invest in carefully screened companies that meet certain social or ethical standards. These also are known as "green funds" or "planet-friendly" funds.

Standard & Poor's   An investment research service that provides a number of market indexes, including the S&P 500. It also provides a rating service for bonds.

Standard & Poor's 500   A weighted index of 500 of the largest stocks. The S&P 500 is the most widely used measure of broad market activity and is often the benchmark to which other investments are compared.

Standard Industrial Classification   A four-digit code assigned to every business. This classification helps the government and researchers identify companies in a particular line of business. Most businesses have more than one SIC code but are required to have a primary one.

statement of cash flow   Part of the annual report that describes the source of a company's cash and how that has changed from the previous year.

stickiness   The quality a Web site has that makes viewers want to stay longer and look at more pages.

stock mutual funds   Mutual funds that invest exclusively or primarily in stocks. The stocks may be broad-based or in one sector. They may include foreign as well as domestic stocks.

stock options   Incentives offered to employees that grant the owner the right to buy the stock at a certain price. These options usually are not transferable or sold on the open market.

stockbroker   Also known as a broker, this is a person licensed and authorized to buy and sell securities. A stockbroker is required to pass examinations and must meet certain standards of conduct set by the National Association of Securities Dealers (NASD).

stop loss order   An instruction to your broker to sell if the price falls to a certain level. This order will prevent further losses.

swing trading   This trading system looks for flaws in the market pricing of a particular stock and attempts to take advantage of the market's correction in the stock's price.

tax-deferred   Refers to investment vehicles that allow principal and interest to grow without paying taxes on the earnings until sometime in the future. Qualified retirement accounts allow tax-deferred growth.

technical analysis   Focuses on the supply and demand for a stock and tries to predict future moves in the price.

the markets   A phrase generally used to mean the collective stock exchanges.

NASDAQ Composite Index   An index that covers the NASDAQ market of more than 5,000 stocks.

New York Stock Exchange Index   An index that covers all the stocks on the NYSE, making a broad measurement of larger companies.

timing the market   An investment strategy to try to pick a stock's low price to buy and a stock's high price to sell. No one can consistently do this with any success.

trade   The buying or selling of stocks, bonds, mutual funds, and other financial instruments. Depending on the usage, it can mean a single transaction or can refer to the total market (as in, trading was heavy).

trailing twelve months (TTM)   A way of looking at a company's ongoing activity rather than just what is reported once a year in the annual report. This is simply a way to look at the past 12 months, no matter when the data is collected.

transaction fees   Fees charged for just about any service provided by a financial institution, including mutual funds.

turnover   The percentage of a fund's holdings that are bought and sold each year. The higher the turnover, the higher the expense ratio and tax liabilities.

unique visitor   An Internet term that represents one visitor to a site during the month. Each unique visitor is counted only once, no matter how often that person may come back during the month.

unit investment trusts   Another hybrid fund that buys a fixed portfolio of stock or bonds and never sells or buys anymore. These are sold by brokers and are traded on the open market.

universal resource locator (URL)   The equivalent of a street address for a Web site. If you know this, you can find the site.

value mutual funds   Mutual funds that look for companies that the market is undervaluing for some reason, with the hope that their fortunes will return and that the stock will experience significant growth.

value stock   A stock that is underpriced by the market, for whatever reason. Often a stock's only sin is not being a part of the current hot sector.

virtual marketplaces   Web sites where buyers and sellers can exchange information and work together more closely. The automakers' marketplace grants vendors' access to users and creates a competitive environment for pricing similar products.

volatile   A stock is said to be volatile if it has wide swings in price each day.

walking dead   Internet businesses that analysts believe won't survive, but that have so much cash from their IPO that they don't know they're dead.

warrants   Entities that give the holder the right, but not the obligation, to purchase a specific number of shares of a stock at a specified price. Warrants often are issued along with new stock as an incentive to investors.

wealth builder   Concepts founded in fact and reason that provide for the accumulation of wealth. Compounding of interest is the best known and most powerful of all wealth-building concepts.

workstations   Terminals used by brokers that are connected to powerful networks and are nothing like your home computer.

yield   Another term for return, but expressed as a percentage. For example, yield is the percent returned to stockholders in the form of dividends.

yield-based evaluation   A model used to value a stock, based on the dividend yield calculation.

Web Sites

This appendix lists the companies mentioned in this book. Most of them are publicly traded and will have a ticker symbol. Use this symbol to look up the stock on an on-line service such as Morningstar.com. If a company is not publicly traded, only be a URL will be included in the listing.

A URL, universal resource locator, is the address on the Internet where you can find the company's Web site. Some browsers require you to put "www." before the URL.

123Jump.com (URL: 123jump.com)

3Com Corp. (ticker symbol: COMS; URL: 3com.con)

About.com (ticker symbol: BOUT; URL: about.com)

Advanced Micro Devices (ticker symbol: AMD; URL: amd.com)

Alta Vista (URL: altavista.com)

Amazon.com (ticker symbol: AMZN; URL: amazon.com)

America Online (ticker symbol: AOL; URL: aol.com)

Apple Computer (ticker symbol: AAPL; URL: apple.com)

Ariba (ticker symbol: ARBA; URL: ariba.net)

AT&T (ticker symbol: T; URL: att.com)

AtomFilms (URL: atomfilms.com)

Atomic Pop (URL: atomicpop.com)

AvenueA (ticker symbol: AVEA; URL: avenuea.com)

Bank of America (ticker symbol: BAC; URL: bankamerica.com)

Barnes and Noble (ticker symbol: BKS; URL: barnesandnoble.com)

Barnesandnoble.com (ticker symbol: BNBN; URL: bn.com)

Bell Atlantic (ticker symbol: BEL; URL: bell-atl.com)

BellSouth (ticker symbol: BLS; URL: bellsouth.com)

Bluetooth (URL: bluetooth.com)

Borders (ticker symbol: BRG; URL: borders.com)

Bottomline Technologies (ticker symbol: EPAY; URL: bottomline.com)

Brilliant Digital (ticker symbol: BDE; URL: brillaintdigital.com)

CDNow.com (ticker symbol: CDNW; URL: cdnow.com)

Cheap Tickets (ticker symbol: CTIX; URL: cheaptickets.com)

Chicago Board Options Exchange (URL: cboe.com)

CIDCO (ticker symbol: CDCO; URL: cidco.com)

Cisco Systems (ticker symbol: CSCO; URL: cisco.com)

CMGI (ticker symbol: CMGI; URL: cmgi.com)

CNET (ticker symbol: CNET; URL: cnet.com)

CNN (URL: cnn.com)

Compaq Computer (ticker symbol: CPQ; URL: compaq.com)

Convad (ticker symbol: COVD; URL: covad.com)

Copper Mountain (ticker symbol: CMTN; URL: coppermountain.com)

DaimlerChrysler (ticker symbol: DCX; URL: daimlerchrysler.com)

Day Trading About.com (URL: daytrading.about.com)

Dell (ticker symbol: DELL; URL: dell.com)

Dilbert.com (URL: dilbert.com)

DoubleClick (ticker symbol: DCLK; URL: doubleclick.net)

Dow Jones (ticker symbol: DJ; URL: dowjones.com)

E*Trade (ticker symbol: EGRP; URL: etrade.com)

E*Trade E-commerce Index Fund (ticker symbol: ETECX; URL: etrade.com)

eBay.com (ticker symbol: EBAY; URL: ebay.com)

Edgar On-Line (ticker symbol: EDGR; URL: edgaronline.com)

Efficient Networks (ticker symbol: EFNT; URL: efficient.com) eGreetings Network (ticker symbol: EGRT; URL: egreetings.com)

Electronic Arts (ticker symbol: ERTS; URL: ea.com)

Elite.com (ticker symbol: ELTE; URL: elite.com)

Exodus Communications (ticker symbol: EXDS; URL: exodus.com)

Firsthand e-commerce (ticker symbol: TEFQX)

Ford (ticker symbol: F; URL: ford.com)

General Motors (ticker symbol: GM; URL: gm.com)

General Electric (ticker symbol: GE; URL: ge.com)

Go.com (ticker symbol: GO; URL: go.com)

Go2Net.com (ticker symbol: GNET; URL: go2net.com)

Goldman Sachs (ticker symbol: GS; URL: gs.com)

Goto.com (ticker symbol: GOTO; URL: goto.com)

Guinness-Flight Internet.com Index (ticker symbol: GFINX; URL: gffunds.com)

Healtheon (ticker symbol: HLTH; URL: webmed.com)

Hotmail.com (URL: hotmail.com)

IBM (ticker symbol: IBM; URL: ibm.com)

iFilm (URL: ifilm.com)

Image Sensing Systems, Inc. (ticker symbol: ISNS; URL: imagesensing.con)

Infonautics (ticker symbol: INFO; URL: infonautics.com

Intel (ticker symbol: INTC; URL: intel.com)

Interactive Week Online (ticker symbol: ZD; URL: zdnet.com/intweek/)

Interactive Wall Street Journal (ticker symbol: DJ; URL: interactive.wsj.com)

Internet Stock Report (ticker symbol: INTM; URL: internetstockreport.com)

Internet Index Fund (ticker symbol: M$-BEHC ; URL: internetindexfund.net)

Internet.com (ticker symbol: INTM; URL: internet.com)

Intuit (ticker symbol: INTU; URL: intuit.com)

Investing for Beginners (URL: beginnersinvest.about.com)

InvestorPlace.com (URL: investorplace.com)

IPO Monitor (URL: www.ipomonitor.com)

323

iVillage (ticker symbol: IVIL; URL: ivillage.com)

iXL Enterprises, Inc. (ticker symbol: IIXL; URL: ixl.com)

K-Mart (ticker symbol: KM; URL: bluelight.com)

Land's End (ticker symbol: LE; URL: landsend.com)

Launch Media (ticker symbol: LAUN; URL: launch.com)

Lucent (ticker symbol: LU; URL: lucent.com)

Lycos (ticker symbol: LCOS; URL: lycos.com)

Major League Baseball (URL: majorleaguebaseball.com)

Market Guide (URL: marketguide.com)

Market Guide—multex.com (ticker symbol: MLTX; URL: marketguide.com)

Maytag (ticker symbol: MYG; URL: maytagcorp.com)

Media Metrix (ticker symbol: MMXI; URL: mediametrix.com)

Microsoft (ticker symbol: MSFT; URL: Microsoft.com)

Microsoft Network Money Central (ticker symbol: MSFT; URL: moneycentral.msn.com)

MicroStrategy (ticker symbol: MSTR; URL: strategy.com)

Morningstar.com (URL: Morningstar.com)

Motorola (ticker symbol: MOT; URL: Motorola.com)

MyPoints.com (ticker symbol: MYPT; URL: mypoints.com)

National Association of Securities Dealers (NASD) (URL: www.nasdr.com)

NetBank (ticker symbol: NTBK; URL: netbank.com)

NetLedger (URL: netledger.com)

NetObjects (ticker symbol: NETO; URL: netobjects.com)

Netopia (ticker symbol: NTPA; URL: netopia.com)

Netpliance (ticker symbol: NPLI; URL: netpliance.com)

Netscape (URL: netscape.com)

Nokia (ticker symbol: NOK; URL: nokia.com)

Nortel (ticker symbol: NT; URL: Nortel.com)

Northpoint (ticker symbol: NPNT; URL: northpointcom.com)

OneSource Information Services (ticker symbol: ONES; URL: onesource.com)

Online New York Times (ticker symbol: NYT; URL: nytimes.com)

Pacific Century Cyberworks (URL: pcg-group.com)

Palm, Inc. (ticker symbol: PALM; URL: palm.com)

Paradyne (ticker symbol: PDYN; URL: paradyne.com)

Peapod.com (ticker symbol: PPOD; URL: peapod.com)

Pollution Research and Control Corp. (ticker symbol: PRCC; URL: dasibi.com)

Priceline.com (ticker symbol: PCLN; URL: priceline.com)

Qualcomm (ticker symbol: QCOM; URL: qualcomm.com)

Quest (ticker symbol: Q; URL: uswest.com)

Radiant Systems, Inc. (ticker symbol: RADS; URL: rads.com)

Red Herring (URL: redherring.com)

Research in Motion (ticker symbol: RIMM; URL: rim.net)

RhythmsNet (ticker symbol: RTHM; URL: rhythms.net)

Salon.com (ticker symbol: SALN; URL: salon.com)

SBC (ticker symbol: SBC; URL: sbc.com)

Sun Microsystems (ticker symbol: SUNW; URL: sun.com)

The Internet 100 (ticker symbol: M$-BDGA URL: usatoday.com)

The Motley Fool (URL: fool.com)

The Standard.com (URL: thestandard.com)

The Wall Street Directory (URL: wallstreetdirectory.com)

The Dow Jones Business Directory (URL: businessdirectory.dowjones.com)

Time Warner (ticker symbol: TWX; URL: timewarner.com)

U.S. West (ticker symbol: USW; URL: uswest.com)

UPS (ticker symbol: UPS; URL: ups.com)

USA Today (URL: usatoday.com)

Value Line Investment Survey (URL: valueline.com)

Value America (ticker symbol: VUSA; URL: valueline.com)

Viacom (ticker symbol: VIA; URL: viacom.com)

VitaminShoppe, Inc. (ticker symbol: VSHP; URL: vitaminshoppe.com)

W.W. Grainger (ticker symbol: GWW; URL: grainger.com)

Wall Street Research Network (URL: wsrn.com)

Wal-Mart (ticker symbol: WMT; URL: walmart.com)

Walt Disney (ticker symbol: DIS; URL: Disney.com)

WebTrends (ticker symbol: WEBT; URL: webtrends.com)

Wells Fargo (ticker symbol: WFC; URL: wellsfargo.com)

Westell (ticker symbol: WSTL; URL: westell.com)

Whirlpool (ticker symbol: WHR; URL: whirlpoolcorp.com)

Wireless MD (URL: wirelessmd.com)

Yahoo! (ticker symbol: YHOO; URL: yahoo.com)

Zacks.com (URL: zacks.com)

ZDNet (URL: zdnet.com)

Index

SYMBOLS

10-K document, 160
10-Q document, 160
123Jump Web site, 160
3Com Corp., 22
  Web site, 259

A

A.C. Neilsen Company,
  266
About.com, 11, 88-89
access point. *See* interface
accessibility, online
  banking, 276
accounts, opening (online
  banking), 276
actively managed mutual
  funds, 186
Advanced Micro Devices,
  25
advertisers, broadband
  access, 256
advertising, Internet,
  265-272
  betting future on
    revenues, 267-268
  media-rich ads, 271-272
  profiling, 269-270
  testing, 266-267
advertising-based sites,
  109-110
advertising-only sites,
  267-268
advice versus fads
  (technology), 154-155

advisory services, online
  resources, 78
  InvestorPlace.com, 79
  Zacks.com, 78-79
allocation systems, IPOs,
  170
  E*Trade, 170-172
Amazon.com, 4, 111, 136
America Online. *See* AOL
analogies, Internet, 264
analysis, day trading, 199
  fundamental, 200
  technical, 200-202
AOL (America Online), 6
  merger with Time
    Warner, 231-234
    benefits for AOL, 233
    benefits for Time
      Warner, 233-234
    broadband future,
      237-238
    competitor reaction,
      238
    financial considera-
      tions, 235-237
    potential problems,
      235
    trouble signs, 237
appliances, network gate-
  ways, 295
application service
  providers. *See* ASPs
Ariba, 288
ASPs (application service
  providers), 31, 287-288
assessing risk, 21-23,
  49-51, 303
  balancing risk, 55

    high risk investments,
      57
    low risk investments,
      55-56
    medium risk invest-
      ments, 56-57
  economic risk, 53
  expectations, 57
  "gee whiz" factor, 23
  inflation risk, 52-53
  market value risk, 51
  risk aversion, 54
  risk tolerance, 53-54
  safety nets, 47-48
ATMS (automated teller
  machines), 277
automakers, virtual market
  places, integration of
  company and Internet,
  228-229
automated teller machines.
  See ATMS
AvenueA Web site, 270
aversion, risk, 54

B

B2B (business-to-business)
  applications, 288-289
B2B (business-to-business)
  services, 5-6
  DoubleClick, 6
back testing, 63
backbone (information
  expressway), 30
balancing risk, 55
  high risk investments,
    57

low risk investments, 55-56
medium risk investments, 56-57
Bank of America, online banking, 279
banking online, 274-276
  accessibility, 276
  bill payments, 276-277
  bill presentment, 277
  cash problems, 277-278
  choices, 279
  deals, 276
  future, 278-279
  history, 275-276
  investing in pure Internet banks, 279-280
  investments, 277
  lack of special services, 278
  loans, 277
  opening an account, 276
  security issues, 280
Barnes and Noble Books. *See* BNBN
Bell Atlantic Web site, 259
BellSouth Web site, 259
Beta (stock volatility measure), 73
Beta versus VHS wars, cooperation in sales, 93
Bigger Fool Theory, 119
bills (online banking)
  payments, 276-277
  presentment, 277
Bluelight.com, 226
Bluetooth, 28, 290
BNBN (Barnes and Noble Books), 110, 136
  Web site, 110
bookstores, 135
  Amazon.com, 136
  BNBN, 136
  Borders, 136

Borders Group Inc., 7, 136
  Web site, 110
Bottomline Technologies, 288
brick-and-mortar companies, 9
broadband, 233, 254-255
  advertisers, 256
  competing technologies for broadband delivery, 256
    cable, 257-259
    DSL, 257-259
    satellite, 258
    wireless cable, 259
  future in mergers, 237-238
  future market, 260
  "Internet everywhere" concept, 261
  regulatory and legal issues, 260
  standards, 260-261
  structuring content for a variety of speeds, 255-256
brokers, day trading, 196-197
  commissions, 197
  space offers, 197-198
business models of companies, integration of the Internet, 224-228
  benefits of Internet presence, 229-230
  Cisco Systems business model, 228
  Compaq Computer, 229
  e-tailers, 225-226
  online selling, 225
  virtual market places, 228-229
business-to-business applications. *See* B2B applications

business-to-business services. *See* B2B services
buying
  holding strategy, 302
  options, 211-213
    reasons to buy, 213-214
  quality investments strategy, 301
  stock, long, 182-183
    limit orders, 182
    market orders, 182
    rolling orders, 183

C

cable, broadband delivery competitor, 257-259
calculators, options, 216
call options, 208-209
  naked, 215
candidacy, mutual funds, 192-193
capital, day trading, 203
cash
  draining from the company, growth, 143-144
  flow, earnings, 107-108
    EBITDA, 107
  problems, online banking, 277-278
  reserves, shrinking, 146
CBOE (Chicago Board Options Exchange), 216
cheap stock, evaluating stocks, 89
Cheap Tickets Web site, 95
Chicago Board Options Exchange. *See* CBOE
CIDCO, 286
Cisco Systems
  business model for integration of company and Internet, 228
  Web site, 228

click and mortar companies, 9
click-throughs, 109
CMGI, 37
CNET
    PSR of a mid-cap company, 96
    Web site, 66
CNN Web site, 65
commissions, day trading brokers, 197
commodities, 242
companies
    change in consumer expectations, 10-11
    changes after going public with IPOs, 43
    Hybrid Internet companies, 6-7
        America Online, 6
        Sun Microsystems, 6
    identifying and evaluating, 8-10
    integration of Internet into business models, 224-228
        benefits of Internet presence, 229-230
        Cisco Systems business model, 228
        Compaq Computer, 229
        e-tailers, 225-226
        online selling, 225
        virtual market places, 228-229
    Internet impact on financial picture, 244-245
    management, 114, 158
        definition of success, 159
        founders stepping aside, 161-162

Internet executives information, 159-161
    profit plans, 114-115
    venture capitalists, 158
    masking themselves as something they are not, 7-8
    Pure Internet, 4-6, 224
        Amazon.com, 4
        DoubleClick, 5
        Yahoo!, 5
    sales, 91
        company connection to the community, 93-94
        cooperation, 93
        Internet standards, 93
        investigating what you are buying, 92
    technology, 112
    traditional mergers with Internet companies, 231-238
Compaq Computer, 8
    integration of company and Internet, 229
competition
    broadband delivery, 256
        cable, 257-259
        DSL, 257-259
        satellite, 258
        wireless cable, 259
    competitor reaction to mergers, 238
Complete Idiot's Guide to Excel, The, 100
components of the Internet, 26-27
    backbone (information expressway), 30
    connection, 29-30
    interface, 27
    software and services, 30-32

computers
    network connections, 293-294
    technology, 284-298
        ASPs, 287-288
        B2B applications, 288-289
        home office revolution, 286-287
        post-PC era, 284-285
        SOHO, 287
        voice recognition, 298-299
connected appliances, 295
consumers, response to Internet businesses, 107
content (Internet), 125
cookies, 265
    profiles, 266-267
cooperation (sales), Beta versus VHS wars, 93
Copper Mountain Web site, 259
copycat business plans, 146
correction (market), 51
cost per thousand impressions. *See* CPM
costs
    going public with IPOs, 40
    lost opportunities, 17
    realistic, Internet strategy evaluation, 244
counting heads (customers), 128
    Media Metrix, 128
    unique visitors, 128
Covad Web site, 259
CPM (cost per thousand impressions), 265
critical mass (portals), 123
custom screens, stock screens, 73-74
customers, 128

counting heads, 128
　Media Metrix, 128
　unique visitors, 128
customer service,
　136-137
　earnings, 108
　trying the service before
　　purchase, 108
　unique views versus
　　unique customers, 129
　unique visitors, 129

D

DaimlerChrysler, 228
day trading, 196
　alternative strategies,
　　204
　　price trading, 204-205
　　swing trading, 205
　analysis, 199
　　fundamental, 200
　　technical, 200-202
　brokers, 196-197
　　commissions, 197
　　space offers, 197-198
　capital, 203
　emotions, 204
　　fear, 204
　　greed, 204
　home traders, 198-199
　Internet stocks, 205
　recommendations, 206
　simulations, 203-204
　tax considerations, 199
deals
　online banking, 276
　venture capitalists, 37
　　incubators, 38
declining sales, 146
decreasing expenses
　strategy, 302
Dell Computer, 10
Dell, Michael, Internet
　strategy, 246

digital subscriber line. *See*
　DSL
digital-divide, 268-269
direct offerings, IPOs, 172
diversification, 20-21, 51,
　303
　employee stock options,
　　220
　mutual funds, 186-187
dot. com economy, 34
DoubleClick, 5
Dow Jones
　Business Directory Web
　　site, 162
　Composite Internet
　　index, 189
　Web site, 189
DSL (digital subscriber
　line), 257
　broadband delivery
　　competitor, 257-259

E

E*Trade
　E-commerce Index fund,
　　189
　IPO allocation system,
　　170-172
e-access providers (Internet
　100 index), 190
e-advertising/marketing/
　media (Internet 100
　index), 189
E-commerce, 11
　Index fund (E*Trade),
　　189
E-economy, 11
e-finance (Internet 100
　index), 190
e-infrastructure (Internet
　100 index), 189
e-new media (Internet 100
　index), 190
e-retail (Internet 100
　index), 189

e-services/solutions
　(Internet 100 index), 189
e-tailers (electronic retail),
　108-109, 225-226
　hybrid, 111
　profits, 134
　walking dead, 108
earnings, 106
　cash flow, EBITDA,
　　107-108
　consumer response to
　　the Internet, 107
　customers, 108
　estimates, 106
　growth, 110
　　expectations,
　　　110-111, 145-146
　　positive signs, 147
　　unsustainable, 111
　　warning signs,
　　　146-147
　sales, 91-94
　　company connection
　　　to the community,
　　　93-94
　　cooperation, 93
　　Internet standards, 93
　　investigating what
　　　you are buying, 92
　　PSR tool, 94-97
　　stock screens, 97-102
earnings before interest,
　taxes, depreciation, and
　amortization. *See* EBITDA
earnings per share. *See* EPS
EBITDA (earnings before
　interest, taxes, deprecia-
　tion, and amortization),
　107
EBPP (electronic bill pre-
　sentment and payment),
　288
economic risk, 53
Edgar On-Line Web site,
　160

education, digital-divide, 268-269

Efficient Networks Web site, 259

electronic bill presentment and payment. *See* EBPP

electronic retail. *See* e-tailers

elements (investments), 49
  amount invested, 50
  length of time, 50
  level of risk, 50

Elite.com, 287

e-mail cons (Internet information source), 61-62

emotions, day trading, 204
  fear, 204
  greed, 204

employee stock options, 219-220
  diversification, 220

enhancing products and services, technology, 151

entertainment
  delivered by Internet, selecting stocks, 124-125
  systems, network gateways, 295-296

entry barriers, 121

environmental systems, network gateways, 294

EPS (earnings per share), 79

estimates, earnings, 106

evaluation
  company connection to the community, 93-94
  Internet strategy, 244-248
    realistic costs, 244
    realistic time frame, 245
    well-defined goals, 244

profits, 117-120
  future visions, 118-119
  patience, 120
  stock market effect, 120

sales as a proxy for earnings, 94
  PSR tool, 94-97

stock screens, 97
  Market Guide, 100
  MSN MoneyCentral, 98-99
  operators, 98
  Power, 100-102

stocks, 81-82
  cheap stock, 89
  growth rates, 88
  New Economy world, 89-90
  numbers, 83-89
  SIC codes, 84-85
  understanding what you buy, 83-86
  Yahoo!, 87-88

trying the service, 108

unique visitors count, 129
  computing market value, 129-132
  percentage of premium converted to sales, 133
  sales per visitor, 131-132

Excite@Home cable service, 259

executives (company management)
  founders stepping aside, 161-162
  locating information, 159-161

expectation bubbles (IPOs), 167

expectations
  growth, 141-142
  risk, 57

expenses, strategy for keeping low, 302

expiration dates (options), 208-211

F

fads versus legitimate advice (technology), 154-155

family information manager. *See* FIM

fat numbers, 147

FDIC (Federal Deposit Insurance Corporation), 48, 275

fear, day trading emotion, 204

FED (Federal Reserve Board), 52, 200

Federal Deposit Insurance Corporation. *See* FDIC

Federal Reserve Board. *See* FED

figuring PSR, TTM (trailing twelve months), 94

Filo, David, 161

FIM (family information manager), 294

financial
  considerations, AOL Time Warner merger, 235-237
  services, 274, 280-281
  Web sites, 75
    Morningstar.com, 75-77
    MSN MoneyCentral, 77-78

fingerprints, IPO myths, 169-170

Firsthand e-commerce, 190

flat growth rates, 146
focused mutual funds, 190
Ford, 228
forecasting growth,
  147-148
fraud, 64
fundamental analysis, day
  trading, 200
funds (mutual), 186
  actively managed, 186
  candidacy, 192-193
  diversification, 186-187
  focused, 190
  index, 188-190
  professional manage-
    ment, 187-188
  TTM, 192
  volatility, 191-192
future
  IPOs, 177
  market, broadband
    delivery, 260
  network gateways, 296
  online banking, 278-279
  visions, profits, 118-119
fyi advisor, MSN
  MoneyCentral, 77

G

gateways, 293
"gee whiz" factor, risk
  assessment, 23
General Electric, 295
General Motors, 228
general news and informa-
  tion (Internet), 65-66
getting out first
  IPO risks, 173
  selecting stocks, 122
Getting Started in Options,
  216
global positioning systems.
  See GPS

goals, Internet strategy
  evaluation, 244
going long (IPOs), 182-183
  limit orders, 182
  market orders, 182
  rolling orders, 183
going public, venture
  capitalists, 36
going short (IPOs),
  183-184
Goldman Sachs E-
  Commerce index, 189
Goldman Sachs Web site,
  189
goodwill, 236
Google, 162
GPS (global positioning
  systems), 296
greed, day trading
  emotion, 204
growth, 110, 140
  draining cash from a
    company, 143-144
  expectations, 110-111,
    141-142
  forecasting, 147-148
  infrastructure support,
    144-145
  prices, 140-141
    unearned cash, 141
  rates, evaluating stocks,
    88
  "scaling" the business,
    143-144
  as substitute for
    earnings, 145-146
    positive signs, 147
    warning signs,
      146-147
  unsustainable, 111
guidelines, 18
  dealing with market
    hype, 20
  diversification, 20-21
  long term investing,
    18-19

risk assessment, 21-23
  "gee whiz" factor, 23
Guinness-Flight
  Internet.com Index, 190

H

high risk investments, 57
history of online banking,
  275-276
holding stocks, strategy,
  302
home
  office revolution
    post-PC era, 286-287
    SOHO, 287
  networks
    products, 292-293
    technology, 155-156,
      292-293
  security, network
    gateways, 294
  traders, day trading,
    198-199
Hotmail.com, 109
hybrid e-tailers, 111
Hybrid Internet compa-
  nies, 6-7
  America Online, 6
  Sun Microsystems, 6
I-banks. *See* Internet,
  banking
IBM, 34, 112
  Internet strategy,
    245-248
impact on companies
  financial picture (Internet
    strategy), 244-245
incubators, venture capitalists finding deals, 38
indexes
  funds, 56
    Internet 100, 56
    Internet.com, 56

mutual funds, 188
  Dow Jones Composite
    Internet index, 189
  Goldman Sachs
    E-Commerce index,
    189
  Internet 100 index,
    189-190
  ISDEX index, 190
  Standard & Poor's 500
    index, 56
inflation risk, 52-53
Infonautics, 98
information
  options, 215-216
  reports and publica-
    tions, Value Line
    Investment Survey,
    79-80
  scams and pitches,
    62-64
  sources (Internet), 59-64
    email cons, 61-62
    financial sites, 75-78
    general news and
      information, 65-66
    newsletters, 60-61
    online research, 74-75
    recommendations
      and advisory
      services, 78-79
    specific news and
      information, 66-67
    stock screens, 70-74
informed decisions, 16
infrastructure
  Internet, URLs, 26
  support, growth,
    144-145
initial public offerings.
  See IPOs
interactive appliances, 295
Interactive Wall Street
  Journal Web site, 65

Interactive Week Online
  Web site, 67
interface, 27
Internet, 273
  100 index, 189-190
  100 index fund, 56
  advertising sales,
    265-272
    betting future on
      revenues, 267-268
    media-rich ads,
      271-272
    profiling, 269-270
    testing, 266-267
  analogies, 264
  banking, 274-276
    accessibility, 276
    bill payments,
      276-277
    bill presentment, 277
    cash problems,
      277-278
    choices, 279
    deals, 276
    future, 278-279
    history, 275-276
    investing in pure
      Internet banks,
      279-280
    investments, 277
    lack of special
      services, 278
    loans, 277
    opening an account,
      276
    security issues, 280
  beginning, 263
  components, 26-27
    backbone (informa-
      tion expressway), 30
    connection, 29-30
    interface, 27
    software and services,
      30-32
  consumers, 107

digital-divide, 268-269
  Index Fund Web site,
    189
  infrastructure, URLs, 26
  as information source,
    60-64
    e-mail cons, 61-62
    financial sites, 75-78
    general news and
      information, 65-66
    newsletters, 60-61
    online research, 74-75
    recommendations
      and advisory
      services, 78-79
    specific news and
      information, 66-67
    stock screens, 70-74
  microprocessors, 25-26
  as a network umbrella,
    289-292
    appliances, 295
    computer connec-
      tions, 293-294
    devices, 294
    entertainment
      systems, 295-296
    environmental
      systems, 294
    futuristic looks at
      everyday life, 296
    home security, 294
    products and tech-
      nologies for home
      networks, 292-293
personal financial
  services, 280-281
sales standards, 93
Service Providers.
  See ISPs
Stock Report Web site,
  66
stocks, 3
  advertising-based
    sites, 109-110

change in consumer
expectations, 10-11
companies to be
weary of, 7-8
day trading, 205
evaluating, 81-82
guidelines, 18
Hybrid Internet
companies, 6-7
identifying and evalu-
ating companies,
8-10
making informed
decisions, 16
market cycles, 13-14
myths, 16
options, 208-209, 217
overpriced, 75
popularity, 11-12
Pure Internet
companies, 4-6
selection, 121
those to avoid,
109-115
strategy, 242-244
commodities, 242
evaluation, 248
impact on companies
financial picture,
244-245
justifying valuations,
245-248
niche markets,
242-243
portals, 243
realistic costs, 244
realistic time frame,
245
well-defined goals,
244
world vision, 243
user growth, 32-33
dot. com economy,
34
offshore opportuni-

ties, 33
"Internet everywhere"
concept, 124-125, 261
Internet.com Index Fund,
56
Internet.com Web site, 67
intraday
activity, 176
prices, 21
intrinsic value (options),
210
Intuit Web site, 275
Investing for Beginners,
11, 243
investment bankers,
pricing IPOs, 41-42
investments
elements, 49
amount invested, 50
length of time, 50
level of risk, 50
high risk, 57
low risk, 55-56
medium risk, 56-57
online banking, 277
strategies, 301
assessing risk, 303
buy quality, 301
buying and holding
stocks, 302
diversification, 303
keeping expenses
low, 302
mutual funds,
302-303
InvestorPlace.com advisory
service, 79
IPO Monitor Web site, 66
IPOs (initial public offerings), 11, 39, 166-178
allocation systems, 170
E*Trade, 170-172
changes in the company
once public, 43
cost to go public, 40

direct offerings, 172
expectation bubbles,
167
going long, 182-183
limit orders, 182
market orders, 182
rolling orders, 183
going short, 183-184
investor dilemma, weak
stocks, 177
long-term holding,
180-181
marketing and issuing,
39-40
misleading reports of
activity, 176
myths, 18, 169
fingerprints, 169-170
offering price, 169
sound retreat, 170
overconfidence, 176-177
predicting the future,
177
pricing, 181
investment bankers,
41-42
primary market, 42-43
quality stock, 178-180
risk, 166-167
volatility, 181-184
ISDEX index, 190
ISPs (Internet Service
Providers), 29
issuing IPOs, cost to go
public, 39-40
iXL Enterprises, Inc., 99

J-K

justifying valuations,
Internet strategy, 245-248

K-Mart Web site, 226
Kam, Alex (director of New
Media for Major League
Baseball), 159

L

Land's End Web site, 152
LANs (local area networks), 290
LEAPS (Long-term Equity Anticipation Securities), 211
legal issues
  broadband delivery, 260
  issuing IPOs, cost to go public, 39-40
length of time (investment element), 50
level of risk (investment element), 50
limit orders, 182
limited partnerships, venture capitalists, 38-39
loans, online banking, 277
local area networks. *See* LANs
long (buying or owning a stock), 182-183
  limit orders, 182
  market orders, 182
  rolling orders, 183
long term investing, 18-19
Long-term Equity Anticipation Securities. *See* LEAPS
long-term
  holding, 180-181
  speculating, Internet stock options, 218
lost opportunity costs, 17
low risk investments, 55-56
low valuations, trading, 146
Lucent Web site, 259

M

Macmillan Teach Yourself Investing in 24 Hours, 200, 301
mail station, CIDCO, 286
maintenance, repair, and operations. *See* MRO market
Major League Baseball Web site, 159
management company, 114, 158
  definition of success, 159
  founders stepping aside, 161-162
  Internet executives information, 159-161
  profit plans, 114-115
  venture capitalists, 158
professional, mutual funds, 187-188
market
  cap (market capitalization), 84
  correction, 51
  crash of 1987, 48
  cycles, 13-14
  hype, 20
  index funds, 56
    Internet 100, 56
    Internet.com, 56
  orders, 182
  value
    computing, MVV, 129-132
    risk, 51
Market Guide screen, 100
Market Guide Web site, 72
market-dominating sites, selecting stocks, 121-122

Market/Viewer Values. *See* MVV
marketing IPOs, cost to go public, 39-40
marriage of corporate America and Internet, 223-228
  benefits of Internet presence, 229-230
  Cisco Systems business model, 228
  Compaq Computer, 229
  e-tailers, 225-226
  mergers
    AOL Time Warner, 231-237
    broadband future, 237-238
    competitor reaction, 238
    trouble signs, 237
  online selling, 225
  virtual market places, 228-229
Maytag, 295
McMillan on Options, 216
Media Metrix (customer counter), 128
media-rich ads, advertising, 271-272
medium risk investments, 56-57
merging traditional companies with Internet companies
  AOL Time Warner, 231-237
  broadband future, 237-238
  competitor reaction, 238
  trouble signs, 237
microprocessors, 25-26
Microsoft Network Money Central Web site, 65
mid-cap companies, PSR tool, 95-97

misleading reports of activity, IPOs, 176

mom-and-pop stores, profits, 135

Morningstar, 75-77
  PSR of a mid-cap company, 97
  Snapshot, 75
  Web site, 97

Motley Fool Web site, 94

MRO market (maintenance, repair, and operations), 227

MSN MoneyCentral, 77-78
  fyi advisor, 77
  screen, 98-99

mutual funds, 186-192, 302-303
  actively managed, 186
  candidacy, 192-193
  diversification, 186-187
  focused, 190
  index, 188
    Dow Jones Composite Internet index, 189
    Goldman Sachs E-Commerce index, 189
    Internet 100 index, 189-190
    ISDEX index, 190
  professional management, 187-188
  TTM, 192
  volatility, 191-192

MVV (Market/Viewer Values), 129-132

myths, 16
  high rollers only, 16
  IPOs, 18, 169
    fingerprints, 169-170
    offering price, 169
    sound retreat, 170
  lose all of your money, 17
  will become rich, 17-18

N

naked calls, options, 215

NASD (National Association of Securities Dealers), 48

National Association of Securities Dealers. *See* NASD

NETA (Network Associates)
  PSR, 97
  Web site, 97

NetBank, online banking, 279

NetLedger, 31

Netopia Web site, 259

Netpliance, 285

Network Associates. *See* NETA

networks
  appliances, 295
  entertainment systems, 295-296
  environmental systems, 294
  futuristic looks at everyday life, 296
  gateways, 293
  home security, 294
  Internet as the umbrella, 289-292
    computer connections, 293-294
    devices, 294
    products and technologies for home networks, 292-293
  market technology, 155-156

New Media for Major League Baseball, 159

newsletters (Internet information source), 60-61

niche markets, 242-243

Nokia Web site, 259, 286

Nortel Web site, 259

Northpoint Web site, 259

numbers, evaluating stocks, 83-89

O

offering price (IPOs), 169

offshore opportunities, 33

old technology versus new, 153-154

OneSource Information Services, 98

online
  banking, 274-276
    accessibility, 276
    bill payments, 276-277
    bill presentment, 277
    cash problems, 277-278
    choices, 279
    deals, 276
    future, 278-279
    history, 275-276
    investing in pure Internet banks, 279-280
    investments, 277
    lack of special services, 278
    loans, 277
    opening an account, 276
    security issues, 280
  personal financial services, 280-281
  research, 74-75
  selling, 225

Online New York Times Web site, 65

opening an account, online banking, 276

operators (stock screens), 98

options, 208-209

buying, 211-213
calculators, 216
call, 208-209
employee stock, diversification, 219-220
expiration dates, 208-211
information, 215-216
intrinsic value, 210
LEAPS, 211
long-term speculating, 218
naked calls, 215
playing the downside, 218-219
premium pricing, 208-210
pricing, 209
put, 208-209
selling, 211-215
short-term speculating, 217-218
strike prices, 208-210
volatility, 211
writers, covered, 214
writing, 208
Options As a Strategic Investment, 216
Options Toolbox, CBOE, 216
overpriced stocks, 75
owning stock, long, 182-183
limit orders, 182
market orders, 182
rolling orders, 183

P

P/E ratio (price/earnings ratio), 13
Palm, Inc. (Palm Pilot), 22
PANs (personal area networks), 290

parachuters, 146
Paradyne Web site, 259
paying bills, online banking, 276-277
PDAs (personal digital assistants), 125, 284-285
perceived risk, 53-54
risk tolerance, 54
risk aversion, 54
percentages, premium converted to sales, 133
personal area networks. *See* PANs
personal digital assistants. *See* PDAs
personal financial services, online, 280-281
personal information manager. *See* PIM
personalization technology, 150
PIM (personal information manager), 294
pitches, 62-64
playing the downside, options, 218-219
portal/information providers
selecting stocks, 123-124
traffic and revenue growth, 123-124
portals, 5, 243
critical mass, 123
Power screen, 100-102
premium (options), 208
pricing, 209
strike prices, 209-210
preset screens (stock screens), 72
prices
growth, 140-141
intraday, 21
IPOs, 181
investment bankers, 41-42

setting in the stock market, 168
strike, 209-210
trading, 204-205
price/earnings ratio. *See* P/E ratio
price/sales ratio. *See* PSR tool
primary market (IPOs), 42-43
professional management of mutual funds, 187-188
profiling, advertising, serving ads, 266-270
profit plans, 114-115
profits, 117-120
e-tailers, 134
future visions, 118-119
mom-and-pop stores, 135
patience, 120
selecting stocks, 121
entertainment, 124-125
getting out first, 122
market-dominating sites, 121-122
portal/information providers, 123-124
stock market effect, 120
prospectus, 160
PSR tool (price/sales ratio), 94-97
mid-cap companies, 95-97
TTM (trailing twelve months), 94
publications, Value Line Investment Survey, 79
Pure Internet companies, 4-6, 224
Amazon.com, 4
DoubleClick, 5
Yahoo!, 5
put option, 208-209

337

Q

Qualcomm, 11, 156
quality investments,
  buying strategy, 301
quality stock, 178-180
Quicken, 280

R

Radiant Systems, Inc..
  See RADS
RADS (Radiant Systems,
  Inc.), 155
recommendations
  day trading, 206
  online resources, 78
    InvestorPlace.com, 79
    Zacks.com, 78-79
Red Herring Web site, 67,
  160
red herrings, 66
regulation
  broadband delivery, 260
  securities, IPO allocation
    systems, 171
reports
  IPO activity, 176
  Value Line Investment
    Survey, 79
research (online), 74-75
  financial sites, 75-78
Research in Motion, 285
resistance, technical
  analysis, day trading, 202
resources
  information sources, 59
  Internet, 60-79
  reports and publica-
    tions, 79-80
  scams and pitches,
    62-64
  Web sites, 321-326

revenue growth,
  portal/information
  providers, 123-124
RhythmsNet Web site, 259
risk
  assessment, 21-23,
    49-51, 303
    balancing risk, 55
    economic risk, 53
    expectations, 57
    "gee whiz" factor, 23
    inflation, 52-53
    market value, 51
    safety nets, 47-48
  aversion, 54
  IPOs, 166-167
  tolerance, 53-54
Road Runner cable service
  (Time Warner), 259
rolling orders, 183

S

safety nets (risk assess-
  ment), 47-48
sales, 91
  advertising, 265-272
    betting future on
      revenues, 267-268
    media-rich ads,
      271-272
    profiling, 269-270
    testing, 266-267
  declining, 146
  company connection to
    the community, 93-94
  cooperation, Beta versus
    VHS wars, 93
  Internet standards, 93
  investigating what you
    are buying, 92
  per visitor, computing,
    131-132
  as proxy for earnings,
    PSR tool, 94-97

stock screens, 97
  Market Guide, 100
  MSN MoneyCentral,
    98-99
  operators, 98
  Power, 100, 102
Salon.com, 98
satellite, broadband
  delivery competitor, 258
SBC Web site, 259
"scaling" the business,
  growth, 143-144
scams, 62-64
screening stocks, 70-71
  custom screens, 73-74
  preset screens, 72
  variables, 71
search engines, 5
SEC, 160
security
  online banking, 280
  regulations, IPO alloca-
    tion systems, 171
selling
  options, 211-212,
    214-215
  stock, short, 183-184
services (Internet), 30-32
short (selling stock),
  183-184
short-term speculating,
  Internet stock options,
  217-218
shorting a stock, 209
shrinking cash reserves,
  146
SIC codes (Standard
  Industrial Classification),
  84
simulations, day trading,
  203-204
sizzle technology, 150
slaves, technology, 153
small office-home office.
  See SOHO

Snapshot,
  Morningstar.com, 75
software, 30-32
  search engines, 5
SOHO (small office-home
  office), 287
sources (information), 59
  Internet, 60-79
    e-mail cons, 61-62
    financial sites, 75-78
    general news and
      information, 65-66
    newsletters, 60-61
    online research, 74-75
    recommendations
      and advisory
      services, 78-79
    specific news and
      information, 66-67
    stock screens, 70-74
  reports and publica-
    tions, Value Line
    Investment Survey, 79
  scams and pitches,
    62-64
space offers, day trading
  brokers, 197-198
speed (Internet), broad-
  band, 254-255
  advertisers, 256
  competing technologies
    for broadband delivery,
    256-259
  future market, 260
  regulatory and legal
    issues, 260
  standards, 260-261
  structuring content for a
    variety of speeds,
    255-256
Standard & Poor's 500
  index, 56
Standard Industrial
  Classification. *See* SIC
  codes
Standard Web site, 67

standards
  broadband delivery,
    260-261
  Internet standards, 93
stickiness, 113
stock market
  crash of 1987, 48
  effect on profits, 120
  setting prices, 168
stock screens, 70-71
  custom screens, 73-74
  evaluating stocks, 97
    Market Guide, 100
    MSN MoneyCentral,
      98-99
    operators, 98
    Power, 100-102
  preset screens, 72
  variables, 71
StockQuest, 100
  Market Guide, 72
stocks (Internet), 3
  advertising-based sites,
    109-110
  change in consumer
    expectations, 10-11
  cheap, 89
  companies to be weary
    of, 7-8
  day trading, 205
  evaluating, 81-82
    cheap stock, 89
    company connection
      to the community,
      93-94
    growth rates, 88
    New Economy world,
      89-90
    numbers, 83-89
    percentage of
      premium converted
      to sales, 133
    profits, 117-120
    sales as a proxy for
      earnings, 94-97

sales per visitor,
    131-132
  SIC codes, 84-85
  stock screens, 97-102
  trying the service, 108
  understanding what
    you buy, 85-86
  unique visitors count,
    129-132
  what you are buying,
    83
  Yahoo!, 87-88
fraud, 64
guidelines, 18
  dealing with market
    hype, 20
  diversification, 20-21
  long term investing,
    18-19
  risk assessment, 21-23
Hybrid Internet
  companies, 6-7
  America Online, 6
  Sun Microsystems, 6
identifying and evaluat-
  ing companies, 8-10
making informed
  decisions, 16
market cycles, 13-14
myths, 16
  high rollers only, 16
  IPOs are gold, 18
  lose all of your
    money, 17
  will become rich,
    17-18
options, 208-217
  long-term
    speculating, 218
  short-term
    speculating, 217-218
overpriced, 75
popularity, 11-12
Pure Internet compa-
  nies, 4-6

selection, 121
  entertainment, 124-125
  getting out first, 122
  market-dominating sites, 121-122
  portal/information providers, 123-124
  those to avoid, 109-115
  volatility, Beta versus VHS wars, 73
strategies
  day trading, 204
    price trading, 204-205
    swing trading, 205
  Internet, 242
    commodities, 242
    evaluation, 244-248
    impact on companies financial picture, 244-245
    niche markets, 242-243
    portals, 243
    world vision, 243
  investing in pure Internet banks, 279-280
  investment, 301
    assessing risk, 303
    buy quality, 301
    buying and holding stocks, 302
    diversification, 303
    keeping expenses low, 302
    mutual funds, 302-303
strike price (options), 208-210
Sun Microsystems, 6, 295
support, technical analysis, day trading, 201-202
swing trading, 205

T

tax considerations, day trading, 199
technical analysis, day trading, 200
  resistance, 202
  support, 201-202
technology, 112, 150
  behind the scenes, 113
  change, 151-152
  computer, 284-298
    ASPs, 287-288
    B2B applications, 288-289
    home office revolution, 286-287
    post-PC era, 284-286
    SOHO, 287
    voice recognition, 298-299
  emerging, 154
  enhancing products and services, 151
  fads versus legitimate advice, 154-155
  home networking market, 155-156
  magnifying flaws with poor customer service, 152-153
  old versus new, 153-154
  personalization, 150
  slaves, 153
  wireless, 289
  Yahoo!, 150
testimonials, 109
testing advertising sales, 266-267
TheStandard.com, 159
Time Warner
  merger with AOL, 231-234
    benefits for AOL, 233

benefits for Time Warner, 233-234
  competitor reaction, 238
  financial considerations, 235-237
  potential problems, 235
  trouble signs, 237-238
Road Runner cable service, 259
timing the market, 17
tolerance, risk, 53-54
trading
  day, 196
    alternative strategies, 204-205
    analysis, 199-202
    brokers, 196-198
    capital, 203
    emotions, 204
    home traders, 198-199
    Internet stocks, 205
    recommendations, 206
    simulations, 203-204
    tax considerations, 199
  low valuations, 146
  price, 204-205
  swing, 205
traditional companies, mergers with Internet companies
  AOL Time Warner, 231-237
  broadband future, 237-238
  competitor reaction, 238
  trouble signs, 237
traffic, portal/information providers, 123-124
trailing twelve months. *See* TTM

trouble signs, mergers, 237
TTM (trailing twelve
months), 94, 192

U

U.S. West Web site, 259
undercapitalization, 114
unearned cash, fueling
growth, 141
unique visitors, 129
counting customers, 128
as method of evaluating
Internet stock, 129
computing market
value, 129-132
percentage of pre-
mium converted to
sales, 133
sales per visitor,
131-132
universal resource locators.
See URLs
unsustainable growth, 111
URLs (universal resource
locators), 26, 321
user growth of Internet,
32-33
dot. com economy, 34
offshore opportunities,
33

V

valuation justification,
Internet strategy, 245-248
value (customers), computing, 129
market value, MVV,
129-132
percentage of premium
converted to sales, 133
sales per visitor, 131-132
Value America Web site, 95

Value Line Investment
Survey, 79
variables, stock screens, 71
venture capitalists, 36
backgrounds, 37
company management,
158
finding deals, incuba-
tors, 37-38
going public, 36
limited partnerships,
38-39
VHS versus Beta wars,
cooperation in sales, 93
viral marketing, 110
virtual market places,
integration of company
and Internet, 228-229
VitaminShoppe, Inc.
Web site, 98
voice recognition,
computer technology,
298-299
volatility
IPOs, 181-184
mutual funds, 191-192
options, 211
stocks, Beta, 73

W

W.W. Grainger Web site,
227
Wal-Mart Web site, 226
walking dead (e-tailers),
108
Wall Street
Directory Web site, 162
Research Network
Web site, 67
WAP (wireless application
protocol), 290
Web sites
123Jump, 160
3Com, 259

advertising-based,
109-110
Ariba, 288
AvenueA, 270
Bank of America, 279
Bell Atlantic, 259
BellSouth, 259
BNBN, 110
Borders, 110
Bottomline
Technologies, 288
Cheap Tickets, 95
CIDCO, 286
Cisco Systems, 228
CNET.com News, 66
CNN, 65
Compaq Computer, 229
Copper Mountain, 259
Covad, 259
DaimlerChrysler, 228
Dow Jones, 189
Dow Jones Business
Directory, 162
Edgar On-Line, 160
Efficient Networks, 259
Elite.com, 287
Excite@Home, 259
financial, 75
Morningstar.com,
75-77
MSN MoneyCentral,
77-78
Ford, 228
General Electric, 295
General Motors, 228
Goldman Sachs, 189
Interactive Wall Street
Journal, 65
Interactive Week
Online, 67
Internet Index Fund,
189
Internet Stock Report,
66
Internet.com, 67

Intuit, 275
IPO Monitor, 66
K-Mart, 226
Land's End, 152
Lucent, 259
Major League Baseball, 159
Market Guide, 72, 100
Maytag, 295
Microsoft Network Money Central, 65
Morningstar, 97
Motley Fool, 94
NETA (Network Associates), 97
NetBank, 279
Netopia, 259
Netpliance, 285
Nokia, 259, 286
Nortel, 259
Northpoint, 259
Online New York Times, 65
Paradyne, 259
portals, 5
RADS (Radiant Systems, Inc.), 155
Red Herring, 67, 160
Research in Motion, 285
resources, 321-326
RhythmsNet, 259
SBC, 259
search engines, 5
Standard, 67
stickiness, 113
Sun Microsystems, 295
U.S West, 259
Value America, 95
Value Line Investment Survey, 79
VitaminShoppe, 98
W.W. Grainger, 227
Wal-Mart, 226
Wall Street Directory, 162

Wall Street Research Network, 67
WebTrends, 111
Wells Fargo, 279
Westell, 259
Whirlpool, 295
Zacks, 106
WebTrends Web site, 111
Wells Fargo, online banking, 279
Westell Web site, 259
Whirlpool, 295
wireless application protocol. *See* WAP
wireless
    cable, broadband delivery competitor, 259
    technology, 289
workstations, day trading, 197
world vision (Internet strategy), 243
writers, covered options, 214
writing an option, 208

X-Z

Yahoo!, 5
    evaluating stocks, 87-88
    technology, 150
Yang, Jerry, 161

Zacks Web site, 106
Zacks.com advisory service, 78-79